NEW BRUNSWICK BEFORE THE EQUAL OPPORTUNITY PROGRAM

History through a Social Work Lens

New Brunswick before the Equal Opportunity Program

History through a Social Work Lens

LAUREL LEWEY, LOUIS J. RICHARD,
AND LINDA TURNER

UNIVERSITY OF TORONTO PRESS
Toronto Buffalo London

Toronto Buffalo London
utorontopress.com

ISBN 978-1-4875-0253-9

Library and Archives Canada Cataloguing in Publication

Lewey, Laurel, 1951–, author
New Brunswick before the Equal Opportunity Program : history through a social work lens / Laurel Lewey, Louis J. Richard, and Linda Turner.

Includes bibliographical references and index.
ISBN 978-1-4875-0253-9 (cloth)

1. Social service – New Brunswick – History. 2. Social workers – New Brunswick – History. 3. Child welfare – New Brunswick – History. 4. New Brunswick – Social policy. 5. New Brunswick – Social conditions. I. Richard, Louis J., author II. Turner, Linda, 1960–, author III. Title.

HN110.N37L49 2018 361.309715'1 C2017-907509-8

University of Toronto Press acknowledges the financial assistance to its publishing program of the Canada Council for the Arts and the Ontario Arts Council, an agency of the Government of Ontario.

Canada Council for the Arts Conseil des Arts du Canada

Funded by the Government of Canada Financé par le gouvernement du Canada

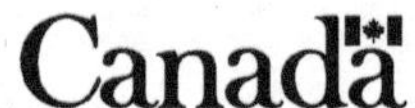

Contents

Foreword: A Landmark in the History of Canadian Social Work

NÉRÉE ST-AMAND

> People sitting on tea boxes and using a tea box for a table, they had nothing. Drinking hot water, heating their feet in the oven, tearing the shingles off the outside of the house in order to heat the water and at the same time losing all the heat out of the house because they tore the shingles off. They had to survive some way and it was tough.[1]

It is impossible to read this book without being deeply touched by the courage and determination of so many people who have lived through desperate conditions of poverty and misery and, at the same time, had to face a multitude of personal and institutional crises. The authors of this book you are presently holding describe a reality that is difficult to imagine today: extreme poverty of the have-nots, unfair treatment of minorities, overt discrimination, no resources for basic needs, and practically no hope of getting out of poverty. Generations of marginalized people were handcuffed by the 1601 Elizabethan Poor Law that led to criminalizing the poor and individualizing poverty. The authors remind us that the province itself was poor, receiving much less than its fair share from the federal government. Furthermore, within the province, there were great disparities between the north and the south, francophones and anglophones, not to mention rural and urban populations, or the Native and Black peoples.

The book demonstrates that social work has come a long way from the overseers of the poor in earlier centuries to the present situation in New Brunswick: hundreds of professional social workers, two university programs, and many private as well as public institutions. Tribute should be given to the authors who had the courage to describe to twenty-first-century readers the immense efforts that past generations of committed social workers have made to establish our current institutions.

We can't help but admire the first generations of social workers, who initiated a profession that is now well established and that has come such a long way from a handful of non-trained dedicated persons to our present-day situation. The book clearly demonstrates that we have evolved from emergency relief to basic rights for all, thanks to Louis J. Robichaud's vision in particular. Readers might wonder to what extent these basic rights are presently endangered by the dismantling of the welfare state and the privatization of social institutions. Thus, the question remains: In an affluent society, with the neoconservative policies of the present era, are we going back to emergency relief? If we continue in the direction social programs are heading now, the following quotation, written in 1939, carries even more dramatic repercussions:

> Another factor that seems clear, although figures are not available to prove it, is this: while among the families on relief, the preponderance is French-speaking, the proportion of these "families of poor quality" in the community, as a whole is English-speaking. Their cost is not so obvious in present outlays on relief, but it shows up in the wasting of educational facilities, expenditures now on medical care, court and police service and payment for dependent children. In the next generation the problems coming from this group will constitute an overwhelming burden, financial, social and moral, if it remains unchecked.[2]

Needless to say, the prejudices about the so-called undeserving people, the women and mothers, the so-called delinquents are still deeply rooted in today's society. Social institutions and progressive people have had to struggle to change people's perspectives on the destitute, the outcast; however, much work remains to be done in a neoconservative era to defend the gains of the past century. This book clearly demonstrates the deep-rooted attitudes and prejudices about the poor and the long-term consequences of the 1601 Poor Law. In such a context, we can appreciate even more the Equal Opportunity Program of the Robichaud era, which had to struggle against prevailing attitudes and prejudices. Add to this cultural and language challenges, geographical inequities, ideological barriers and unfair judgments based on religion, race, gender, etc., and we can appreciate how much the province of New Brunswick and its first generations of social workers had to deal with to bring about some significant changes.

It also brings to light the fact that the work around this book has to be continued in at least two areas:

1) Since the book stops in the 1960s, more work could be done to present the last half-century of developments. Has our society evolved? If so, in what way? Does the Equal Opportunity Program have any impact today? Are we facing more inequalities and ethical challenges, based on the same contradictions and structural biases as the pre-1960 era?
2) Since we seem to have lost, in New Brunswick and elsewhere, the vision of Robichaud's Equal Opportunity, we need other courageous visionaries to redress the problems of our lost equality ideals, but this time reinforced with a sense of justice and compassion. Who is presently doing this? Who defends the poor and silent minorities, people who are discriminated against in terms of gender, race, class, rurality?

This is a very well documented book, with plenty of invaluable information provided by several people who have had firsthand experience of these dire conditions. Some of the persons interviewed are still alive, others not, making their historical testimonies even more precious. It is the same with the authors who initiated this project; the early departures of Brian Ouellette and Katherine Marcoccio, who worked extensively on this project, have left a great void in New Brunswick's social work scene.

This book constitutes a very valuable document for both the general population and future generations of New Brunswickers. Needless to say, it should be adopted as a textbook for social-work courses, not only in New Brunswick but in other Canadian provinces as well, since the New Brunswick provincial situation resembles many others at a time when the consequences of the 1601 Poor Law were still very present. It should also be adopted in other courses as well: for instance, in history and political science.

Finally, there are underlying questions that emanate from this book. Here are a few:

- What if social workers had taken a more holistic approach to intervention to change social programs and society's attitudes, rather than dealing with individual victims?
- What if instead of giving meagre pittance to the poor and destitute, social workers had adopted a structural approach?

- What if we, past and present, worked on eliminating violence and poverty rather than just offering a helping hand to its victims?
- What if decent housing were a right rather than a privilege?
- What if decent working conditions were protected by law?
- What if we had taken another approach rather than relying on Mary Richmond's charitable philosophy? In this vein, it could be argued that the poor have been, and still are, more courageous than the people helping them, as this quotation suggests:

> *We cannot sit down to our own attractive meals, comfortable surroundings, knowing that just a short distance away people are living so miserably. Poverty is not a disgrace to them, but it is to us who have plenty.*[3]

I hope you find these pages as compelling and informative as I did.

Nérée St-Amand
Professor, School of Social Work, University of Ottawa
Former child-welfare worker (Campbellton) and Professor, Université de Moncton, New Brunswick

Acknowledgments

The authors acknowledge Brian Ouellette, whose commitment to New Brunswick's pioneers in social work generated interviews that led to the collective decision by social work faculty from St. Thomas University and Université de Moncton to write this book; also to Anne Ouellette for granting permission after Brian's death to use his intellectual property. We also acknowledge our colleague Katherine Marcoccio, who diligently devoted herself to the research and creation of a poster honouring New Brunswick's earliest social workers.

We would like to thank the following people for their important assistance: Nérée St-Amand, University of Ottawa, who contributed the foreword to the book; Sandra deVink of St. Thomas University and Isabel Lanteigne of Université de Moncton for reviewing early drafts of the book and providing welcome encouragement and suggestions; and Emeritus Professor Philip Doucet for kindly reviewing a chapter. Also thanks goes to retired Professor Jos Laviolette for sharing information on La Patente; to Emeritus Professor Phyllida Parsloe (Bristol) for suggesting a study on the earliest Acadian social workers; and to Dr Brenda LeFrançois for help in the final editing stage of chapter 8; and additionally to the twelve Acadian social workers interviewed in 1992 for their generosity in sharing their work experiences and also for their patience. Appreciation goes to Veronique Brideau, Deborah Cammack, Judy Teakles, and Andrea Watson as research assistants and to Melanie Melanson for her transcribing.

We were assisted in this research by Library and Archives Canada in Ottawa, the Provincial Archives of New Brunswick, le Centre d'études acadiennes and la Bibliotheque Champlain, both on the Moncton campus of Université de Moncton.

Monies for research and/or future translation of this book were gratefully received by (in no particular order): the New Brunswick Association of Social Workers; School of Social Work, St. Thomas University; Senate Research Committee, St. Thomas University; New Brunswick and Atlantic Studies Research and Development Centre (NBASRDC); École de travail social, Université de Moncton; Le Consortium national de formation en santé, Université de Moncton; and Dr Neil Boucher, Université de Moncton Academic Vice-president's office. We appreciate Jeanne Chiasson's skill and expertise translating the book into French.

We are extremely grateful to the University of Toronto Press team, including Acquisitions Editor Stephen Shapiro and Eric Carlson, who was the first to read and affirm the value of our work. The sustained high calibre of the reviewing process, including the work of the conscientious peer reviewers, greatly improved the manuscript. We are very grateful to Catherine Plear for outstanding copyediting and indexing services, and we thank Lisa Jemison, Associate Managing Editor, for solid guidance bringing the book to press.

Laurel Lewey thanks her daughter for her encouragement and sustained interest in the project. Louis Richard thanks his daughter, Dominique; friends Jean-Marc and John; and Mr Alfred Losier and Ms Jacqueline Bernard. Linda Turner thanks Louis Chiasson for perennial support.

We thank our many colleagues and social-work students who shared enthusiasm for the history over the years as this project became a reality. Finally, deep gratitude is extended to the many social workers of New Brunswick who appear in one way or another in the pages of this book.

NEW BRUNSWICK BEFORE THE EQUAL OPPORTUNITY PROGRAM

1

Introduction

LAUREL LEWEY, LOUIS J. RICHARD, AND LINDA TURNER

New Brunswick has a rich and complex history. It remains Canada's only officially bilingual province, having achieved this status with the Official Languages Act on 18 April 1969. We cannot speak about the history of New Brunswick without acknowledging the histories of three major social groups: the Mi'kmaq and Maliseet peoples, the Acadians, and the United Empire Loyalists. However, as will be revealed in this book, any discussion of social work in New Brunswick will talk mostly about anglophone and francophone groups originally represented by the United Empire Loyalists and the Acadians.

The Mi'kmaq and Maliseet are discussed far less frequently in this story because of the legal dynamic imposed by the federal government. Federal fiduciary responsibility for Indigenous people, implemented in the consolidated Indian Act in 1876, put them outside the provincial organizations for social caring. It is possible, however – and this is done in chapter 5 – to describe and critically analyse the experiences of New Brunswick's Indigenous peoples in some depth, revealing the negative effects of assimilationist policies that resulted in inadequate education, standard of living, and access to health care and social programs compared to what the United Empire Loyalists enjoyed.

It is also not possible to speak of New Brunswick's history without addressing the prevalence of poverty and speculating on its evolution and persistence, as well as the inability to counter these forces, yet we can speak of the ways in which social workers tried to mediate them. The authors describe some of the contexts within which social work found itself in this province, while highlighting who the earliest social workers were and how they saw and experienced the environments in which they worked. The authors critically analyse the often-harsh conditions and discrimination such as the poverty, racism, linguistic oppression, classism, ableism, religious repression, ageism, and gender discrimination experienced by some New Brunswickers. We describe how this research project began and some of the strengths and limitations of this contribution to foundational knowledge about social work in New Brunswick. The period covered by this study focuses on social work's origins, which have roots in both the English Poor Laws dating back to Edward III's Ordinance of Labourers (1349) and Statute of Labourers (1351)[1] and to religious institutions from England and France.

A common complaint in New Brunswick, as in other areas of Canada, was the perennial lack of social workers from the beginning, but especially during the 1940s and 1950s. For example, in 1948 at the first meeting of the New Brunswick–Prince Edward Island branch of the Canadian Association of Social Workers (CASW), fourteen social workers were listed as members of the CASW. By 1964 there were only fifty-three social workers in New Brunswick who were members. Fred Whalen, an interviewee for this research, reflected:

> We had our first professional association formed (mid-1960s), so in the 1950s you had a mish-mash of people trained as social workers and people functioning as social workers and there was a real mixture of individuals doing social work.[2]

Qualified social workers were often sought out for administrative positions because the various levels of government expanded due to the introduction of social programs in the post–Second World War period. However, gender discrimination rewarded men returning from war with administrative positions, even if they were not qualified social workers – a practice that occurred throughout Canada. Interviewee Archie Smith shared his experience with Brian Ouellette:

> I worked as a case worker, and one day I asked her why she (Bernadine Conlogue, his supervisor) had hired me, because I didn't have a full degree. I had taken university courses while working at the reformatory but didn't have a full degree. In fact I took three or four courses at St. Thomas [University] and a number from UNB [University of New Brunswick]. Her answer was that the reason I hired you was that you were a male. I was the first man they hired. The problem was that there was eighteen women and no men to go out on a night call when a child has been abused.[3]

The lack of social workers meant that many people who were not social workers were hired as agents of Children's Aid Societies (CASs) or into other positions related to social welfare. Until services were centralized and standardized through the Equal Opportunity Program, these welfare workers negotiated the parish system and the overseer of the poor for each parish to procure the most basic provisions for families. Richard Duffy, a pension inspector, reported the following in an interview with Brian Ouellette:

> I ran into a gentleman down there in the sixties, and he lived right down here in ______ and he was the last child handled by the overseer of the poor from Gagetown. He was sold to a family down in Kennebec, I think it was for five hundred and eighty dollars or something like that. I interviewed him for the Old Age Assistance at the time ... He kept telling me his story and he showed me some of the papers he had and they were all signed by the overseers of the poor from Gagetown ... He said he was the last one that he knows of, this happened in the twenties. So they used to take any orphan children and they would find a farm family that would guarantee to feed them, clothe them, school them, and look after them until they were twenty-one.[4]

A history of the provision of social welfare in New Brunswick within the Poor Law mentality reveals that the various private charitable organizations, often dependent on volunteer labour, significantly augmented the meagre level of social well-being available to New Brunswickers. Readers of this book will decide for themselves the relative importance that this province placed on the well-being of children, mothers, families, and those rendered dependent due to war, disability, and poverty. Archie Smith reminds us that for single mothers struggling in the context of poverty and discrimination, "either you had the money to look after the child or you lost the child."[5] Donald Richard, another interviewee, echoed the idea that injustice pervaded the systems: "At that time, during the sixties, the social worker was 'supreme' in court to settle family situations, as there were no lawyers representing either the Crown or the plaintiff, oftentime a parent. You defended your case as best you could, and I suspect, in some cases, that the parents' rights were not always respected."[6]

Louis J. Robichaud's Equal Opportunity reforms of the 1960s represent a transformation of society in New Brunswick that is arguably without precedence and that has not occurred since in Canada. The Royal Commission on Finance and Municipal Taxation (1962), chaired by Edward Byrne and known as the Byrne Report, outlined the eventual program of Equal Opportunity. The essence of this report was articulated in the White Paper on the Responsibilities of Government (1965). The social reforms introduced under Robichaud's leadership from 1960 to 1970 have become known as the Equal Opportunity Program, which aimed to ensure that francophone and anglophone New Brunswickers received the same quality of services in the areas of education, public health, justice, and welfare. The Indigenous people, however, were not intended beneficiaries of these reforms because of the consolidated Indian Act (1876). Child welfare services that would place the responsibility for Mi'kmaq and Maliseet in the hands of their own communities would not begin until 1979, when chiefs from four reserves began the process leading to the formation of Indigenous child and family service agencies.

Before the idea for this book germinated in 2004, two of the original authors, Brian Ouellette and Louis J. Richard, who shared a warm, professional relationship, were already pursuing their passion and respect for early social workers. In 2000, Brian had taken a one-year sabbatical from his position as a professor of social work at St. Thomas University to interview some of the earliest-known social work practitioners in the province, and discovered the names of many more. Louis, meanwhile, had carried out his doctoral research, which focused on the first professionally trained Acadian social workers and their experiences and challenges. In 2002 they presented their findings in the same session at an international social work conference in Halifax. Soon afterward, appreciation for the significance and value of this material grew among colleagues and students exposed to it, along with the desire to transform the stories and the perspectives into a book. As a result, the first official meeting of the authors occurred in December 2004, which led to the group expanding to include fellow social work professors Laurel Lewey, Katherine Marcoccio, and Linda Turner, who shared the commitment to capturing and publishing the history of social work in New Brunswick. This early group of authors represented a collaboration between social work educators at the Université de Moncton and St. Thomas University, the only two universities offering social work degrees in New Brunswick.

The team created an educational poster naming the pioneers of social work in New Brunswick through support from the New Brunswick Association of Social Workers (NBASW). The poster was presented at a Canadian social work conference in 2006 and then presented to the premier of New Brunswick during National Social Work Week in March 2007. With the untimely deaths of Brian in 2005 and of Katherine in 2007, the remaining three authors opted to carry on, staying committed to preparing and publishing this reader.

A number of methodologies were used to gather data. Louis Richard's doctoral study on the first Acadian social workers used a mail-out questionnaire, followed by a taped two-hour face-to-face interview with the participants. Some respondents to that study have consented to their materials being sent to the Centre d'études acadiennes Anselme-Chiasson, located at the Université de Moncton, where the documents are available to the general public. Most of the interviews that were not part of the Acadian social worker study were conducted initially by Brian, with additional ones by Laurel, Katherine, Linda, and Louis using the same interview questions as more potential interviewees were identified. All of these audiotaped interviews are stored at the Provincial Archives of New Brunswick. A genuine spirit of generosity was demonstrated by the willingness of the social work pioneers to share their time and views in this format. The authors also received funding for this project from a variety of sources. Funding was granted by the New Brunswick and Atlantic Studies Research and Development Centre (NBASRDC) and the Senate Research Committee at St. Thomas University. A substantial amount of funding for translation of the book was gratefully received from the Université de Moncton through the Consortium National de Formation en Santé and the NBASW, and the Department of Social Work (now the School of Social Work) at St. Thomas University.

Dr Lewey played a predominant role in the numerous hours spent combing through historical documents doing archival research, assisted by several research assistants.[7] A portion of that work was completed at Library and Archives Canada in Ottawa, in the Provincial Archives of New Brunswick, the office of the NBASW in Fredericton, and at St. Thomas University with numerous documents that had been donated to the Department of Social Work through the years. Examples of types of documents include the CASW's earliest records (New Brunswick and Prince Edward Island branches), minutes of meetings, and organizational records.

The ten chapters in this book address the historical, economic, and political contexts and the evolution of social caring for the three major groups and also point out the lack of equality, the degree of poverty, and the lack of access to social services and education, especially for Acadians and even more so – virtually a total lack of services – for Mi'kmaq and Maliseet people.

This exploration examines New Brunswick's political and economic history in order to contextualize the environments where the province's first professionally qualified social workers and their colleagues in positions of social service provision lived and worked. Dynamics, tensions, realities, and outcomes in the province can best be understood and appreciated through a critical-theory lens. Founded in the Frankfurt School and born in (but departing from) some aspects of Marxist theory, critical theory "is interested in the radical transformation of society and human emancipation, and it conceives of itself as an active element in a process leading to new social forms."[8] Critical theorists pay attention to the perpetuation of injustice and oppression and view social dynamics as immersed in conflict and power struggles.

Structural social work theory as developed by Maurice Moreau in 1990 and by Robert Mullaly in his seminal textbook *Structural Social Work: Ideology, Theory and Practice* enables an even deeper analysis. According to Merlinda Weinberg, structural social work "is part of a critical, progressive tradition that has been concerned with the broad socio-economic and political dimensions of society, especially the effects of capitalism, and the impact of these influences in creating unequal relations amongst individuals."[9] This research study revealed that in New Brunswick's history lie all ingredients for a recipe for disaster and hardship for entire communities and for individuals cursed with misfortune. While many faced harsh and dehumanizing living conditions and disrespect for their humanity, a small but very privileged minority reaped benefits not legitimately earned nor deserved. They were allowed and encouraged to continue amassing wealth while the majority, many of whom provided the labour, were robbed of the dignity of having sufficient means to provide for themselves and their families.

The work presented in this book reveals a pattern through which three threads are woven:

1 The first thread was that specific groups were impacted in varying ways by politicians and decision-makers who assumed power and imposed systems that reflected their own values and which also blatantly ignored and denied equally credible systems and values. As United Empire Loyalist culture asserted itself with this ruling-class mentality, the Indigenous people, the Acadians, Black New Brunswickers, and the Irish experienced marginalization and

disadvantage. People whose life circumstances made them vulnerable and dependent likewise experienced the burden of oppression.

2 Another thread central to the pattern was natural-resource exploitation by the profit-driven capitalists. Spurred by greed and affirmed by a culture that praised individualism, mechanisms to allow proliferation of wealth were enabled and the benefactors were congratulated, despite the injustice of inequality and resultant suffering.
3 A third thread, by no means less important than the others, is the assortment of religious, non-government, and charitable organizations that have picked up the pieces from the beginning. Admirable when at their best, despicable when causing harm, they were dominated by the ideology and values of the period. Social work as a profession cut its teeth and experienced adolescence in this environment, until government positions began to emerge in the 1950s. The contributions of the agencies and institutions cannot be underestimated.

A critical-theory framework with a specific emphasis on structural social work analysis provides a valuable lens through which to examine New Brunswick's history. Chapters of this book will highlight one or more of the three threads that are woven into the history, and each chapter includes discussion to highlight links between the content and the framework.

Chapter 1 provides an introduction to this collection. In chapter 2 three population groups whose histories are integral to New Brunswick are presented, along with information about additional groups who made the province their home. Chapter 3 examines the historical, economic, and political contexts of service provision in New Brunswick. In chapter 4 the uniqueness of the province is noted, in that the vestiges of the English Poor Laws dating to the fourteenth century lasted longer in New Brunswick and Nova Scotia than elsewhere in Canada. Chapter 4 also looks into the nature of poverty experienced by New Brunswickers. Chapter 5 includes a brief history of the agencies that provided social care and describes services available to the anglophone, francophone, Mi'kmaq, and Maliseet populations. The reader will observe that the network of social care differed among the three groups.

Chapter 6 portrays a history of the evolution of child welfare in New Brunswick up to and including Equal Opportunity. The following three chapters contain stories on various aspects of social work from social workers and Children's Aid Society agents that give us an idea of how things really were. The first of these chapters, chapter 7, describes the perspectives and experiences of professionally qualified social workers portrayed in many different roles. Chapter 8 is the result of doctoral research and examines the first Acadian social workers in the province. In chapter 9, we hear stories from those who were responsible for the protection of children in the province. Chapter 10 describes the nature and importance of the changes brought about through Equal Opportunity. The final chapter, chapter 11, provides concluding discussions of some tensions and factors that blocked change as well as areas that remain to be researched. Lastly, we have included two appendices: Appendix 1 provides a brief history of the New Brunswick Association of Social Workers, and Appendix 2 provides biographies on the social workers and social welfare workers who were either interviewed or whose names were found in archival materials.

Historical accounts will always vary depending on the location, perspectives, and biases of the person who is speaking or writing, and this book is no different. We invite readers to consider the views or perspectives we provide in each chapter, whether they represent our interpretations and analysis or those provided through quotations from the people who were interviewed.

Our hope is that future researchers will benefit from our collective work as a starting point for further and deeper investigation into social work's history in New Brunswick. The authors also take responsibility for any errors or omissions of more important historical events that may be uncovered through readers' expertise, experience, and knowledge. Viewing the comments and materials considered during our research through a lens of critical inquiry revealed that the dominant and inherently discriminatory or disadvantaging social and economic structures that prevailed in earlier times influenced social work thinking and practice.

This book grew out of the realization that little of the social services of earlier days was researched and documented. The authors have endeavoured to provide sources of insight and reflection while reinforcing the notion that social work occurs in particular historical, economic, political, and social contexts. Social work is not, and has never been, an easy profession, as Fred Whalen insisted during an interview:

> Of course social work is a very difficult occupation. It almost seems to me that social workers have to deal with the tragedies that society produces over which the social worker has no control ... But it (social work) was not

> really very identifiable, I don't think if you said you were a social worker people would know what you were talking about. Well not many, anyway.[10]

As educators of the next generation of social workers and despite widely varying origins and backgrounds among our group, we are proud to provide readers with this examination of the evolution of social services in early New Brunswick. It is but a first look at the earliest-known practices in the general field of social services in the province of New Brunswick.

2

A History of the Peoples of New Brunswick

LAUREL LEWEY, LOUIS J. RICHARD, AND LINDA TURNER

Indigenous people had lived for centuries in what today is known as New Brunswick before Europeans arrived in the region and began to claim areas of the land as their own. In this chapter we introduce the original inhabitants and what occurred as cultural groups from across the Atlantic Ocean arrived and settled. We then share a history of the Acadian people, including their challenges and successes in this part of Atlantic Canada. The United Empire Loyalists were the major population group to impose cultural systems and structures that asserted and maintained their dominance and power. In the last part of this chapter, we provide narratives of additional groups who made their way to and settled in New Brunswick.

Brief History of Indigenous Peoples in New Brunswick upon Settler Influx

Origins of traditional lifestyle and cultural practices

Oral history passed through elders indicates that the Mi'kmaq, Maliseet, and Passamaquoddy people have lived on Turtle Island (North America) since time immemorial. The Mi'kmaq ("our clan" or "our relations") were called Micmacs by European settlers; however, the Mi'kmaq also call themselves L'nu or "the people." Maliseets (Malecite), as they were referred to by settlers, refer to themselves as Wəlastəkwewiyik,[1] or "people of the beautiful river." All groups are members of Eastern Algonquin speakers, while the Maliseet and Passamaquoddy peoples of southwestern New Brunswick and Maine are "the most closely related, both culturally and linguistically."[2] In fact, the Passamaquoddy were never officially recognized by the New Brunswick government, even after two lots of land were reserved for them in the early 1800s, and so we know little of what they experienced. The Mi'kmaq traditionally lived in coastal locations, while the Maliseet traditionally lived close to the Saint John River along the most northerly point at Madawaska to the most southerly point of the river. Olive Dickason notes a type of cultural adaptation unique to both groups: "that of an agricultural people reverting to hunting and gathering. According to their traditions, they were descended from people who had migrated from the south and west."[3] Both groups had transactions with Europeans through the fisheries and fur trade; however, "it was their role as guerillas in the colonial wars that ensured their survival in their ancestral lands until the defeat of the French in 1760."[4]

Both the Mi'kmaq and Maliseets were traders. The Mi'kmaq likely served as "middlemen between the hunters of the north and the agriculturists of the south."[5] They were also fish farmers.[6] With respect to the Maliseet,

> their prowess in trade and warfare lay in their expert canoe navigation of the upper river and lake systems drained by the St. Croix and Saint John rivers by which they could reach the St. Lawrence valley in eight days. With the coming of European trade, first with Basque, Breton, Norman, and Portuguese fishermen, and later with French, Dutch, and British colonists, semi-permanent Malachite [sic] settlements arose to reach the benefits of such exchange at the mouths of major rivers flowing into the Atlantic.[7]

According to Andrea Bear Nicholas,[8]

> unlike Europeans, Maliseets used all parts of their territory in a pattern of seasonal migrations from headwaters for hunting and trapping in the winter, to village sites for fishing, planting, and meetings in the spring, to more coastal areas in the summer for saltwater sources, then back to the village sites for harvesting, fishing and preparations for the winter.

Spirituality was an organizing feature of their cultures, with egalitarianism a prominent value; roles among men and women were complementary; and medicinal knowledge was honed over the centuries.[9] At the time of contact with Europeans in what is currently known as the Maritime provinces, the Mi'kmaq relied upon the Grand Council, composed of district organizations that were represented by seven grand chiefs and captains. The Grand Council met once a year in order to ensure that each family had adequate fishing stations for spring and autumn, hunting ranges for winter, and gathering grounds for summer. Where there were disputes among families that went beyond a given community, the Grand Council would serve as an arbitrator. With an expanding population, the Council ensured that families' traditional rights to certain hunting grounds and fishing waters were balanced against the needs of the Mi'kmaq people as a whole.[10]

The Maliseet also relied upon a Grand Council. Carolyn Ennis, an elder and activist from Nekotkok (Tobique), described the governance and care structure:

> There was no such thing as an organization for social workers so it was all part of the Grand Council operation, and the Grand Council was the governing body and that governing body started from the family. If I had something that needed to be resolved, it started with my family, my immediate family, and if it needed to go farther and if someone did something that involved the community, then it would go farther into my clan. Then my clan would bring it to the whole community – the community would come together and then eventually they would resolve their problem one way or another. It worked better than the way things work now.[11]

Effects of contact

The French Jesuit missionaries had contact with the Maliseet by the late 1600s, and so any conversion to Catholicism occurred after this time. Mi'kmaq historian Daniel Paul[12] uses the term "pre-Columbian" rather than European to acknowledge that contact previous to the Europeans in this phase had occurred, yet an exact time frame is difficult to determine. Jesuit contact among the Mi'kmaq also had a lasting legacy in that the Mi'kmaq Grand Chief Membertou converted to Catholicism in 1610 along with twenty-one additional members of his band.[13] The Wabanaki Alliance of 1701 consisted of the Maliseet, Abenaki, Passamaquoddy, Penobscot, and Mi'kmaq Nations[14] and reflected their aversion to British authority in their lands and in what was called the colony of Acadia. Although the French may have believed that they were sharing land with the Mi'kmaq, and the British may have believed that the colony of Acadia had been relinquished at the Treaty of Utrecht (1713) – implying that the lands now belonged to King George I – the Mi'kmaq had not consented to this arrangement: "The Mi'kmaq responded in no uncertain terms that they did not come under the Treaty of Utrecht, would not recognize a foreign king in their country and would not recognize him as having dominion over their lands."[15]

The Mi'kmaq and Maliseet of New Brunswick could thrive as long as they were able to pursue their traditional ways of living. Although their ability to do so was compromised somewhat by French settlers, the Mi'kmaq and Maliseet experienced even greater threats with the increasing influx of British settlers. The "settler imperialism"[16] that began in the late 1700s (marked by the capture in 1758 of the French fort at Louisbourg) dispossessed Indigenous people in the region of their lands when, following the American Revolution (1775–83), immigrants loyal to King George III arrived. After New Brunswick separated from Nova Scotia to become a colony in 1784, the first inhabitants, having no protection, found that much of their lands had been granted to the Loyalists and that they were further displaced by squatters. Indian commissioners were not paid at this time, and lands were granted on an ad hoc basis to settlers.[17]

Although the intent of the Royal Proclamation in 1763 was to protect against the theft of Indigenous land by settlers, "the theft of Amerindian land did not abate, nor did anyone try to stop it."[18] New Brunswick did not recognize a land grant that had been made to John Julian and his Mi'kmaq band of 20,000 acres in 1783 on the Miramichi River, and as a result, "by the time the grant was confirmed in 1808, it had been reduced by half."[19] Further, the population was reduced so much so that by 1830, "New Brunswick counted an even smaller Aboriginal population than Nova Scotia: less than 1,000 Mi'kmaq, Maliseet and Abenaki."[20] The 1844 Act for the Management and Disposal of the Indian Reserves in this Province stipulated that each family was to be allotted fifty acres and any surplus was to be sold "for the benefit of the Indians."[21] By 1838, 61,293 acres of land were divided among fifteen Mi'kmaq and Maliseet reserves in New Brunswick. It should be noted that much of the land allotted to Indians was not of good enough quality for agricultural purposes.[22]

Leslie F.S. Upton believed that

> the only economic interest that the Empire had in the Indians was to arrange for the peaceful transfer of the land to which their possessory title had been acknowledged by the Proclamation of 1763. This process was going ahead to the complete destruction of the Indians' economic, social and cultural life. And to ease this process the British Colonial Office adopted a new policy after 1830: to assimilate the Indians into white society. It was a

> policy that was later generalized across the Dominion after 1867 and has guided the official conduct of Indian Affairs down to the present day.[23]

And further:

> To those who formulated Canadian Indian policy in the 1830s, protection and civilization were part and parcel of the same process. The protection of the Indians' accustomed way of life was never contemplated, for that would have meant imposing severe restrictions on the expansion of white settlement. The Indian could not be protected unless they were assimilated. But the government had no intention of putting public money into the venture; rather, the Indian was to pay his own way and so indirectly relieve the Treasury of the expense of a special department to minister to his peculiarities. And the missionary, who financed himself, came to be seen as an increasingly important agent of assimilation.[24]

Despite the many ways employed by the settler society to eliminate Indigenous people in New Brunswick, they remain a strong and visible presence. Statistics from 2014 show more than 15,000 First Nations persons living in the province, with two-thirds living on reserve.[25] The average age of Maliseet and Mi'kmaq people is much younger than found in the general population.[26] There are fifteen Mi'kmaq and Maliseet communities located throughout the province. Aboriginal organizations in the province have included the New Brunswick Aboriginal Peoples Council, the Joint Economic Development Initiative, the Indigenous Women's Association of the Maliseet and Mi'kmaq Territory, Gignoo Transition House, and the Union of New Brunswick Indians, to name a few.

Aboriginal economic enterprises continue to develop and grow. First Nations social workers have partnered with St. Thomas University to develop opportunities for bachelor of social work education for Mi'kmaq and Maliseet people from New Brunswick, Nova Scotia, and Québec. This initiative continues to attract steady enrolment and interest. At University of New Brunswick, the Mi'kmaq-Wolastoqey Centre[27] (formerly the Mi'kmaq Maliseet Institute) is one example of how Mi'kmaq and Maliseet culture is being promoted in the oldest university in the province. Another initiative is the *Mi'kmaq Maliseet Nations News* community newspaper.[28] Demonstrating leadership in environmental issues even in the face of government and police opposition, people from Elsipogtog First Nation led a massive resistance initiative in 2014 that rallied

Aboriginal and non-native people to protest the risks of water contamination due to shale gas exploration.[29]

More discussion of the social caring of Indigenous people in New Brunswick will ensue in chapter 5.

Brief Overview of the Acadians

Genesis of a people, 1604–1755

Acadians trace their origins to a small contingent of French explorers led by Pierre Du Gua de Monts (and which included cartographer Samuel de Champlain)[30] who, arriving in 1604 on Ste Croix Island near what is today St. Andrews, claimed the territory for France.[31] Their arrival forged the way for early settlers who would quickly recognize that they needed to turn to the Mi'kmaq and Maliseet peoples to learn essential New World survival skills, including cooperation.[32]

Descendants of the French settlers acquired the name *Acadiens*, and they developed relationships with the groups around them: the Mi'kmaq and Maliseet; the French society and soldiers in Louisbourg, whose language – but not culture – they shared; and the English-speaking New Englanders, with whom they maintained a north-south trade.[33] They were so adept at developing and maintaining useful liaisons with everyone, except the British rulers, that they became known as the French "neutrals." They led a peaceful life that revolved around family and church, meeting their needs through farming and fishing. However, the defining moment in the history of their people was about to happen: their deportation.

The events leading to the Acadian Deportation are numerous and complex and are not reviewed here in detail. Instead the reader is provided with glimpses of the times, glimpses that suggest why "ethnic cleansing" of the Acadians took place between 1755 and 1763.[34]

Since the beginning of colonization there had been frequent conflicts between the two European powers as well as among the fourteen colonies. During the period from 1690 to 1710, hostilities between France and England were rampant, disrupting lives in the British colonies. Acadians became aware of their powerlessness in determining their future.[35] To hold political aspirations was not realistic; the British-based parliamentary system of electoral processes related to representative and responsible government was slow to emerge in Halifax, where governing authority for New Brunswick still lay. Participating in and sharing political power were out of reach for Acadians because Roman Catholics could not hold office in either the judicial or the legislative branches of government. A half century later, in 1749, the arrival in Halifax of thousands of settlers represented a turning point in British colonial policy: London had adopted a more imperialist bent by which the need for new markets was replaced by the aggressive focus on possession of territories.[36]

Events in different areas of the British colonies suggest that their residents had begun to express increasingly hardened positions towards Acadians. Three particularly significant events took place during the fifty years prior to the deportation, which began in 1755. First, the Massachusetts General Court "criminalized the intercolonial trade" in 1696 as a "severe measure" designed to threaten Acadian life and property.[37] Trading opportunities with the British colonies had been essential for survival, development, and defence. Being unable to trade for needed goods likely threatened and intimidated Acadian people.

Simultaneously, an influential merchant group, also from Massachusetts, proposed the conquest of Acadia as a means of defending "their acquired rights."[38] A third indication of animosity towards Acadians in the colonies was the appearance of the following in the *Pennsylvania Gazette* newspaper, only weeks before the beginning of the deportation:

> We are now upon a great and noble Scheme of sending the neutral French out of this Province, who have always been secret Enemies, and have encouraged our Savages to cut our throats. If we effect their Expulsion, it will be one of the greatest Things that ever the English did in America; for by all Accounts, that part of the Country they possess, is as good Land as any in the World: In case therefore we could get some good English Farmers in their Room, this Province would abound with all Kinds of Provisions. (*Pennsylvania Gazette*, 4 September 1755)[39]

The French literary critic and essayist Henri d'Arles (nom de plume of Henri Beaudé, an Acadian descendant and a Dominican priest) is recognized as a scholar intimately familiar with the body of historical literature about the deportation of Acadians, according to John Mack Faragher.[40] D'Arles reported that "critical parts" were played out by the Yankee members of the Governor's Council of Nova Scotia; by Governor William Shirley of Massachusetts; and by Major General John Winslow, his officers, and men.[41] However, the ultimate responsibility for "the violent climax of a long history of double-dealing"[42] belongs to the "government ministers and colonial authorities."[43] In the opinion of the respected French scholar, the violent campaign of expulsion that continued for nearly a decade was "conducted with the official approval of the British government."[44]

The deportation, 1755–1763

The deportation or expulsion of Acadians began in 1755. It occurred in several locations over months and years. Lieutenant-Governor Charles Lawrence perceived them as a threat and was more than displeased that despite several attempts dating from the early 1700s, "the Acadians refused to swear an oath of allegiance to the British Crown unless the oath was qualified by recognition of their freedom of religion, their neutrality in case of war, and the right to emigrate."[45] After initially imprisoning two groups who were meeting him in Halifax to appeal confiscation of their boats and guns, and getting nowhere with his request that they sign an unconditional oath, he made the decision and gained approval for the plan to deport the population. Among those entrusted to carry out his orders was Lieutenant-Colonel Robert Monckton, for whom the city of Moncton was named. Throughout August and into December at many locations, hundreds of men and boys were taken prisoner; homes, farms, and crops were burned; and in total 6,000 Acadian people were forced out of their lands. Some who escaped fled and hid on what is today Prince Edward Island, as well as in northern New Brunswick. Beaubears Island, in the Miramichi region, became a hiding place for a couple of hundred. Fifteen hundred more are said to have fled to northern New Brunswick after Fortress Louisbourg was captured in 1758, but as many drowned aboard overloaded refugee ships.

Thus the fate of some 10,000 Acadians who were apprehended during the seven-year period from 1755 to 1762 was widespread dispersion, resulting in death, starvation, and imprisonment for many. The survivors were scattered along the Atlantic seaboard in states that included North and South Carolina, Maryland, Pennsylvania, and Virginia; however James E. Candow notes that

> the Acadians were not welcome in the colonies. Anti-Catholicism was widespread, as was hatred of the French in the wake of Braddock's defeat in the Ohio valley; the colonists were reluctant to assume the financial costs of supporting the Acadians; and in the southern colonies, there was fear that the Acadians would unite with slaves in a general uprising.[46]

Some were kept prisoners in either Halifax or England, or were returned to France. A group made its way to Louisiana after Spain gained that territory from France. A few took part in a short-lived settlement project from France to the Falklands.[47]

There is evidence that in some parts of the region Mi'kmaq people came to the assistance of the Acadians during this tragic time:

> The Mi'kmaq faithfully stuck by their Acadian allies to the bitter end. Some of the Acadians tried to escape and were aided and protected by the Mi'kmaq to the best of their ability. Many Acadians went into hiding among the Mi'kmaq and remained with them until the British and French ended their hostilities in 1763. A group of several hundred were hidden by the Mi'kmaq in the area known today as Kejimkujik National Park.[48]

The names of thousands of New Brunswickers and other Atlantic Canadians identify them as descendants of Acadian people who survived the deportation and expulsion and found both strength and courage to persevere, and to return to re-establish themselves as citizens of this part of Canada. History also reveals, however, that many family groups disappeared forever, as confirmed by the following source:

> Nearly three-fourths of the families whose names comprise this list did not reappear in Acadia after the Dispersion (1755). Of these, a certain number disappeared naturally either because the couple in question had no surviving children at all (Gisé, Lambourt, Poupart, Racois for example), or at least no surviving sons (Belou, Bézier, Flan, Forton, Gadrau, Gentil, Gouzille, LeJuge and so forth). Others perished as a direct result of their deportation (Apart, Froiquingont, Oudy, Tillard), especially in group disasters such as shipwrecks and epidemics. Other families saw their numbers drastically reduced in these tragedies, but were not entirely extinguished (Arcement, La Vache, Le Prieur).[49]

The resettlement, 1763–1860

When Acadians were forced to flee from what is today the Grand-Pré region of Nova Scotia, many who were not put on ships found refuge in the woods, even while the British continued to hunt for them. However, beginning in 1764, British authorities allowed Acadians to exist once again, without threat of expulsion, in the territory called Nova Scotia (which at this time still included New Brunswick). Acadians were required to meet certain conditions: for example, they were forced to "take the oath of allegiance, and with the stipulation that they be spread out in small groups only, in certain designated places."[50] The new areas where they were permitted to settle (in today's Nova Scotia) included St. Mary's Bay, Chéticamp, Cape Breton, and an area of Guysborough county on the Atlantic shore. They were also allowed to settle in parts of Prince Edward Island and northern and eastern sections of New Brunswick. It was a significant moment in Acadian history, as it reflected the start of a very lengthy process of legal repatriation, during which many Acadians would gradually return and resettle.

When displaced Acadians returned to Acadie over the next hundred years (the process was very gradual; their determination to return to their settlements despite the challenges and length of time it could take is noteworthy), they could not stay on the lands they had cultivated earlier, for these had been given away as free land tracts to those loyal to the British. Thus the deportees settled in remote areas and became reacquainted with the few Acadians who had escaped deportation. They practised an existence of subsistence and marginality while maintaining their language and culture.[51] Their presence appears to have gone unnoticed during this period. They were not participants in the historic meeting of the Fathers of Confederation in Charlottetown in 1864, nor were they mentioned in the British North America Act, 1867, the act that created Canada.

During this period Acadians concentrated on three basic units: the family, the local community, and the Catholic parish. The economy was simple, local, and based on cooperation. Throughout the twentieth century, Acadians demonstrated economic and social strength in cooperative development: from as early as 1915 with a fishermen's cooperative in Chéticamp, Cape Breton, Nova Scotia, and a caisse populaire (similar to credit unions) in 1916 in Richibuctou-Village, New Brunswick. The 1976 work of Father Anselme Chiasson, *Petit manuel d'Histoire d'Acadie de 1867 à 1976*, provides a history of the cooperative movement in Acadian communities. Contact with English-speaking outsiders was minimal and relegated mainly to the small-business class.

The renaissance, circa 1860–1880

The period of the Acadian renaissance began during the last half of the nineteenth century. This period marked significant steps taken by Acadians in the area of post-secondary education in the French language, the adoption of an independent stance vis-à-vis Québec, and the selection of their own symbols of nationality.

The Roman Catholic Church through its priests and nuns provided the exclusive avenue to higher education in the French language in l'Acadie. Among the most lasting of those initiatives is the work begun by Father Camille Lefebvre, a Holy Cross priest from Québec, who laid the groundwork for the Collège Saint-Joseph in Memramcook in 1864. A century later, another significant achievement of Acadian culture would be the creation of the Université de Moncton, described by its founder, Clément Cormier, as a step that represented for Acadians an "access to maturity."[52]

In 1880 in Québec city, Acadian leaders asserted their independence from Québec nationalists by declining to adopt the symbols of Québec, such as the fleur-de-lys, and Saint-Jean-Baptiste Day as their national holiday. Shortly thereafter, Acadian leaders selected their very own symbols. The conventions nationales, consisting of large gatherings of Acadians from all corners of Maritime l'Acadie, played a crucial role in solidifying Acadian nationalist spirit. The earliest ones were held in Memramcook, New Brunswick (1881); in Miscouche, Prince Edward Island (1884); and in Pointe-de-l'Église – or Church Point – Nova Scotia (1890). It was during the first two of these conventions that Acadians adopted the French tricolour (red, white, and blue) flag with a gold star representing the Virgin Mary as guiding light, the Acadian national hymn, "Ave Maris Stella" (Latin for "Hail, Star of the Sea"), and the national feast day, August 15, honouring their patron saint, Our Lady of the Assumption. An interesting twist of Acadian history is that the American literary work, *Evangeline*, by Henry Wadsworth Longfellow, was embraced as an Acadian cultural symbol, becoming popular in 1847 even before Acadians chose their own symbols.

French language education

Leading up to the introduction of the Equal Opportunity program, legal, social, and political realities had an impact on education for New Brunswick's Acadians. Among the legal aspects was the British North American Act (BNA Act) of 1867. According to the BNA Act, French and English are the two official languages of Canada. Renowned Acadian educator Frère Léopold Taillon points out that although language may have been designated a federal responsibility and respect for the two languages was declared, the teaching of language did not fall under federal jurisdiction. Under the terms of the act, education was a provincial responsibility and the Canadian government held no official authority in matters that pertained to education.[53] The Common Schools Act of 1871 replaced the Parish Schools Act of 1858. Its goal was to abolish church-run schooling in New Brunswick and to replace it with a system of government-run "common schools." This act was opposed by the Roman Catholic Church and its adherents, and a series of clashes between New Brunswick Catholics and the provincial government resulted in the fatal shooting of two people during the Caraquet riots of 1875. The act was subsequently amended to implement a joint religious-secular schooling system.[54] Principal accommodations included the fact that religious persons could wear their order's or the congregation's habit and could offer religious instruction on condition that it be outside school hours and beyond the prescribed program of studies. Another part of the context was ongoing interest by authorities in the provincial capital of Fredericton to find ways to anglicize the Acadians as well as to bring them over to the Protestant fold.[55]

With regard to the social positioning of Acadians, Senator Pascal Poirier observed that Acadians of the day were "submissive" and "obedient," towards the English in civil matters.[56] Frère Léopold Taillon was of the view that unless Acadian children were taught in their own language it would not be possible to rid them of their "illiteracy."[57] Noted Acadian educator and administrator Calixte-F. Savoie, explained how a position of "inferiority" was assigned to the Acadian child by the public education system; this, he argued, was accomplished by leading the child to believe that the study of French was unimportant compared to the study of English.[58] He associated that belief with a school system that was "anglicised" and "anglicising."

Frère Léopold Taillon[59] reported on a speech given by the Honourable C.H. Blakeney, New Brunswick education minister, during the third congress of L'Association Acadienne de l'Éducation, held in Edmundston in 1943. The elected official acknowledged an illiteracy problem in the province and was of the opinion that it originated, to a large degree, in the French schools.

The Acadian population of New Brunswick of the nineteenth and twentieth centuries faced considerable odds in its journey towards equality and justice; some obstacles originated in structural arrangements, unchanged and unchallenged over the years, as seen above. In response, an elaborate network private institutions, consisting of convents and colleges, was established to prioritize education; these were organized and administered by religious communities, female for the most part.

Some fifteen such institutions were founded in New Brunswick between 1864 and 1924.[60] (See chapter 10 for a list.) The initiative was carried out by the Roman Catholic Church alone, and it had also assumed the responsibility for educating Acadian children through a private system until the arrival of province-sponsored schools from the 1960s onward.[61]

Acadian women

While the end of the nineteenth century saw the feminist movement inspire action to achieve the vote and for greater freedom for women to participate throughout society, Nicolas Landry and Nicole Lang indicate that Acadian women were on the sidelines in those efforts, due to the firm expectations in Acadian society that their place was in the private domain of the home.[62] The role of Acadian women appears to have been prescribed as predominantly mother and educator. According to Cécile Gallant, a leading Acadian newspaper, *le Moniteur Acadien*, published the viewpoint that women were not born for politics or a political life, but rather should be content to be queen of the domestic domain.[63]

Yet, Emilie LeBlanc Carrier, using the pen name of Marichette, dared to publish from a feminist perspective in the 1890s in the daily Acadian newspaper *l'Evangeline* and wrote of her vision of starting her own newspaper with an all-female editorial staff. She is said to have also voiced support for women gaining the vote and to have written on topics of social injustice and political issues.

A perspective that brings to light leadership and strength among Acadian women in general has also emerged. As preparations for the Congrès mondial acadien were being finalized in the province in 1994, Acadian women took stock of their contributions, accomplishments, and goals. In an article entitled "Les Acadiennes font entendre leur voix" (Acadian women make their voices heard) by Michèle Berthelot,[64] Antonine Maillet reflected on her appreciation for Acadian women's contributions, too long invisible. For Maillet, there is no doubt that it is the women who have ensured that l'Acadie survived; her character Pélagie in *Pélagie-la-Charrette* symbolizes the painful struggles as families returned to the land from which they had been deported. She maintains that throughout Acadian history, it was the women who maintained morale, kept hope and hearth going, and took care of the family; and through doing so, ensured their future.

Contributions made throughout the eighteenth, nineteenth, and beginning of the twentieth century are beyond measure, Maillet says. The period from 1880 to 1914 saw a strengthening of women in religious life through an expansion of convents. Among the locations of congregations of nuns in New Brunswick were the Sainte-Famille Convent in Bathurst; l'Académie Notre-Dame du Sacre-Coeur in Memramcook; l'Académie de Saint-Basile; the Congrégation de Notre-Dame in Saint-Louis in Kent county and Caraquet; l'Immaculée-Conception in Bouctouche, Dalhousie, and Rogersville; and l'Académie Sainte-Famille in Tracadie. These numerous educational institutions came about through the Sisters of Charity, Congrégation Notre-Dame, the Notre-Dame du Sacre-Coeur congregation, the Religieuses Hospitalières de Saint-Joseph, and the Filles de Jésus. As authors Landry and Lang explain, "These communities contributed in an exceptional manner to the Acadianization of the Church and to the taking responsibility of the educational sector for the Acadian minority."[65]

Isabelle McKee-Allain, sociologist, has written of the importance of the institutionalized role played by Acadian women in affirming and contributing substantially to the developing Acadian identity through education.[66] Maillet also highlighted the leadership and commitment to education provided by nuns, especially Mother Marie-Jeanne de Valois of the Congrégation Notre-Dame that ensured young women, in 1946, could access post-secondary education for the first time in French in New Brunswick. Women also brought Acadian culture to national and international stages, notes McKee-Allain, citing Edith Butler, whose career began in the early 1960s. McKee-Allain affirms that Acadian women deserve to be seen as subjects in history beyond the important role as protectors of home, language, and religion, in order to represent the diversity and extent of women's involvement. While occupational roles were limited to vocations of nun, nurse, teacher, and mother, many nonetheless ventured into roles that had been reserved for men. These include architect (Sister La Dauversière), educational administrator (Marguerite Michaud), founder and director of a caisse populaire (Anna Lavoie Perron), founder of a newspaper (Rachel Vandardaigue Guérette), union leader (Mathilda Blanchard), and a national organization president (Blanche Schofield Bourgeois).

Towards the end of the 1960s the first gatherings of Acadian feminist groups were speaking out about the rights of women, including employment discrimination and lack of maternity leaves, daycare, and kindergartens.[67]

Sustained political power beginning in 1960

By the 1960s, cohesive, well-organized, and structured activities that were part of the Acadian fabric would create favourable conditions for political power and would propel Acadians to seek to occupy the same general space as anglophones and on an equal footing. These included a focus on education, development of an elite, creation of Acadian institutions, and leadership by the Catholic Church.

Until that time, the Acadian presence in the mainstream political arena had been isolated and rare. As examples, Dr L.N. Bourque was the first Acadian elected to the Moncton City Council in 1890[68] and although Pierre-Jean Veniot was appointed premier of New Brunswick for a few months in 1923, he was never elected. In June 1960 New Brunswick Acadians made a big leap forward by electing the first Acadian premier of their province, five years after they had marked the bicentennial of the deportation. Louis J. Robichaud served as premier from 1960 until 1970. His political career and contributions and their significant impact, particularly on francophones, are discussed in further detail in chapter 10.

United Empire Loyalists

The immigrant group that wielded and retained the most significant power and influence was the United Empire Loyalists. The group consisted of men, women, and children who had been living in the Thirteen Colonies, were loyal to the British Crown, and found themselves unwelcome after the battles led to a victory by the American side. The exodus began when "six major fleets of Government-provided vessels ... carried loyal exiles from New York to the mouth of the River St. John in 1783. Five of these were composed primarily of Refugees of the Bay of Fundy Adventurers. The sixth fleet was composed almost entirely of disbanding Provincials and their families."[69]

In the initial fleet of ships that spring, close to 2,400 loyalists are believed to have arrived, followed by nearly 4,500 more between June and October. While earlier ships brought civilians fleeing the turmoil, among those arriving in the fall were the defeated soldiers of thirteen distinct regiments.

The loyalists found much cause for disappointment and disgruntlement: "arrangements ... for the reception of this vast army of people were sadly inadequate ... an unpardonable delay in the surveying and allotment of lands ... privations and sufferings which many of the refugees suffered were piteous ... women and children, died from cold and exposure and insufficient food."[70]

Grants of land were not evenly distributed. Those first to arrive were allotted the largest parcels. In 1784, the year following the first influx of loyalists, New Brunswick became a separate province, with Governor Thomas Carleton in charge. As will be seen throughout this book, the parish system that government leaders soon implemented became more and more problematic, particularly due to limitations that resulted in the vast inequalities, injustice, and misery that Robichaud's Equal Opportunity legislation would attempt to combat. Full credit for imposition of the parish system Poor Law mentality, with its inherent inequality and oppressive characteristics, can be placed squarely with Governor Carleton: "His most singular tactic in the drive toward oligarchy ... was to make the parish, with its associations of obedience and pastoral order, the unit of local government and to make it completely subservient to the county ... as in England, the county was to be a conduit for royal and parliamentary power."[71]

Whereas the first inhabitants of New Brunswick had lived with and on the land successfully while maintaining their culture and traditions, the several shiploads of United Empire Loyalists arriving in 1783 brought with them strongly held assumptions that their style of civilization and systems were "superior" to the ways of life practised in Indigenous or Acadian communities. As Ronald Rees notes,

> Although uprooted and debilitated by a long and, for them, unsuccessful war, they came with expectations or, as we might say now, with attitude. Far from being ciphers ready to do the bidding of colonial officials, the Loyalists arrived in Nova Scotia – of which New Brunswick was then a part – with a blueprint of the world they intended to inhabit. The rough and heavily treed land might have given them pause but the leaders were in no doubt as to the kind of political and social patterns they intended to impose upon it.[72]

In neighbouring Québec, René Lévesque, that province's premier from 1976 to 1985, would describe the handful of loyalist families in his Gaspé-coast hometown of New Carlisle as powerful. According to Lévesque "They (Loyalists) treated the French Canadians like the white Rhodesians treated their blacks."[73]

Establishing access to higher education appears to have been a priority. The University of New Brunswick, founded in 1785, is the oldest

English-language post-secondary institution in Canada. On its website today, credit is given to its historical loyalist connection, reflecting the forced migration of defeated British subjects:

> As the American Revolutionary War drew to a close, thousands of Loyalists gathered in New York City to await transportation to homes in other British colonies. Among these Loyalists were Charles Inglis, a former interim President of King's College, New York (Columbia University); Benjamin Moore, later President of Columbia; and Jonathan Odell, minister, poet and pamphleteer. These men were the visionaries of their day. In the midst of war, privation and exile, they drew up a plan for the future education of their sons in the wilderness. Recognizing that the new American nation would provide instruction only in revolutionary "Principles contrary to the British Constitution" and that the cost of an overseas education would be prohibitive, they urged the representatives of the British government to consider the "founding of a College ... where Youth may receive a virtuous Education" in such things as "Religion, Literature, Loyalty, & good Morals ..."[74]

Among the settlers were Black loyalists: some had come as slaves of the loyalists, while others had gained promises of freedom in exchange for choosing to fight on the British side. History tells us that they faced discrimination and far greater challenges than their White loyalist counterparts: "At the opposite extreme, socially and economically, from the smug (sic) gentility of Felicity Hall was a large class of Loyalists whose life was marked by oppression, failure or disarray. Most identifiable among this group were the free Blacks."[75]

Jim Freedman, an author well versed in African history, wrote a book based on a true story, entitled *Sissiboo River Redemption.* The narrator of the book provides an important portrait:

> The Governor of New Brunswick cared nothing for the free Blacks. At a whim, he would ignore the British commitment to give them provisions in the initial years and if he gave land to the black settlers as agreed, these lands were located so far from River St. John the black settlers could reach them only at their peril. James Langford picked out a plot. He walked upriver for three days past homesteaders living in abysmal circumstances, through bush until, by his reckoning, he had arrived, though it was near impossible to be sure. Wherever he asked for directions the response from white settlers was surly and led him astray, wandering until provisions were gone.[76]

Examples of systemic racism towards the Black population included exceptional delays in surveying their land grants, assignment of smaller and less valuable land, failure by Saint John to award municipal-freemen status to Black tradesmen, and the denial of the right to vote in the 1785 election. It is assumed that only White loyalist males were able to vote.

An early source citing population statistics in New Brunswick in 1901 claimed that among the 331,000 people, the number of Black New Brunswickers was close to 1,400, with substantial communities evident at Otnabog (the area known today as Elm Hill), which was settled in 1812 and traces its origins to Black Loyalists from Virginia. Another substantial community of Black New Brunswickers was Willow Grove (near what is today Rothesay), which was settled in 1817.[77]

Even in the face of discrimination and marginalization, notable members of the Black community demonstrated their capabilities and determination to overcome barriers. Abraham Beverley Walker (1851–1909), born on the Kingston Peninsula in the province, was among the first students at the Saint John Law School (which later became the UNB Law School). He became a lawyer in 1881 and shares (with two others) recognition as the first Black lawyer in Canada.[78] It would be another seventy years before another Black student would enrol in the UNB Law School.[79]

Segregation endured in various social settings. The Royals Baseball Club of Saint John in the early 1920s provides an example from the field of sports, and segregation was also visible in teams from specific occupational groupings, such as train conductors, dyers, and longshoremen.[80] Given the engrained racism of mainstream churches, Black communities formed their own church communities, developing their own congregations and clergy to meet their social and spiritual needs. Denise Gillard describes, for example, a very early experience in maritime history in her article on the Black church in Canada:

> For example, most Blacks believed that baptism in the Anglican Church would make them "one and equal with whites." However, even when Dr. John Breynton, Rector of St. Paul's, baptized many hundreds of them, Blacks found that while they could attend services and receive communion, they were segregated from White parishioners and forced into galleries set apart for Blacks, the poor, and soldiers. By 1815, Black worshippers were kept behind a partition. Ultimately, Blacks were excluded when White parishioners grew in numbers. Furthermore, they were advised to gather in their own private homes.[81]

Additional Groups

In addition to the Mi'kmaq and Maliseet peoples, the Acadians and the 10,000 United Empire Loyalists, there were several other cultural groups who settled in New Brunswick. Between 1759 and 1768 several thousand people known as "Planters" (a word for colonists) from New England accepted offers of farm land that the Acadians had been forced to give up. In 1760, several families from Massachusetts established themselves in a twelve-square-miles area in what is today Maugerville, soon expanding when more families came to the area after the 1775 American Revolution. Meanwhile German-speaking settlers referred to as the Pennsylvania Dutch immigrated in 1776 after having first settled for more than ten years in Pennsylvania. Originating in Germany and not the Netherlands (it is believed use of "Dutch" was applied because they spoke "Deutsch," which is the word for German), the group consisted of eight families bearing surnames still apparent among their descendants in Moncton today, such as Jones, Somers, Lutes (originally Lutz), Steeves (originally "Stief"), and Trites (originally Treitz).[82]

The Irish also established a strong presence in New Brunswick, arriving in greater numbers than any other group in the first half of the 1800s. Originally many came on ships that were part of the timber trade and made ongoing voyages across the Atlantic, bringing new settlers on the return trip. By 1850, Irish made up more than 50 percent of the colony.[83]

Dan Soucoup has also written about the Irish famine in the years 1845–9 leading to the proportionately higher numbers of immigrants to New Brunswick, noting they settled in greatest numbers in Saint John (more than 14,000 in one year alone) and Miramichi, but also in significant numbers in other areas, such as Woodstock. He describes religious and cultural conflicts that arose:

> The influx of destitute Catholics escaping poverty and famine, combined with a downturn in the province's lumber trade, set the stage for violent confrontations between these new citizens and the existing Protestant workers, farmers, and tradesmen. The Protestant reaction to the new immigrants involved the expansion of the Orange Order.[84]

Violence and riots, particularly on Irish feast days, became part of New Brunswick's history, with the worst incident being the Saint John riot of 1849, in which a dozen were killed and hundreds injured as members of the Orange Lodges from the country and city invaded York Point, the area of the city where the Irish predominantly lived.[85] As will be seen later in the book the earliest social workers in New Brunswick would be conscious of the Irish Catholic and English Protestant divisions even a hundred years later.

At the age of twenty-five, William Davidson, one of the first Scottish immigrants, settled in the Miramichi area in 1765. He would gain notoriety through roles as lumberman, shipbuilder, and politician. While there were numerous smaller groups of Scots who settled throughout the province, some rural areas attracted larger numbers, such as in Restigouche County near Campbellton and in Victoria County, in a community known as Kincardine.[86]

Lebanese communities have also existed in New Brunswick for more than a century. The following story is not unique:

> In 1911, 15-year-old Ibrahim Kassouf left his home in the Mount Lebanon area of Syria. By the time he arrived at the train station in Newcastle, NB, he had become, according to the tag on his chest, Abraham Asoyuf. His brother, Charles, who had immigrated to New Brunswick in 1897, came to collect him. The very next day, with no English and a few words of French, Abe Asoyuf set out to peddle a pack of dry goods and notions from Charles' store in Eel River, near Baie Ste. Anne on Miramichi Bay. Charles was already on his way to becoming a successful merchant, and Abe followed his lead. Before long, Abe owned a fish packing plant. When it came time for him to have a wife, his parents arranged his marriage to a cousin, Zakia, from home. He met her boat in Montreal and brought her home.[87]

The first Danish immigrants arrived in 1872, bearing the surnames Carlsen, Christensen, Clausen, Johansen, and Neilsen, and accepted government offers to settle and farm in New Brunswick. Their community of New Denmark, a rural farming community, today has a population of about 1,700 people.

New Brunswick's Jewish community traces its history to 1858, when the Solomon Hart family arrived.[88] Saint John was a bustling urban centre, the population of which gave it standing as third largest in British North America at that time. The population would be bolstered around 1900 with large numbers of Jewish immigrants passing through Saint John from Eastern Europe, followed closely by many driven from homelands such as Austria, Hungary, and Russia because of persecution and hardship. The first Jewish Immigrant Aid Society in Canada was formed in 1896 in Saint John as a response to that dire need. (The society would be established in Toronto more than twenty years later, in 1920, and was legally incorporated two years after that.)[89]

As early as 1915, records of mine workers in the Minto area, situated in central New Brunswick, reflected a diversity of ethnic origins, including Belgian, Germans/Austrians, Italians, and Russians, and expanded in the 1920s and 1930s to include Polish and Hungarian people.[90] In the 1940s, as the Second World War was unfolding, seven hundred Jewish men and youth were held at the only internment camp in Atlantic Canada – at Ripples, thirty kilometres east of Fredericton – as a favour to the British government, which feared that some of them were spies. The camp then housed prisoners of war, including German and Italian people, as well as people who spoke out against the war. Camillien Houde, mayor of Montreal, was forced to stay at Camp Fredericton for two of the four years of his internment, transferred from Camp Petawawa where RCMP had imprisoned him in August of 1940 after he spoke publicly against conscription.[91]

New Brunswick has not achieved as much growth in ethnic diversity of its population as Central and Western Canada. According to statistics for 2011, in New Brunswick, 64.9 percent of the population identified English (only) as their mother tongue, while 31.6 percent claimed French only for the same category. The next three most common mother tongues were Mi'kmaq (0.3 percent), German (0.3 percent), and Korean (0.3 percent). Nationally, the most common mother tongues next to English and French are Punjabi (1.4 percent), Chinese (1.3 percent), and Spanish (1.3 percent).[92]

In this chapter we have offered an account of three population groups with a significant historical presence in New Brunswick: the Mi'kmaq and Maliseet peoples, the Acadians, and the United Empire Loyalists. The arrival and settling by additional ethnic groups and communities was also described.

In chapter 3, the historical, economic, and political contexts within which New Brunswickers lived, and the environments upon which provincial government service provision would eventually be displayed, are described.

3

Historical, Economic, and Political Contexts of Service Provision

LINDA TURNER

Examining the history of social welfare organizations, programs, and legislation in any province or territory will reveal complex and unique contexts and influences. In New Brunswick this is indeed the case, particularly given this province's adherence to laws and practices born centuries earlier but operating into the 1960s. However, New Brunswick is also unique in terms of the way its resources and industries created opportunities and provided the province with assets to exploit. Its forests, rivers, and ocean coasts were critical to its development. We begin, therefore, by acquainting readers with the natural-resources industries (agriculture, forestry, fishing, and mining). In the second section, some key aspects of New Brunswick's economic development are discussed. The third section of the chapter places an emphasis on power and politics. We share how the Irving and McCain industrial empires influenced life in the province, as well as where resistance and radicalism surfaced in the decades leading into the 1960s.

Agriculture

Agriculture has always played a predominant role in New Brunswick's economic development. The region of Sussex, still a thriving dairy farming community, boasts the oldest agricultural society in the world,[1] although already by 1860 there were twenty-four agricultural societies across the province. Sussex would also become, by 1910, the location for a provincial dairy. Reports in 1900 speak of crops such as hay and oats, and products such as flour of high quality, cheese (fifty-four cheese factories existed), and abundant amounts of milk and butter production, with thirty-three creameries in the province and export activity to England.

Acadians also took part in farming in early times in the area they had settled. However, even in agriculture, United Empire Loyalist domination had negative effects. One source, referring to Acadian farmers, noted, "The difficulty of language made their rigid social order and religion their only supports. There was no information available to them in their own language and only small access to education. The Loyalist influence was still strong and dominated the official policy and thinking of the provincial leaders."[2] Perhaps that explains a very noticeable and steady decline in agricultural production in Gloucester, Restigouche, and Kent counties through the 1920s and into the 1950s, while crop acreage in Kings, Queens, and Westmorland counties saw increases.

New Brunswick is strongly associated with potato production: "New Brunswick grew 8.3 percent of Canada's potato acreage in 1929, but through the efficiency of the producers, accounted for 12.8 percent of the yield. In that year, the crop was worth $8.2 million to the farmers."[3] Ten years later: "In 1940 the potato crop reached the 11.4 million bushel mark for the first time with the yield average well above the rest of Canada. Certified seed, under the inspection system begun in the 1915 crop year, showed 12,667 acres under production with a yield of 3.4 million bushels."[4]

From the 1950s farms grew larger but had fewer people working on them. Leaders in the cooperative movement and farming in general advocated for creation of an umbrella organization, the New Brunswick Federation of Agriculture, which came into being in 1952.

Equal Opportunity and its radical transformation of the taxation system was every bit as significant to farmers as it was to people in other occupations in the province:

> Based on the "Byrne Report" on taxation in the province, the planners under Premier Louis Robichaud between 1960 and 1965 put together a package of programs known as "Equal Opportunity" ... For the farmers, the change meant a good deal. For the first time taxation applied universally across the province and for the first time, government programs could be used by everyone. New Brunswick had come of age in a real sense and it represented the first major revamping of the political structure in over a hundred years.[5]

Certainly farmers would have been discouraged that their hard work to support families and earn a livelihood in New Brunswick were not producing dividends, and like many others including social workers, they would have held hope that Equal Opportunity reformations would improve their lot:

> Farming, as such, had not held its own with other facets of the Canadian economy from 1951 to 1967. Farm prices had risen only 6 percent during the period while the costs of farm operation had gone up over 25 percent. More efficient, mechanized farms were producing more agricultural production than all the small farms together but the income was dropping and future progress looked bleak in view of the lack of capital for new land, machinery or buildings.[6]

Lodged in the history of agriculture in New Brunswick is the Women's Institute movement. It began after Mrs James E. Porter, wife of a Victoria county MLA, accompanied him in 1911 on a field trip to Ontario, where she learned more about the organization that had started there in 1897. At a time when women did not yet have the vote and when political discussion by women was not encouraged, the institutes would become a place where rural women's voices could have a forum. The first institute began in Andover with 19 members, and in only three years there were sixty-one branches and more than 1,900 members. The organization led to numerous community improvements and services, as well as being a place where women's leadership could be nurtured and developed. The organization also had highly active francophone chapters from 1927 onward (l'Institut féminin).[7]

Forestry

New Brunswick's economic history is intertwined with its forests and the capitalists' fierce determination to wring out as much wealth as they could from this natural resource. From its earliest beginnings, interest in New Brunswick was associated with how capital could be extracted from its forests. By 1812, timber exports increased more than twenty times the 1805 level, and in ten years forestry had become the province's primary industry.[8]

New Brunswick's forests provided pine for the masts of the Royal Navy during the American Revolution. Harvesting was conducted to such an extent that it caused Captain John Munro to observe that in the port of Saint John in 1783, there were enough masts to fill ten ships.[9]

Bear Nicholas also reported how the timber merchants "seized control of great tracts of land and sent in gangs of cutters."[10] By the mid-1820s the forests and animal habitats were so disrupted that for the Maliseets, hunting for survival was in peril. In addition, the Nashwaak River, a tributary of the Saint John River that is known for its abundant salmon population and which flows 113 kilometres from the west-central part of the province to Fredericton, was so polluted with sawdust from the sawmills that the salmon had disappeared from the river.[11]

Graeme Wynn notes that a subtle shift in the nature of the forest industry, and in particular its economic dynamics, would gradually create a large wedge between workers and owners, resulting in an eventual loss in independence for the common man, a situation that would heighten vulnerability and powerlessness for decades to come.

The same author further clarifies the significance of the transformations:

> Between 1800 and 1850, the scatter of small lumbering and commercial enterprises that characterized the timber trade in its early years was gradually replaced by a more tightly integrated system in which a handful of larger concerns were dominant ... Especially in the northeast of the province, the lines of entrepreneurial control over the trade were firmly drawn by mid-century. These broad changes were still only dimly perceived for what they were – early stages of transformation that would eventually recast the very nature of life in the province – but as they occurred, the social and economic differentiation of society in New Brunswick increased.[12]

By 1875, timber reserves, land set aside for use for the forestry industry, covered 9,375 square miles of the province,[13] a full third of the timber reserves held in Ontario, a province much more vast in size. Impressive increases in exports of lumber products from the Miramichi region in one year, from 1878 to 1879, speak to the ongoing productivity and aspirations of the industry:

> The lumber and timber exports from the port of Miramichi, for seven months as compared to 1878 were: 69,291.759 cubic feet vs. 76,293,375 cubic feet in 1879. Most of this product went to Ireland, London, and the Continent ... The port of Miramichi also shipped 287 tons of birch lumber for 1879 as compared to 27 tons in 1878. Pine was up to 247 tons vs. 45 tons in 1878.[14]

Dan Soucoup's history of New Brunswick's logging days reveals that wages were paid monthly to those woodcutters who were also provided with their lodging and meals in the camps, and he notes that the ban of alcohol in the province in the 1860s would have ensured even more money went home with them in the spring.[15] Opportunities for rural men supplying the labour for the industry were abundant; in 1880, a prominent Miramichi lumberman named William Richards was running twenty-five lumber camps that employed 480 men.[16]

Change was inevitable, however, and with a greatly reduced need for ties for railway construction and decrease in demands from overseas, the foundations for the industry had destabilized by 1920. Forestry was not about to decline as a central industry, however:

> Pulp wood into newsprint and paper products now became the next big thing … Everyone clamored to build a pulp and paper plant and International Paper was now the largest papermakers in the world. It was planning to build three plants in Canada including one on the east coast … in the end, Dalhousie with its deep harbour and some financial incentives from town council, was able to beat out Campbellton as the location for the giant new plant.[17]

The decision was indeed a fortunate one for the northern New Brunswick community of Dalhousie and the surrounding area, given that the Depression years would soon be upon the region. With the opening of the New Brunswick International Paper Mill on 1 March 1930 came jobs and new workers. Within a year fifty-five tons of newsprint were being produced and as many as 1,000 workers found employment there. The mill became a community economic asset that would endure eighty years.[18]

Fisheries

The cooperative movement played a fundamental role in New Brunswick's fisheries. A commission set up by the federal government in 1927 examined the fisheries crisis in the Maritimes. Important outcomes were the birth of the cooperative organization, the United Maritime Fishermen, and the recommendation by the Honourable Pierre J.A. Cardin, Canada's head of the Department of Marine and Fisheries, that Dr Moses Coady be appointed to organize cooperatives:

> Within that large association, Fr. Livain Chiasson of Shippagan and Martin J. Légère of Caraquet set up local fishermen's associations along New Brunswick's Acadian coast. Those associations were based on coop

> strategies consistent with the ideal of the movement spearheaded by Rev. Moses Coady and Fr. Jimmy Tompkins of St. Francis Xavier University in Antigonish. Those strategies sought to extricate the fishermen from their problems by helping them find efficient methods of acquiring fishing equipment at better cost and selling the fish they caught.[19]

The following provides an outline of significant developments in New Brunswick's fisheries:

> During the post-war era, in the mid-1940s to be precise, John McNair's government, Fisheries Minister André Doucet and civil servant Hédard Robichaud worked with federal authorities to industrialize New Brunswick's fisheries. Traditional fishermen were being squeezed out: it was time for fishermen to gain their share of fishery resources and supply the coastal processing plants. The provincial government set up the Fishermen's Loan Board of New Brunswick, which later became the New Brunswick Fisheries Development Board (1978). Through that board, the fishing fleet was rejuvenated and trawlers were added to it. Traditional fishermen were strongly critical of trawlers, which had been dubbed "sea scavengers" 25 years earlier. The Gloucester, Chaleur, and Charlotte type trawlers were built in Bas-Caraquet, Blacks Harbour, and Port Greville. Launched in the late 1940s and early 1950s, they performed as anticipated by taking in larger catches.
>
> Now that the fleet had been upgraded, the impact of those increased catches was not long in coming. In 1968, the province reached a new peak in fish landings (upwards of 244,000 metric tonnes). Catches of herring and snow crab soared, offsetting low catches of cod and lobster. Those larger catches not only filled the needs of the processing plants; they also brought about the construction of refrigerated warehouses, an example being the Shippagan warehouse, in which the federal and provincial governments and Connors Brothers Limited invested. The Fishermen's Loan Board also took an interest in diversifying the species fished and in training for fishermen. So it was that the School of Fisheries opened in Caraquet in 1959.[20]

In the late 1940s, New Brunswick had powerful advocates who spoke in favour of Newfoundland joining the confederation, while some provinces such as Nova Scotia voiced opposition. The cod industry at the time was important in the northeastern Acadian Peninsula. If cod had been a more predominant industry in English communities, or if the many Acadian families who relied on cod fishing for a living had held vocal and political power, a greater resistance to Newfoundland might have emerged, as it did in Nova Scotia. However, there was "no contest" for the economically and politically powerless Acadian community, as Corey Slumkoski aptly notes, "Acadian concerns would have counted for less in 1940s New Brunswick than the endorsement of a prominent senator and industrialist."[21]

New Brunswick's source of pride late in the 1940s became, instead, its long-established sardine industry of loyalist origins[22] in the south:

> Charlotte county accounted for 98 percent of New Brunswick's annual sardine catch in 1948. In 1947 the Sardine was New Brunswick's most lucrative fish resource, with the market value for the province's canned sardines being $5,683,213. When the $926,339 received for the fresh and salted sardines is added to that figure the total value of the New Brunswick sardine fishery in 1947 was $6,609,552, displacing the lobster industry as the province's most lucrative fishery.[23]

Sardines success notwithstanding, it is worthy to note that at the beginning of the 1940s, Saint Andrews, New Brunswick, had earned the title "Live Lobster Capital of North America" and hosted the first lobster "ranch" in the world.[24]

Mining

According to Gwen Martin, author of a comprehensive text on the history of mining in New Brunswick, Indigenous people living in New Brunswick "used and traded various types of rocks and minerals for at least nine thousand years before European contact."[25] When Champlain arrived in 1604, it was with orders from the funder of his voyage, King Henri IV of France, to look for and extract gold, silver, copper, or other metals and minerals from mines. An Indigenous man named Messamouet is said to have led Champlain to the area of Beaver Harbour where rich copper deposits were found; however, the harsh winter didn't allow for further exploration.[26] As early as 1643 there is recorded evidence in the journals of Governor John Winthrop of the exportation of coal from what is believed to be Grand Lake, New Brunswick, to his home port of Boston. Coal mining in central New Brunswick, in the Minto and Chipman area, would see rapid and extensive development and investment in that industry and endure throughout the twentieth century. From its early days it attracted labourers, with the required experience and skills, from other countries.[27]

The province's (and Canada's) first provincial geologist was Abraham Gesner, who took up the position in 1838 and produced a geological survey within two years. After only four years the ruling government, unconvinced of the value of supporting such a position, dismissed him. According to Gwen Martin, Gesner's reports

> identified scores of potential mines and quarries and brought curious investors to the colony. Some of those deposits were developed almost immediately, while others were explored following his death. And in the 1950s, just as he predicted, the New Brunswick mineral industry achieved worldwide recognition after a long rite of passage marked by intrigue and foolishness, tragedy and farce.[28]

Martin describes the dramatic transformation of landscape in the name of profit, similar to the trajectory in New Brunswick's forestry industry, where resources were extracted and sent across the ocean to England on behalf of investors:

> Tetagouche Falls today is a lovely site with steep cliffs bracketing the river before it spills over the rock ledge into a swirl of foam and mist. In the early 1800s it was called *Tootoogoose,* meaning *squirrel jump* in Mi'kmaq, referring to how squirrels leap between overhanging branches to cross the gorge. Stevens arrived early in 1841 and broke the wilderness with a vengeance. His men excavated a sluiceway through solid rock. They built and installed a waterwheel to harness the falls and drive the mine machinery. They blasted an adit into the cliffs and raised 130 tons of manganese ore which was shipped to England over the autumn and following spring.[29]

The province has a long history of interest and exploration in various types of mining, but a significant point was 15 January 1953 when "news broke in the *Northern Miner* about a colossal base metal deposit near Bathurst. Its discovery prompted the largest staking rush in Canadian history, spawned a galaxy of lucrative mines and rekindled mineral exploration throughout the province."[30] Writing of the Belledune metal smelter and the especially large Brunswick No. 12 deposit that began producing in 1964, Martin refers to "political and corporate writings, the cacophony of accusations and counter-accusations" that accompanied the mine's and smelter's openings. Significant players included

> a ring of contestants, the most prominent being Premier Louis Robichaud, J.J. Boylen, industrialist K.C. Irving, St. Joseph's Lead Company of Missouri and Noranda Mines Ltd. Noranda eventually gained control of BMS in 1967 with the help of Robichaud and over vehement protests from the Irving faction in a battle of the titans that left J.J. Boylen anxiously wringing his hands, caught in the midst of what degenerated into a personal feud between Robichaud and Irving.[31]

Economic Development

The three Maritime provinces – Nova Scotia, New Brunswick, and Prince Edward Island[32] – witnessed a doubling of populations in urban areas from the late 1800s through to the first decade of the 1900s, while the rural population decreased by 25 percent.[33] Ernest Forbes and Del Muise point out that in the first decade of the 1900s the urban populations in New Brunswick increased by 22,262. For those who stayed on the land, the range of activities for subsistence included cutting pulpwood or involvement with the maple-syrup industry, barrel building, gardening, and woods work, employment in mills or work on road and railway.[34]

An examination of New Brunswick's fiscal realities from the era reveals substantial challenges, in part due to geography and the need to build roads and bridges across its many rivers, along with ever-deepening debt. Those factors in turn made poverty an inevitable reality for many who, had they lived in most other provinces, would have received higher levels of financial assistance when in need and had more opportunities for work.

Rural and urban settings differed in many ways. In 1930, two-thirds of the province's citizens were living in rural areas, sanctioned by government strategy nationally and provincially to direct certain groups to remain or to settle there. Programs of "relief" appearing in the 1930s coincided with efforts of the government to strongly encourage people reliant on welfare to settle in rural areas.

A 1931 federal initiative, intended to insert monies previously used for relief into shifting people to rural areas with scant populations, initially received an enthusiastic response in New Brunswick, particularly among Acadians. A roadblock arose, however: "when the municipalities learned that their share of the capital required to outfit the farmers was much more than they were paying for relief in other forms, they refused to participate. The unemployed took out land but did so under nineteenth-century settlement legislation, with only a fraction of the support provided by the national program."[35]

Work projects were quickly developed to ensure that those receiving assistance "earned" it through road construction and forest-related initiatives:

> The provincial government built roads, gave the settlers a few implements, supplied $4.07 worth of groceries four times a year, paid bonuses for land cleared and planted, and periodically allowed settlers to cut and sell timber from Crown lands. By 1936 new families were taking out land at a rate of about 600 per year. Concentrated in the northern counties, they created a few dozen communities, including Allardville in Gloucester county, Trout Brook in Madawaska, St. Arthur in Restigouche, Alnwick in Northumberland, and Bronson in Queens. By 1939 the new settlers remaining on their land grants totaled 11,165.[36]

New Brunswick's forests provided many of its residents with at least a subsistence livelihood over the centuries, yet lumber-related industries have always been impacted by the ups and downs of the marketplace. Dramatic variation in prices was experienced in this sector during the 1930s: when pulpwood prices sank from $9 a cord to $4.50 or $5, worker salaries dived from $2.50 to less than $1. The winter season employment by a hiring office out of Moncton of anywhere from five to eight thousand men for lumbering shrank to only three to four hundred individuals being hired.[37]

Demographics are another highly relevant contextual consideration. Data reveals that "on March 31, 1943, there were 11,818 old age pensioners. There were also more blind pensioners in relation to population than in any other province. The average old age pension payment was only $15.27 monthly, less than that of any province except Prince Edward Island."[38]

Meanwhile Saint John, a bustling city for more than a century, was facing stresses unique to its characteristics: "as the largest commercial and industrial centre of the province and the major port of entry for immigrants, its residents had to provide for a larger number of transients, pauper immigrants and parish paupers, than any other area of the province."[39] Immigrants suffering from disease or those especially destitute were sometimes assisted through the Provincial Emigrant [sic] fund, which began in 1832 and was still operating in 1859. The provincial funding was given to overseers of the poor and health officers to respond to requests.[40]

As part of the Antigonish Movement in Nova Scotia, New Brunswick, and Prince Edward Island, cooperatives flourished during the 1930s. Fishing, farming and credit unions were common particularly on the east coast and the north shore where Acadians lived.[41] While governments at provincial and federal levels were failing rural New Brunswick citizens, some economic strategizing and hope could be found in the blossoming Antigonish Movement that spread education about creating cooperatives and credit unions throughout the province, particularly among Acadian communities. Amid counties where illiteracy among francophones prevailed in the 1930s, fishing, farming, and other cooperatives as well as credit unions emerged, with more than 180 in existence by 1939 in the six counties where the Roman Catholic religion and Acadian heritage were most extensive.[42] Promoting values of mutual aid, self-sufficiency and education of members, the contribution of the Antigonish Movement to regional development is undeniable.

Regional disparity is another important background variable to consider when reflecting on New Brunswick in the first half of the twentieth century:

> Taxable valuations per capita of population vary greatly from county to county and from town to town. The counties and towns in the northern part of the province are very poor, by contrast with those in the lower Saint John Valley. The provincial government, in its submission to the Rowell-Sirois Commission in 1938, pointed out the difficulties that the poorer municipalities had in supporting schools and in meeting social service charges.[43]

Marcel Arseneau, a social worker interviewed for this research, affirmed that in his role as a social worker at the Campbellton Provincial (psychiatric) Hospital[44] he was very aware that certain counties were richer than others, which meant that certain counties were more generous with amounts provided to residents. However, he emphasized that amounts given were minimal, no matter the county of origin. Only strict essentials were provided: he spoke of being in a position at times of providing food or wood and oil for home heating. He also mentioned that to his knowledge, medical prescriptions continued to be made available to patients through the hospital pharmacy, were paid for by the hospital, and delivered through the mail when necessary.[45]

As late as the 1960s, taxation levels affected rural living. In a study entitled "Life and Poverty in the Maritimes," by Pierre-Yves Pepin (1968), interviews with a parish priest in Kent County revealed that "taxes were a serious problem for the farmers – $400 to $500 on a gross income of $2,000. Everything was taxed: land, buildings, animals. The farmer would even pull down an unused barn in order to decrease his assessment."[46]

Power and Politics

To understand New Brunswick and the reasons why outmoded social welfare structures (discussed in the next chapter) pervaded for so long, one must consider the part played by the cultural mores of the two settler populations. Hugh G. Thorburn noted that

> economically, socially and therefore politically, New Brunswick is one of the most static provinces in Canada. The two traditions from which it sprang, the Loyalists and the French Acadian, show respect for the past and suspicion of change. The province, while remaining relatively poor, has been spared the full impact of the violent economic fluctuations that stirred radicalism in the west. Also, as there is so little immigration, new political ideas and methods from outside have made very little impression.[47]

Although the desperate financial needs of many New Brunswick families were apparent to social welfare advocates, other issues were preoccupying the provincial governments in the forties and fifties. For one thing, the period following the Second World War saw conflict and competition with neighbours Nova Scotia and Prince Edward Island, according to Slumkoski, who notes that "the internecine competition among the Maritime Provinces for what limited funds were available meant that the region emerged from the conflict fragmented and in an even weaker position relative to the rest of Canada than it had been in during the Depression."[48] The same author suggests that Liberal Premier John McNair focused budget expenditures on road development and hydroelectric facility creation. Don Hoyt gives a description of McNair's achievements: "Reform-minded and progressive, McNair greatly expanded the role of Government in the life of the province, created a

Civil Service Commission, instituted a large-scale rural electrification program, built a consolidated school system in rural New Brunswick and made Fredericton the centre of operations for the Government and New Brunswick Electric Power Commission."[49]

Federal-provincial political negotiations during this period clearly required savvy and intelligence, particularly in a context in which individual provinces, even neighbouring ones, did not share a collaborative spirit:

> J.L. Ilsley's budget speech announced the federal government's intention to negotiate ad hoc tax rental agreements with the provinces. New Brunswick Premier McNair was quick to enter into an agreement with Ottawa, but he soon saw the error of his hasty actions. When provinces that had delayed entering tax rental agreements with Ottawa, such as Nova Scotia, received better terms as enticements for their cooperation, New Brunswickers called for a renegotiation of their deal, and McNair was eventually granted terms on par with Nova Scotia. All of this points to the lack of regional cooperation that prevailed in the Maritimes in the years immediately preceding Newfoundland's Confederation.[50]

While there are examples of federal funding coming to the province during McNair's time as Premier, the following illustrates a decision fraught with frustration:

> Following his victory at the polls in New Brunswick in September 1952, Progressive Conservative Premier Hugh John Flemming began an aggressive campaign to develop "power for industry." When the St. Laurent government – already committed to mass capital infusions to build and maintain the St. Lawrence Seaway – refused to provide assistance for the Beechwood power project on the Saint John River, Flemming was outraged.[51]

In the first half of the twentieth century most New Brunswickers made their living from occupations that saw them working directly with the land or in industries that profited from natural-resource exploitation. However, the reliance on resource-based industries would not last:

> During the 1950s alone, the numbers of people working in agriculture dropped by 49 per cent, in fishing and trapping by 37 per cent, in forestry by 24 per cent, and in mining by 22 per cent. The exit from primary pursuits continued through the 1960s. Each sector had its own cycle, but

all were reshaped to meet the demands of an increasingly bureaucratized, centralized, mechanized, and, ultimately, computerized world.[52]

Irving and McCain: New Brunswick's Industrial Giants

New Brunswick industrialists Kenneth Colin Irving and brothers Harrison and Wallace McCain developed empires that continue to be substantial on an international scale at the time of this writing. Numerous biographies have been written about the life of Irving. John DeMont's work uncovered that

> for years Irving had grown rich by playing the various municipal councils off against one another, enabling him to get the best possible tax deal for his companies. Irving Pulp & Paper, J.D. Irving, Ocean Steel, Brunswick Mining and Smelting, Saint John Shipbuilding and Dry Dock and the Irving refinery all enjoyed juicy tax breaks with fixed rates, regardless of inflation and changing land values. The amounts were often absurdly low in comparison with taxes paid by private individuals. Under the original agreements, taxes for the $50-million refinery, for example, moved from $51,000 in 1960 to a projected $75,000 in 1990 – a fraction of what the usual business taxes would have been for an operation of that size. Irving Pulp & Paper paid a fixed rate of $65,000, about one-quarter of what it would normally have forked out.[53]

In the years immediately preceding the political-landscape transformation inspired by Robichaud's era in the 1960s, New Brunswick witnessed much government assistance devoted to making Saint John a port of distinction. Meanwhile, entrepreneurs with tremendous power and influence had taken centre stage, notably the McCains and the Irvings. In his recent book *New Brunswick: An Illustrated History*, Ronald Rees entitled one chapter "The Oligarchs," referring to the two entrepreneurs. Conrad and Hiller lament the fact that "K.C. Irving moved to Bermuda to avoid Canadian taxation even though his oil, transportation, and media empire benefited greedily from government assistance."[54]

The McCain brothers, Harrison and Wallace, embarked on a joint business venture in their home community of Florenceville in 1957, benefitting from their parents' seed potato business. Donald Savoie, in his biography of Harrison McCain, refers to the close and respectful relationship between McCain and Louis Robichaud. Savoie cites an interview in which McCain says he wrote a letter to Robichaud in the period when newspapers, including the *Saint John Telegraph Journal*, were giving the premier very negative coverage. McCain says he wrote words of reassurance to Robichaud, telling him he was not alone, that he was doing the right thing, and that he should tell the other voices to "go to hell." Support from an anglophone business leader appears surprising for the time:

> Robichaud's reform package unleased a firestorm of protest. Some Anglophone business leaders, the economically strong urban areas, and the English-language media went at Robichaud with all the determination and venom they could muster ... The 1967 provincial election was a critical moment for Robichaud's plan. If he won, he would be able to implement the ambitious program. If he lost, the plan was doomed. The province's largest private sector firms were joined against Robichaud. They financed the return of flamboyant, fluently bilingual, fiery orator and high-profile Tory politician J.C. Van Horne in one of the most hard-fought campaigns in the province's history. Harrison McCain stood tall for Robichaud.[55]

Voting and Politics

Gaining the right to vote is an essential step toward affirmation of equality for individuals and for entire population groups. The right to vote symbolizes recognition and sharing of power through voicing preference for candidates, parties, and policies. Eligibility criteria were blatantly discriminatory:

> Up until 1830, Catholics could not vote in the province of New Brunswick. After this year, it was possible to vote after swearing allegiance to the King and his Protestant heirs. Catholics who were not willing to swear in allegiance to the King and his Protestant heirs were not allowed to vote. Since French Canadians were usually not land owners and were mostly Catholics, they were more often than not excluded from the voting process.[56]

In New Brunswick, reaching the right-to-vote milestone varied dramatically. Historian William Spray maintained that

> Carleton and his Council took it upon themselves to issue special instructions in October 1785. These instructions to the sheriffs of the various counties informed them that "the votes of Blacks are not to be admitted." This practice of excluding the Blacks from voting was to continue for many

> years and there are no records of when Black people were first allowed to vote. This is difficult to determine since they were not excluded by any law or act passed by the legislature. They were simply prevented from voting in early years by special instructions issued by the Lieutenant-Governor and the Executive Council. This practice still continued in 1820 and certainly went on in Saint John until at least 1840.[57]

Women were excluded specifically by the Elections Act of 1849. By 1886, if a woman owned property, she could vote in municipal elections – but only if she was single. Women won the right to vote in 1919, but it wasn't until 1934 that they became eligible to run for election to provincial office; Frances Fish was the first woman who ran provincially, in 1935. It would be 1967 before New Brunswick would see its first woman elected to the Legislative Assembly, Brenda Robertson.[58]

The last group to receive voting privileges were Indigenous peoples, who would need to wait one hundred years after Canada became a country:

> In 1963, the section of the 1952 Elections Act which had disqualified from voting, "every Indian person ordinarily resident on an Indian reservation except one who has served or is serving in Her Majesty's armed forces" was repealed. It had originally reflected the federal Indian Act through which native Indians living on reservation lost their native status if they chose to vote during elections other than for band council.[59]

Until 1935 New Brunswickers voted for candidates rather than parties in provincial elections: "For many years, electors seemed to vote based on the candidates' personal inclinations, such as religion, place of birth, social class, drinking habits, and family ties. The only specific divisions [sic] that seemed to exist were between the 'government' and the 'opposition.'"[60]

Historically, Conservatives and Liberals are the two parties that dominated the political landscape and its electoral process in New Brunswick. However, as in other parts of Canada, social and economic conditions drove some citizens to not only question but indeed to challenge that domination, particularly when faced with blatant inequality. An example is that in 1910 Maritime socialists became members of the Socialist Party of Canada. They comprised 10 percent of party membership nationally, a surprisingly high proportion, when one considers that the Maritimes represented only 13 percent of the Canadian population.[61]

New Brunswickers supported the Cooperative Commonwealth Federation (CCF) in New Brunswick in the greatest numbers in the 1940s, despite a largely anti-labour climate and opposition to the CCF by entrenched power structures. Allen Seager referred to John Babbitt McNair, Liberal premier of the province from 1940 to 1952, as an anti-labour "hardliner," comparing him to Mitchell Hepburn in Ontario (1934–42) and Maurice Duplessis (1936–9; 1944–59) in Québec as "violent opposers of communism and industrial unionism."[62] McNair did introduce the Labour Relations Act in 1945, in recognition of the popular wartime labour reforms that had begun, thus co-opting the political left.[63]

George Castleden (member of parliament for Yorkton, Saskatchewan) was sent to New Brunswick by the national CCF office before the election in 1944 to help the party. He observed that people in New Brunswick were "almost completely ignorant of the policies, the principles, program or organization of the CCF," although he did allow that those involved in labour organizations, pulp and paper industries, and the railways were well-informed.[64] However, despite this, in the 1944 election, the CCF won 68,248 votes, which amounted to 13 percent of the total votes in the province.[65]

The CCF was unable to elect anyone to the Legislative Assembly because the party faced many challenges. The party lacked funds, as it eschewed contributions from business, but fundraising from the average person in one of the poorest provinces in the country was challenging. Experienced candidates were difficult to find, and were not privy to the internal workings of the government. The CCF had scant funds for advertising, and similar to experiences in other provinces, they were scorned by the media. For example, the editor of both Saint John newspapers refused to even print advertising paid for by the CCF or anything related to it.[66] As George Castleden noted, relatively few New Brunswickers were aware of the CCF policies and platform, likely could not afford the price of the printed materials, and given the high rate of illiteracy, were unlikely to be able to read the materials if they could afford it.[67] In this anti-labour, anti-CCF climate, a person might jeopardize their employment if known to be associated with the CCF. In contrast, McNair's power and party machinery provided a formidable opponent. He enjoyed much support from both anglophone and francophone voters for various reforms that were implemented for civil servants, including the Labour Relations Act in 1945, and for introducing the Adoption Act in 1947 – along with his achievements in modernization that were substantially aided by the injection of funding from the federal government for regional development.

New Brunswick was also affected by class divisions. The second chapter of this book sheds light on the imposition of culture and political structures by the United Empire Loyalists who were granted land that would be called New Brunswick. Inherent in the sense of superiority held by many of the people with a Loyalist background was a belief in the maintenance of their privilege and rights, as well as an assumption that the working class and minority groups, including Acadians and Mi'kmaq and Maliseet peoples, were inferior or "second class." Such attitudes spelled dire consequences for people with the least power.

An unsettling story recounted by a man in the first half of the 1930s, revealed that "middle management" had significant roles and used power in abusive ways, which contributed to the destitution of non-unionized employees and their families. We are told by the story's author (himself a manager of unionized employees at Canadian National Railway in Moncton, and thus in a different type of employment environment) that an unofficial "club" of fifteen to twenty men with management-level responsibilities in key companies of the province would gather socially on a regular basis in the Miramichi region for fishing and hunting. A scenario similar to the following would often ensue during these "meetings":

> We'd be sitting around and one would say something like, "Well, Bert, I'm going to trim off some more fat this week." This might have been a foundry or a sawmill. Bert would ask how many, and the other fellow would say five, three, six, whatever, and Bert would say, "Okay, Harry, if you can, I'll wait a week and match you," or he'd say, "That's the way you see it, eh? Okay, let me know if there's a ruckus, and if not, I'll do the same." This type of thing went on, week after week, and I saw maybe fifteen or twenty of my good friends dealing in men's lives, their wives' lives, the very futures of their children, maybe two dozen children, and doing it just like they were raising each other at stud poker. Some guy in lumbering would say, "I'm asking my sawyers to take an eight percent cut." He meant he was *telling* them they would be cut eight percent. No ifs, ands or buts. No union, so bugger you. If it worked out – and there was no such thing as work-to-rule and that in those days, not really – then the next guy would do it, and in a month, the whole industry in southern New Brunswick would have sawyers making less a shift, and in another month, that rate would be standard throughout the Maritimes. See how easy it worked?[68]

This narrative provides a clear demonstration of the class-based oppression that took place, with dire consequences for the individuals and families whose subsistence and quality of life would be severely affected. To the powerful it seemed little more than a game. An observation by historical geographer Graeme Wynn provides a relevant analysis of the situation:

> Capitalist and workman became ever more distinct. Cash and contract increasingly defined the relationship between master and man, and for aspiring immigrant and native son alike, the possibilities of achieving yeomanly independence in New Brunswick ended with the emergence of a nascent proletariat in the Province.[69]

Such scenarios create environments in which disgruntled and desperate workers become motivated to look to new ideas and political philosophies in hopes of change. H.H. Stuart (1873–1952) had been one of the founders of the Fredericton Socialist League in 1902 and, at the Moncton meeting convened by the Federation of Labour on 23 June 1933, he would become one of the first officers of the New Brunswick branch of the CCF. On that date 1,000 people at the Moncton Stadium listened to the guest speaker, J.S. Woodsworth (1874–1942), one of the founders of the national CCF movement and its first national leader.[70]

This chapter began with a description of the forestry, fisheries, agricultural, and mining resources that one could say have defined economic development in New Brunswick. It then shifted to a chronological exploration of shifts and transitions related to the populations and opportunities that unfolded. The latter part of the chapter contrasted the powerful industrialist influences with attempts at radical political movements. In the next chapter, we examine poverty, inadequate living conditions, and marginalization alongside the haphazard social welfare approaches and systems constructed to respond to social issues.

4

Poor Law Legislation and the Poverty Experience

LINDA TURNER AND LAUREL LEWEY

Having described significant components of New Brunswick's historical, economic, and political contexts, this chapter turns its focus to a consideration of the "Poor Laws" legislation and how they affected the day-to-day life of New Brunswickers. The Poor Laws established structures such as the "parish system," the "overseer of the poor" and "poorhouse commissioners," and institutions where the destitute were sent, including the "almshouse" (often called the "poorhouse" and later known as the municipal home) and the "workhouse." "Contracting out" of people unable to provide for their own needs to other New Brunswickers who fed and supported them in exchange for their labour, a transaction sometimes achieved through public auctions, is also described. The first section concludes with a critical analysis of how the continued existence of the Poor Laws up to the 1960s affected the establishment of a progressive social welfare system in the province.

The second section of this chapter offers a preliminary background into governmental responses to the needs of New Brunswickers unable to provide for themselves. It is accompanied by glimpses into the experience of poverty through several decades, from the 1920s to the 1960s, when professionally qualified social workers are known to have been practising in the province.

Living under the Poor Laws

A unique feature of New Brunswick's social service origins is the influence on daily life of laws born six centuries earlier; they remained in effect until Equal Opportunity legislation was created in the 1960s. For example, aspects of the 1351 Statute of Labourers persisted, such as the power of a governing body to mandate workers into employment and to set parameters around who they could work for. In Great Britain in 1601, forty-three sets of laws pertaining to the government's responsibility for residents and related issues became what are referred to as the Elizabethan Poor Laws of 1601.[1] The loyalist influx from New England transported philosophies and practices arising from those laws to New Brunswick. With the passing of "An Act for Preventing Idleness and Disorders and for punishing Rogues, Vagabonds, and other Idle and Disorderly Persons" at the opening legislature's first session in 1786, the Poor Law model was established. According to James Whalen, "The New Brunswick Poor Law of 1786 closely resembled the New England legislation based on the Elizabethan Poor Law of 1601 and contained provision for compulsory assessment on the residents of each parish for relief of their own poor."[2] It is noteworthy that neither Upper Canada nor Lower Canada relied on the Poor Laws. Therese Jennissen and Colleen Lundy suggest that in Ontario, although civil law was adopted from Britain, the Poor Laws were not. Rather, individuals had to rely on themselves, their family, or community and then ultimately seek help from voluntary agencies or organizations. In Lower Canada, or Québec, the Roman Catholic Church looked after the poor.[3]

Harry Cassidy was a high-profile figure who was dean of the University of Toronto's School of Social Work in the 1940s. In his seminal Canadian social policy book *Public Health and Welfare Reorganization*, he offers a clear portrait of the way New Brunswick attended to health and welfare needs through the local government. He explains:

> The province is divided into fifteen counties, whose councils levy taxes and carry on the main functions of local government in the rural districts. The rural areas are further divided into 152 parishes, which have administrative and financial responsibilities for poor relief. In addition there are three cities (Saint John, Fredericton, and Moncton), twenty towns, and three villages, which share the usual powers and responsibilities of local government with the counties in which they are situated – except in the case of Fredericton, which is quite independent of its districts.[4]

Carol D. Proctor, a social worker practising in the early 1950s, shares the following description of parishes in the region where she was employed. The term parish in the Poor Laws context refers to civic subunits of the county rather than subunits in a religious sense:

> They had names like Tormentine Parish, Botsford Parish, Sackville Parish, and Dorchester Parish, and there would be at least two overseers of the poor

> in each one of those parishes that went to the county council meetings. The seat of our government was in Dorchester for Westmorland County. There would be two people. They would always be men in those days. They would go to have these county meetings and they would decide how county taxes were going to be collected and spent ... the actual tax money gathered in that area stayed there to do what was needed ... it would have to cover educational costs and so on.[5]

One aspect of the Poor Laws was a residency requirement: the stipulation that people must reside in a parish for a set period of time before that parish became responsible for the cost of supporting them. This law appeared in 1876, when one year of residency in a particular parish was needed to qualify for relief. By the 1940s, a minimum of three years of residency in a parish or city or town was required.[6]

Overseers of the Poor and the Almshouse Commissioners

Each year, three individuals were selected for each parish by justices of the peace or later by county councils to fulfil the role of "overseer of the poor." Their role was to be the provider of services, money, or goods to poor and sick members of the community, as outlined by the statutes in place. Fines were given to individuals who refused to accept the role or were found to be neglectful in their duties. Responsibilities were said to be "extensive and their powers discretionary."[7]

Within their respective jurisdictions, overseers of the poor primarily attended to the non-institutional care of poor persons, while "Municipal Home Commissioners," under Section 205 of the Revised Statutes of New Brunswick (1927), held responsibilities primarily with poor individuals inside almshouse establishments, where they had the authority to make and enforce rules and regulations.

Each year, overseers of the poor presented a statement of the needs of those living in poverty in their area: how many individuals and families required support, and to what degree. The county council assessed the submission and subsequently demanded that the assessors collect enough money in taxes to provide for the care of those in need in that area for the next year.

A commentary on the discretionary powers of persons occupying the role of overseer of the poor is provided by Carol Proctor:

> They were well-meaning people but they did have a lot of prejudices. Often, the overseer would refuse to assist the children of alcoholics or to assist an

unwed mother because of the values they held towards these people. I had to do a lot of public education around their prejudices and found it very challenging as a social worker to work under this system.[8]

Richard Duffy, a welfare administrator in the Saint John area who participated in this research, shared a story of meeting an older gentleman in the 1960s who believed himself to be the last child handled by the overseers of the poor from Gagetown. He was sold to a farm family for a sum of money and in exchange was clothed and kept until the age of twenty-one.[9]

Interestingly, within the British new Poor Law of 1834, the term overseer of the poor officially disappeared, yet in New Brunswick the role with title continued, another reflection of the conservative continuation of earlier practices.

In some communities, such as St. Andrews, the persons acting as overseers of the poor were simultaneously the "Almshouse (or Poorhouse) Commissioners," meaning they maintained all responsibilities related to "Indoor Relief," literally the support of people who did not have the means to support themselves, by giving food and accommodation in exchange for service inside a "Poorhouse" or "Workhouse."[10] They held a firm stance against "outdoor relief" – that is, providing support to poor people living anywhere other than the poorhouse – based on a belief that it would result in people not wanting to work and would be extravagant for the parish. Yet outdoor relief was provided in other counties.

Correspondence between a municipal inspector for Northumberland County and the alms house commissioner, dated 1937, reveals a preoccupation with ensuring that assistance was being given only to those whose life circumstances indicated extreme need. The commissioner was asked to record names of families in the parish who were receiving alms assistance and the reason it was necessary. Acceptable reasons were disability, illness, widowed status, or another cause. The inspector concluded, "Real honest-to-goodness paupers must be looked after, that is granted, but there are always some who are willing to enter this class who can very well look after themselves if they make the effort; it is these that Commissioners must protect themselves and the County against."[11]

Almshouses (Municipal Homes)

Gerard Boychuk provides an excellent overview of New Brunswick's strong adherence to the Poor Laws and of its practices regarding care of people in need. He notes that the way assistance was provided resembled the principles underlying the (British) new Poor Law of 1834, particularly because it so firmly insisted that people should be maintained within municipal homes. He refers to the Canadian Welfare Council's observation that New Brunswick adhered to outdoor relief (supporting people to continue to live in the community) far less often than most other provinces. Even as late as the 1940s, Boychuk has noted that in Saint John, if there was space for people in need inside the almshouse, then "outdoor relief" or providing support for individuals who wanted to live in their homes in the city was not an option.[12]

Comparing situations among provinces, Alvin Finkel observes that

> distinctions were made between the "deserving poor," that is, individuals whom social custom argued could not be expected to be in the labour force, and the "undeserving poor," that is, the able-bodied unemployed. The latter were treated in the Canadas as slackers and denied outdoor relief, while in Nova Scotia and New Brunswick, practically all impoverished people, whether regarded as unfortunates or idlers, ended up in the workhouse.[13]

In many areas of the province, local authorities opted to build institutions to house those without the means to support and care for themselves. These were known as "almshouses" and later as "municipal homes." A "workhouse" referred to similar institutions; however, individuals who were deemed in need of correctional services would be sent there, as Whalen explains: "...the almshouse provided food, shelter and protection to dependent persons while the workhouse afforded accommodation for indolent who needed some form of correction or detention."[14] However, people were supposed to work in both institutions. As mentioned above, New Brunswick (and Nova Scotia) consistently shied away from assistance to people who were capable of (and may have preferred) staying in their homes. As Boychuk explains,

> By providing assistance in the poorhouse the state did acknowledge responsibility for care of the poor; however, indoor relief appeared most clearly geared to reinforcing the market and family by providing a visible reminder to participants in those institutions of the fate that awaited them should they require assistance. Not only was indoor relief stigmatizing, it actually posed significant dangers to the health of the unfortunate residents (especially through infectious diseases). Work even at sub-subsistence wage levels or life even within a dysfunctional family were probably more attractive alternatives.[15]

Residents of an almshouse, including children, were given duties and roles to contribute to the functioning of the home and to the feeding and housing of its inhabitants. Saint John was the site of New Brunswick's first almshouse in 1801, followed by four county almshouses during the nineteenth century: York County Almshouse and Workhouse, Fredericton (1823); Saint John City and County Almshouse and Workhouse, built in the Parish of Simonds (1843); Northumberland County Almshouse and Workhouse, erected in the Parish of Chatham, (1869); and Kings County Almshouse and Poor Farm in the Parish of Norton (1899).[16]

Alvin Finkel notes the ideological problem arising from the mixing of people who were unemployed with people whose life circumstances or personal capacities imposed limitations:

> The place of the "dissolute" within the same subgroup as the merely unemployed speaks volumes to the mindset of the elites who framed social policy. Upper Canada's governor, Sir Francis Bond Head, commented that "workhouses should be made repulsive" so that anyone capable of eking out a living any other way would avoid them.[17]

This view is embedded in the current neoconservative ideology that ensures that public social assistance is sufficiently inadequate, thereby coercing people to seek any kind of work. From their earliest days, almshouses were characterized by overcrowding, questionable administrative practices, inadequate and unsatisfactory provision of nourishment, limited activity offerings, and a mingling of adults and children with diverse and unrelated issues, including disability, poverty, mental illness, unmarried parental status, and intellectual limitations. Numerous times, in the absence of a medical facility, people who were deathly ill with such diseases as cholera and typhoid were brought in to reside among the other residents, creating additional outbreaks and death.[18]

Criticism from the New Brunswick Child Welfare Survey from 1927 to 1930[19] focused on the lack of differentiation of needs and realities among people who found themselves living in an almshouse. As the conservative social worker Charlotte Whitton notes,

> the children share the life of the adults, aged, and infirm, who are in the almshouse, eating in the same rooms and sharing the same sleeping and toilet accommodations. In many cases aged men and women; the feeble minded; the senile; crippled and incurable; unmarried mothers;

> dependent families; children and infants were all found in the same home, separated only by one broad classification of sex.[20]

Moncton's municipal home in this period was said to be on a thirty-four-acre plot, located two-and-a-half miles from the city, with one large dormitory for men and a separate one for women. While lacking a sitting room of any kind, the building was said to "avoid the bleakness of the average institution," and though designed to accommodate thirty-five persons, it had seen as many as fifty-two residents, including children, at one time.[21] In 1938, a statistical analysis of causes of resident intakes included thirty-seven for "destitution," one pregnancy, two boys aged fourteen and fifteen through parental neglect, five unable to care for self, two due to "drink," one deportation from the U.S., one (TB) [tuberculosis] sanitarium discharge, one "bad" boy, aged fourteen, one illegitimate baby, and one "deserted (feeble-minded) wife." Ethnic background data showed thirty-two Roman Catholics, twenty Protestants, twenty-nine French Canadians, twenty-two British Canadians, and one German. Thirteen were included as having "obvious mental defects." Almost two-thirds of the residents had lived there for more than one year.[22]

An interviewee who recalls visiting such an institution in Saint John shared the following description. He talked about clients he had seen living at the "municipal home," which was the more common term for the almshouse by the mid-1940s, and describes their desperate situations, seemingly unchanged since the late 1920s:

> in some cases they ended up there because they had no place to live and no money, no income, no nothing ... whole families would end up there. Those were the days when they used lye soap and that sort of thing for disinfectant, and they would wash and scrub them all when they went in there, took all their clothes off and gave them used clothing ... this ritual ... was mandatory ... there were all ages and disabilities of all different kinds, blind and deformities and everything like that. Then there were just people who were mentally challenged and in poor health and no one to look after them.[23]

A report on New Brunswick's system of welfare written in 1949, by Bessie Touzel, a social worker with twenty-one years of experience at that time and assistant executive director of the Canadian Welfare Council, offers the reflection that the time had come, was even overdue, for a transformation of the enduring Poor Laws system of institutions as they existed:

> The Municipal Homes were provided for at a time when institutional care was considered the best solution for the "support of the poor" on the grounds that it provided shelter and some degree of physical care for those who were unable to care for themselves in the community, and at the same time provided a work-house for those who were considered "work-shy" or who were felt to need a mild form of detention. They were provided at a time when no other type of care was known, and when the special treatment and training now recognized as necessary for particular groups, such as the defective, was unknown also. Although they are now out-dated, they have survived in New Brunswick and in many instances the devotion of the staff has done much to minimize their defects.[24]

"Pauper Auctions" and "Contracting Out"

Another aspect of the Poor Laws was that unemployed people deemed to be "able-bodied," and therefore capable of working, could be forced by two or more overseers and justices of the peace to work for any person ready to hire them, under the threat of imprisonment with hard labour for refusing.[25]

Individuals and families unable to support themselves or facing barriers or challenges of any kind could be assigned by the "overseer of the poor" to live with other members of the county willing to accept the least amount of money drawn from taxpayers' pockets to house and feed them while simultaneously making them work for it. This contract system prevailed in these regions up to the late 1920s in numerous counties in the province.

Some parishes of New Brunswick participated in auctioning off to the lowest bidder – to spare county taxpayers unnecessary expense – people without the means to support themselves, so that the buyer could benefit from whatever labour they could extract from the person in exchange for room and board. One historian describes the inhumane nature of this phenomenon:

> Over the years the selling of the poor by auction degenerated to the place where no inspection was made of the homes of their purchasers, with the result that the lot of these unfortunate people, in some cases, was unbelievably

hard. They were grossly mistreated and forced to work beyond their ability. For clothing they received cast-off rags, insufficient to keep them warm. They were often hungry. Old men slept in barns; old women in woodshed lofts or on a pallet of straw on the floor of a cold room with a ragged quilt or piece of old carpet for covering. Worked beyond their strength, children became drudges.[26]

An account of such a "pauper auction" in Sussex, Kings County, is said to have appeared in a Saint John newspaper in 1884;[27] the last one is believed to have been held in Sussex in 1898.

Critiques of the Poor Laws System

The Poor Laws contributed to meagre and substandard realities for people who faced hardship and misfortune. In this section, we offer some of the criticisms articulated by advocates who were able to see the injustice of the system.

Outside observers who took up the cause of critiquing New Brunswick's care of its citizens spoke of the weaknesses incurred as a result of the longevity of the Poor Laws. Harry Cassidy described the public health and welfare system as "much weaker than those of most provinces,"[28] and went on to say that "from an administrative standpoint, the poor law system of the province has two basic weaknesses – the use of the smallest local units (parishes, towns and cities) as administrative and taxpaying units and the total lack of provincial supervision. These are two defects of the Elizabethan poor law in England which were remedied a Century ago."[29] New Brunswick wouldn't be addressing these defects until the 1960s through Equal Opportunity.

People in need could not expect representatives of their local municipal governments to look kindly or generously upon them, as intense moral judgments were lodged deeply in societal and community perceptions of people who could not meet their own needs:

Under the municipal system, local prejudices were inbred. Some of the moral fixations that came into play kept financial input for welfare assistance at a low standard. Whether someone was a good citizen or not was a criterion for providing social services or financial help. The people felt that the money to feed or to care for the disadvantaged came out of their pockets; and why should they have to assist them? "After all, God helps

> those who help themselves," was the call. Social welfare, apparently, was not seen as a virtuous act.[30]

Nova Scotia and New Brunswick's situations paralleled one another's social welfare history in many ways: "the larger incidence of destitution in the region meant that NS and NB, despite their harsh reliance on the poorhouse for dealing with indigents, spent more per capita on social assistance and services than the Canadian average. Indeed, in 1945, only BC and Saskatchewan outspent these two provinces on a per capita basis."[31] Newfoundland, however, presents a contrasting portrait with regard to perspectives of blame and responsibility as it

> had per capita incomes as low as the Maritime provinces. Yet, early on, because of its independence on precarious fishery, it developed the practice of treating poverty as structural rather than the fault of individuals. While public assistance was never generous, it was offered to most destitute people in their homes without efforts to categorize them as deserving or undeserving, and without the erection of poor houses or the imposition of work requirements. In the winter of 1932–33, perhaps one quarter of all Newfoundlanders received public relief.[32]

In an address to representatives of the Children's Aid Societies of New Brunswick, the president of the Queen's County Society acknowledged the strain on county councils as well as on those who owned property: "in these pressing days the limited quota that we have for raising money is from taxation placed directly upon the real estate as principal factor, and anyone who has experience in the field of municipal taxation will appreciate the hardship the farmer, the laborer and real estate owner is passing through today."[33] While assistance rates were comparable among New Brunswick's three largest cities, people living in rural areas relying on their local parishes received far less.[34]

Living under the Poor Laws meant the province lacked the administrative ability to tax all New Brunswickers, and this in turn meant it did not have ultimate responsibility to provide for the social and economic needs of its citizens. New Brunswick earned the title of being the last province to repeal its Poor Laws, after Nova Scotia had done so. Margaret Strong notes the decision to no longer adhere to Poor Laws, which some governments adopted, "appears as a distinct advantage in the development of organization and technique in the public welfare field."[35] Whalen is another author who provides an analysis of why a system such as that imposed by the Poor Laws fell short of responding to needs: "Under this decentralized system the varying resources of the local units were not considered and a wide divergence in the treatment of the poor took place because this was left to the whim of local authorities."[36]

Organizations from within and outside the province that provided essential social welfare service to New Brunswickers were required to spend much administrative time invoicing the various county councils rather than following a more efficient procedure, such as billing a provincial agency. For example, in 1955 the Halifax regional office of the Canadian National Institute for the Blind, which maintained contact with the forty-eight blind persons living in Northumberland County in New Brunswick and also provided services to "indigent persons – mainly children," requested an annual $500 grant for their services, noting that "despite all efforts the cost of these services is increasing from year to year and it is only with your generous financial assistance along with that of the public that we are able to maintain our services and even increase them where necessary."[37] A vulnerability of access to services such as this by New Brunswickers and dependence on the benevolence of a council back in their home province that hopefully recognized the various needs as priorities for spending were characteristic of the system in place.

Flora Jean Kennedy, a social worker in child welfare, shares her views of those welfare workers who were in the role of approving assistance requests in the late 1950s and early 1960s: "The assistance program operated under the Poor Law and welfare was provided by the counties, throughout the province. They were all staffed by men in the county who knew how to save a dollar. Not only did they provide indoor assistance, but they also provided living accommodations and some dollars, not too many, just a few dollars."[38]

Another weakness inherent in Poor Laws policy was the issue of determining residency and which parish was to pay for residents of almshouses or recipients of other services. Overseers of the poor had the power and responsibility of ensuring that children without parents who could care for them would be assigned to other families or individuals, but at a rate that would not be costly for the taxpayers of the parish. Carol Proctor's recollection of the 1940s and 1950s reinforces the potential implications of this framework:

> we actually would write to the overseer of the poor where apprehended children came from and ask if they would accept responsibility if we could

> prove that they really had come from there … you had to trace back all the relatives and make sure the grandfather really did live there, and then they would assume some responsibility. In some cases you could leave them where they were if the money amounts weren't going to be too great, and they would send money for the care of those children. But they often made you send them back, and the husband and wife might have been away from there a long time. So the shuffling of people around was bad.[39]

Up to this point, this chapter has explored Poor Law Legislation's impacts on residents including the parish system, the "overseer of the poor" and "commissioners," the almshouse, public auctions, and the practice of "contracting out." Adherence to Poor Laws unique to New Brunswick and Nova Scotia resulted in an ineffectual safety net for the poor of the province. When the workhouses were closed as late as 1956, children were still found among their inhabitants. Francophone citizens suffered from the regional disparity. They did have access to outdoor relief. It is clear that any citizen who experienced poverty also experienced accompanying shame. It is also obvious that being English-speaking and Protestant in New Brunswick in its earliest years meant better access to health, education, wealth, resources, land, and economic opportunities.

Poverty's Prevalence in the Early Twentieth Century

The experience of poverty within New Brunswick's historical, economic, and political contexts, particularly in the face of the demeaning and harsh Poor Law legislation's influence, was not easy. In this section of the chapter, government policies, programs, and services in response to economic and social hardship are described. The limitations of "relief," a system intended to provide temporary measures for meeting basic needs, are discussed. Vivid descriptions of the realities of poverty reflect what life was like for many New Brunswickers from the 1920s through the 1960s. These realities provide the context for understanding the environment experienced by the earliest social workers.

The period leading up to the 1920s

During the nineteenth century, provincial governmental responses to social welfare needs were characterized by short-term, situation-specific responses rather than comprehensive programs. For example, when crop failures occurred in the first half of the 1800s, the province developed a funding scheme that allowed farmers to buy seed grain and potatoes. Likewise, members of the Loch Lomond community of Black residents were offered provincial aid between 1838 and 1848 for sick and indigent persons, and for the education of children. When fires such as the major Saint John fire in 1877 occurred, the provincial government would have responded.[40]

New Brunswick could be characterized as an economically disadvantaged province from the start of the twentieth century and as such, "the need for health and welfare services in the province is much greater than average and the very cause of that need, poverty, precludes the province and its municipalities from meeting it."[41] Forbes and Muise affirm that financial problems in the Maritime provinces were not exaggerated, citing "taxes in relation to their resources to be the highest in the country. By 1929 New Brunswick and Nova Scotia were devoting respectively 28 and 26 per cent of their revenues to the servicing of the public debt, compared to about 15 per cent for all provinces." In less than five years New Brunswick had to devote 55 percent of its provincial revenue towards debt payment. If the province had more money to put into program funding, incoming federal funding would have been higher, because of the formula used.[42]

Seasonal shifts in available employment resulted in salary interruptions and disparity in amounts paid depending on where one lived:

> The stronger municipalities in New Brunswick, such as Moncton and Saint John, paid comparable amounts through the winter, but reduced payments when the province cut off funding during the summer months. In the poorer municipalities, payments were much lower. In Gloucester, for example, in the winter of 1936, the twelve thousand people on relief received little more than a dollar a month. In Prince Edward Island, residents of Charlottetown averaged almost four dollars while the others secured less than two. That province, too, cut off most relief payments through the summer months.[43]

A further challenge was that New Brunswick had a very limited capacity to generate revenues through taxation compared to its peers, and its provincial debt (the third highest in Canada) plagued the government on a large scale. New Brunswickers found themselves in one of the poorest areas of the country and receiving the least assistance because the province could not match federal funding.[44]

In the midst of generalized economic conditions of this sort, it goes without saying that to be unemployed or to find oneself in dire need resulted in great vulnerability and uncertainty, as well as a stigmatized identity. Gender served to deepen the disadvantage. "Houses of Industry" emerged in the mid-1830s in urban centres such as Montreal, Québec, Toronto, Kingston, and Saint John. In these institutions women were primarily trained to work in the homes of the rich. Accounts from Upper Canada reveal diets of only milk and bread, and high numbers of people being sheltered there: "One in twelve residents of Toronto lived in the House of Industry at some point during its first half-year of operation"[45]

In rural areas, food and clothing were rationed to mothers in need through the overseers of the poor in the various parishes. Women living in a town or city approached municipal officials for aid or went through an agent of the Children's Aid Society (CAS) as early as 1914 in Saint John, 1916 in Fredericton, and 1917 in Moncton, to broker their requests for aid.[46] Various policy stipulations determined receipt of these rations: children had to have been born in wedlock and birth certificates produced for each child; the husband had to be unable to work due to disability or hospitalization. If the mother was sick and the father worked, presumably family or neighbours looked after the children, according to Ruth Brittain who worked with the widows' allowance program in Saint John.[47] If the breadwinner could not provide for his family the CAS agent would approach the alms commissioner to take a mother and children into the county home.

The 1920s

Visitors with a mandate to survey the welfare needs of the province during the late 1920s made the following observations:

> with its old settlements, its vast hinterland and long period of serious economic depression, the province could not help but have deplorable housing conditions. This was particularly so in the larger cities and poor, rural areas. In the cities there was serious overcrowding in ramshackle buildings while in the country house after house scarcely fit for animals to occupy, let alone human beings, was visited, where panels in doors were patched with cardboard, walls were papered with newspapers, broken window panes stuffed with old clothing.[48]

Deplorable social conditions were of concern to many Protestant church denominations in the Maritimes just as they were across the country. The Social Gospel Movement, "a Christian movement for change that spread through the major protestant denominations in Canada from the 1890s to the 1920s,"[49] was visible in many initiatives that responded to needs of New Brunswickers. It stirred many social workers with religious affiliations and social justice principles to speak out against poverty, oppression, and illegal activities. Belief in a moral obligation to create social change through institutions and institutional transformation was a hallmark of the movement that emerged from Christian religious congregations.

Harry A. Renfree, writing about the participation of Baptists in the movement, points to the creation of the Interprovincial Home for Young Women in Riverview, near Moncton.[50] It was a correctional facility for females over age sixteen, and came about through the organized efforts of Presbyterians and Methodists, as well as the Baptist and Anglican communities. One of New Brunswick's first professionally qualified social workers, Jennie Robinson, was its first superintendent. The institution is an example of an organized collective response achieved in the Maritime region through cooperation between leaders of several church organizations and motivated by a shared commitment to improving living conditions for women.

In the 1929 *Annual Report from the Acting Superintendent of the Interprovincial Home for Young Women*, the author, identified only as "Miss Walker," describes a homeless woman, no doubt suffering from a sexually transmitted disease, who was admitted to the institution that year:

> Our door was opened one midnight to admit a Peace Officer bringing a girl who could be likened to nothing else but Lazarus, whose body the dogs licked. She was covered with sores from her eyes to her toes. There was no place for her to stay – no work in that condition. She appealed to a Peace Officer, who told her there was one place that would take her in – The Interprovincial Home. Pleading guilty to a charge of vagrancy, she was sentenced to one year in the Home. Already there is hopeful reaction to treatments. We can only hope that the grace of God will bring cleansing to a soul as diseased as her body.[51]

The 1930s

At the time of the Depression, poor relief was the major source of assistance outside the family and, to some extent, the church. The Canadian Council on Child and Family Welfare in 1932 described "relief" as the provision of food, clothing, fuel, shelter, gas, light, water, insurance and loans, and health services.[52] Those who lacked the barest of necessities had to meet demeaning criteria and often faced abusive treatment from the gatekeepers of relief. The Maritime provinces in 1933 were receiving only 3.5 percent of federal funds distributed to municipalities (despite representing 10 percent of the national population) to try to deal with extreme poverty and need. By 1938–9 this amount was reduced to 2 percent. Municipalities were required by policy to come up with the first third of the funding for direct relief as well as to administer the program. The funding raised was matched by provincial and federal governments.[53] The systemic structure thus worked more effectively for municipalities that were better off than more strapped neighbouring communities.

The only alternatives for the destitute were subsistence on poor relief or the almshouse in those counties that had one, as discussed previously in this chapter. Resorting to relief (a term we know today as "welfare") was avoided at all costs – it was humiliating and degrading to face the overseer or volunteer committee in one's parish knowing that "… it was their responsibility to stretch as far as possible the limited funds accorded them. In Northern New Brunswick, where people were starving, they sometimes arranged loans on their own credit.[54] They also prosecuted for the crime of bastardy, directed at those who illegally created new mouths to feed outside of marriage."[55]

In her scholarly work, Elizabeth Blaney spoke of her own grandmother's experience of relief:

> from the time I was eleven, I had to work for my board. I had no place to live or nothing to wear. Just old stuff people had given me, shoes too big for my feet. The Parish was supposed to help. It didn't give you much – just got by, that's all. To eat at somebody's table kept you alive. The people who looked after you didn't get money. If you lived you lived; if you died, you died.[56]

Blaney's grandmother also spoke of the pain of decaying teeth and not having one new dress until the age of sixteen.

In the 1930s, when New Brunswickers faced major economic devastation with far-reaching implications, the systems born of the Poor Laws were inadequate to meet the demand. Nationally, an unemployment-relief program was desperately needed. When the federal unemployment relief program was established through the Employment and Social Insurance Act of 1935, New Brunswick needed to restructure itself so that New Brunswickers could benefit from it, although initially the overseers of the poor administered the support.

What means of support were available to people who undoubtedly found themselves living in highly discouraging housing situations, including the elderly and people living with disabilities? Even though the federal government introduced the Old Age Pension in 1927, New Brunswick was not prepared to share the cost equally (required in the first four years of the program's existence), nor was it ready when in 1931 the federal government took on 75 percent of the cost of the program. New Brunswick was only the eighth province to agree to participate, with the first payments issued in 1936. Only British subjects (and notably not individuals of Aboriginal ancestry) with twenty years of residency in Canada, aged seventy and over with incomes less than $365 per year (including the pension) were eligible. No one received more than $20 per month or $240 per year.[57] Within that system were pensions for blind persons, instated in 1938.

Once federal monies dried up, the premier announced in August 1937 that New Brunswick was "off relief," and the Relief Office was renamed the Employment Office. The practice of workfare was implemented beyond the almshouses and workhouses where it was already occurring. While these measures were but fleeting evidence of provincial commitment to citizens in financial need during the Depression, it was a first as it represented a province-wide program for which provincial government had responsibility.

Examples of allowable provisions for those who qualified for relief can be found in this note from a municipal inspector to an almshouse commissioner in a central region of the province in 1935: "a list of the provisions which it is proper to provide under the regulations governing direct relief ... potatoes, tea, sugar, flour, molasses, rolled oats, pork (price not to exceed 15c per lb.) beef (price not to exceed 10c per lb.), fish, salt, butter, lard, beans, yeast cakes, milk, kerosene oil, soap."[58] A comparison of amounts allotted to families of five in eight cities across Canada in 1938 revealed that those in Moncton were receiving at least $2 to $3.75 less per week than their counterparts of other provinces.[59]

Research on welfare services in Moncton in 1939 was conducted by the Canadian Welfare Council and clearly exposed the over-representation of French-speaking persons on relief. At that time, *inside* relief meant staying at the municipal home, while *outside* relief meant provision of some kind of basic goods. A contrast in approaches was evident in eastern Canada in general, compared to Upper and Lower Canada.

It appears that French-speaking individuals were more likely to receive outside relief. However, in 1938 it was noted that twenty-nine French

Canadians, compared to twenty-three others, had what were considered lengthy stays in the Moncton home;[60] yet at that time Acadians represented only 30 percent of the population. In that same year francophone children needing institutional care received almost half of the expenditures of English-speaking children. However, the author of the report noted that

> another factor that seems clear although figures are not available to prove it is that while among the families on relief, the preponderance is French-speaking, the proportion of these "families of poor quality" in the community, as a whole is English-speaking. Their cost is not so obvious in present outlays on relief, but it shows up in the wasting of educational facilities, expenditures now on medical care, court and police service and payment for dependent children. In the next generation the problems coming from this group, will constitute an overwhelming burden, financial, social and moral, if it remains unchecked.[61]

The governments in the maritime colonies were less willing to develop separate institutions that would cater to the particular needs of various groups of poor people, and forced most of the destitute into workhouses, as discussed earlier in this chapter. Gradually in Upper and Lower Canada, state aid to charities allowed the insane and the aged to leave the workhouses for other institutions, turning workhouses increasingly into homes for destitute single men. Charities and poorhouses tried to keep families in their homes. As an example, the Annual Report of Toronto's House of Industry in 1857 claimed to have helped three thousand individuals. Most had lived in the house at some point during the year, but the house had also distributed 200 cords of wood and 3,176 loaves of bread to the homes of indigent families.[62]

The Canadian Welfare Council's suggestion was to place a bilingual family worker in the municipal home. It was expected that being thorough and treating francophones and anglophones alike "will tend to decrease any undue French proportion on 'outside relief.'"[63] Interestingly, even though the author of the report noted that in many cities unfortunate groups lived in specific parts of a city, for example the north end in Regina, Saskatchewan, or "the ward" in Moncton, she attributed, "the contributing circumstances as community and economic rather than racial in their origin."[64]

The "dirty thirties" saw Western Canadian farmers facing dramatically declining wheat prices, drought, and locust infestations; thousands of people "riding the rails" from coast to coast to find employment and food; shanty towns being built in cities by people who had lost everything in the collapse of the stock market; and endless line-ups for work and food. Not unlike the situation today, those who were forced to rely on relief during the 1930s were cast as either undeserving or unwilling to take work offered to them. The prevalence of such attitudes is a testament to the conservative hegemonic dynamics made possible through a class structure that enabled an elite ruling class to deny the unemployment crisis and hardship that were occurring throughout the nation. These realities were countered in the 1938 Family Welfare Association Report on Families on Relief in Saint John whose authors lamented:

> It has been charged that quite a few undeserving heads of families have obtained assistance, but from direct observation, we can state that their children, who outnumber the adults four to one, are innocent sufferers and cannot be ignored ... It is fairly easy to dismiss this great need by the careless remark often heard, "that these people would not work if it were offered to them, and would refuse it." We are convinced that choice has nothing to do with the present condition of a large majority, and even if it were true of a minority, their children cannot be named.[65]

In 1939, throughout the province, poverty continued to be a challenge. The following images acknowledge grim living conditions:

> a great many of the families were living in quarters actually unfit for human habitation, there was overcrowding, suffering from cold, lack of clothing, bedding, cooking, utensils, and food. There was plain evidence of slow starvation among many adults and little children in this group, and the ravages of disease were apparent as attested by their medical and hospital records ... from records of families on relief and those in a similar condition not on relief, there is evidence that there must be 1,000 families in Saint John in greatly depressed circumstances, unable to gain the meanest living in employment, without assistance.[66]

The realities experienced by people who found themselves in the penal system is worthy of mention for a number of reasons. If the head of the household was jailed, the family, including children, was required to go to the poor house before they could receive municipal aid. One is reminded that among those imprisoned at this time were New Brunswickers who were unable to pay their debts, given that the Poor Laws considered poverty a crime. Indeed it was estimated that in Moncton in the late

1930s, eight to ten cases of families of prisoners being provided municipal assistance were situations of the main breadwinner being imprisoned for debt.[67]

Conditions of the prisons were lamentable as well:

> There is no provincial jail in New Brunswick, prisoners being detained in common jails operated by the counties without governmental supervision ... The Dominion Royal Commission to Investigate the Penal System was outspoken in its condemnation of the local jails of the Maritime Provinces in its report of 1938. The Commission said: The jail system in the Maritime Provinces is entirely inadequate and ... the manner in which prisoners are treated in these jails can only result in degrading them morally and physically. Generally speaking, the jails are overcrowded, unsanitary, poorly lighted and ventilated, and provide very limited opportunity for outside exercise. There are no facilities for classification or segregation, and no workshops to provide useful employment ... Young offenders must spend their sentences under these conditions, indiscriminately mixed with older and hardened criminals, many of whom have long prison records.[68]

The 1940s

In the nineteen forties hardship and poverty continued to be evident throughout the province as people struggled to meet their needs. Limitations and constraints imposed by Poor Law legislation persisted. The following personal account from Richard Duffy, who eventually worked in providing assistance, describes growing up poor in Saint John in the early 1940s:

> I remember our grocery bill ... for my grandmother, my aunt, my sister, myself, and my dad and ... all living on a ten-dollars-a-week grocery order. Mrs. Osgoode's store would give us credit every week, and we would go down and get a quarter pound of butter, ten cents worth of baloney. Ten cents worth of baloney in those days would get half a pound of baloney. You would get three pounds and you would go up to that city store and you would get three pound of stew meat for a quarter, you would get a whole roast, a four-pound roast for a dollar, twenty-five cents per pound, pork roast. Then we used to go along the tracks and pick up the coke from the trains and we used the coke. Then we went up to the McCavers, who used to get all the tea boxes from the tea company, and we used to pack the fish in the tea boxes. We went up there during the war especially when everything

> was rationed and we used to empty the tea boxes out and we got a dollar a pound for tea when all the rationing was going on. You could get maybe a half an ounce out of each box but you really shook them and made sure that there was none left in them. The people who were poor and who had no furniture, they used the tea boxes for chairs and tables. [69]

Antonine Maillet, the first winner of the Prix Goncourt by a non-European and the author of *La Sagouine,* created a character beloved by Acadians – a charwoman (housekeeper) for wealthy families. Maillet's work provided readers with an understanding of the poverty experienced by many Acadian families in New Brunswick's fishing villages in the first half of the twentieth century. In a CBC interview she speaks of one particular woman, a real-life "sagouine," whom she met in her youth who acknowledged the tragic and devastating realities of poverty and disadvantage while offering them up through the vehicle of humour. Maillet also explained that to access a career, there was only one college option for Acadian women. If she wanted to be a school teacher, for many years the only route through which that aspiration could be realized was to become a nun with a religious order.[70]

The following commentary reflects a kindness of attitude among some storekeepers of the period, perhaps remembered as "unsung heroes" by those struggling to feed their families while living without sufficient income:

> All those little stores, it just amazed me how they could do it, these little corner stores; they gave everyone credit. They knew most of the time they would never get it. Someone would owe them a hundred dollars and would come in and say, could I get five dollars' worth of groceries? They would say yes. "I'll pay you next week"; next week never came.[71]

The use of vouchers meant it was easy for store personnel and the public to identify who was receiving relief assistance. As Archie Smith, employed at the Boys' Industrial Home, indicates, recipients had little freedom to choose how to spend the vouchers:

> Everything was done in a voucher form … If your rent, say it was twenty dollars or twenty-five dollars, whatever it might have been, then you got that, you didn't like they do today: receive a cheque for a gross amount of money and you divide it up. The money was controlled … controlled by the city

and by the department, the Welfare Department. There was so much allotted for each child for food. There certainly wasn't any money allowed for luxury items that is for sure: deodorants and things like that, they wouldn't have been considered in those days.[72]

Smith further explains:

some stores would say, "You can cash your voucher if you spend 10 percent here." The fellow that used to run it, what he would do is that they would hold that voucher, it might be for a hundred dollars, and he would call me and he would say we have got a voucher here, we are suspicious of this one. The guy doesn't look like he is old enough to have four kids. And I would go check it out and find out: "Yeah, it is good money, go ahead." They would say okay, you can spend twenty-five dollars now, and we will hold the voucher here in the store and you can come back next week and get another twenty-five or whatever. They would divide it up maybe in two-week periods, fifty dollars a period and then come back on the 15th ... a lot of stores did that to get the business. Some did it to take 10 percent of the profit.[73]

Whether in the city or in rural areas, store merchants played a very large and important role in the day-to-day attempts of individuals and families to feed and clothe themselves and in the ways they experienced spending their welfare vouchers. Generosity and kindness on the part of some store owners contrasted sharply with the prejudice or insensitive practices of others.

Any insurance from the death of a husband would have to be used up before a mother would be considered eligible for Mothers' Allowance.[74] The funding allotted if a woman was married but her husband was ill, deceased, or disabled consisted of six dollars a week maximum – even if one had fifteen children! Interviewee Richard Duffy noted that

if you had less than that you would get a lot less. Six dollars a week, that is for everything ... at that time they were paying fifty cents a day for rent at some of those places down the south end down there, no floors just barns is all they were. People sitting on tea boxes and using a tea box for a table, they had nothing. Drinking hot water, heating their feet in the oven, tearing the shingles off the outside of the house in order to heat the water and at the same time losing all the heat out of the house because they tore the shingles off. They had to survive some way, and it was tough.[75]

The 1950s

Throughout the 1940s and into the 1950s assistance continued to be distributed by welfare officers or relief officers not as cash or cheques but as vouchers to be brought to stores and verified. The following is a picture of what one municipality provided to families needing external resources in the early 1950s:

> We also provide "Outdoor Assistance" to families in temporary circumstances of want. Food is given through an open voucher on a store, the amount varying from $4.00 to $8.00 per week. One half ton of coal a month is provided but no clothing, rent, water or light. Oil is provided for cooking purposes. Insofar as rent is concerned, the municipality operates "Emergency Housing" shelters available at very low rental to families in need of a low-rental house.[76]

At times when all the money set aside for alms in a given year had been depleted, families got nothing, as the following story illustrates:

> I went to see the Alms Commissionaire, the councillors and the secretary of the county. Mr. Teed said he could do nothing about it as all the money rated for alms had been spent and the stores would not wait longer than a month for their money. The councillors told me the same but said for the children would go to the county home until something was worked out for them.[77]

A "pension inspector" provided a look at differences in aspects of the Old Age Security, the Blindness Allowance, and the Disabled Person's Allowance programs during the fifties:

> Old Age Security, you couldn't get until you were seventy. But it was only forty dollars a month. That's all there was. There was no means test on it so you didn't have to worry about that. But in 1955 they decided that they would help people out who were blind. They started the Blindness Allowance. It was on a means test. Then in 1955 they also started the Disabled Person's Allowance, which was on a very strict income and you had to be totally and permanently disabled according to the Act they set down. Then in 1958 the Federal government decided that they would bring the Old Age Security down from seventy to sixty-five.[78]

The Saint John Social Welfare Workers' Association produced a brief on relief in 1950[79] and presented it to the municipal council; in it the welfare workers highlighted high levels of unemployment and poverty and criticized outdated eligibility requirements. The high prosperity experienced after the war had evaporated, and when unemployment ran out, people were forced to turn to private and public agencies for help. The brief spoke of those who did not have the minimum amount of food to maintain health, nor enough fuel to prevent children from contracting pneumonia; of those who could not pay the rent, for even the worst hovels, or clothe their children. The brief stressed that private agencies could not meet these basic needs in the midst of unworkable municipal policies. For example, if a married man in his fifties with dependent children was refused employment because of his age, he was too young to receive pension yet he was not eligible for assistance. Many men were turned down for work if they were known drinkers, even though they worked steadily when work was available. Applying for relief was truly a last resort.

A great amount of literature can be found about the city of Saint John, with its bustling population and organized responses to social welfare needs. The following passionate description in 1957 by Mildred Bridgeford, executive secretary of the Family Welfare Association in that city, reveals the poverty evident in this urban setting:

> It is appalling to see homes in Saint John where living conditions are just as bad, worse I would venture to say, as I saw 25 years ago on the Lower East Side of New York, where at least the buildings were stone. Here, they are flimsy wooden structures, many without foundations built on the ground, damp, cold, and can only breed all the ills of life, and this is where we see children live; how can we expect them to have good health with no opportunity for normal development. All Family Agencies must clamour harder than ever for low rental housing. We cannot sit down to our own attractive meals, comfortable surroundings, knowing that just a short distance away people are living so miserably. Poverty is not a disgrace to them, but it is to us who have plenty.[80]

A phenomenon of the 1950s described by a resident of Bathurst at the time was in all likelihood commonly practised in many communities in the province. A description of what they referred to at the time as "beggars" (as he notes was the term used at the time) would come to the door of their family home for handouts or small change and glasses of water, with "regulars" arriving at certain times on a weekly basis.[81]

In the 1950s social workers in Saint John must have been frustrated by the numerous roadblocks to relief that were created by eligibility requirements. For example, a person would be turned down for relief if he or she had not paid taxes for three years, even though that stipulation was not included in the Act Respecting Settlement of the Poor; all property owners were refused relief without considering that their debt might be greater than their assets; mothers of young children were advised to go to work if the husbands couldn't "even though it is known in advance that the Municipal Home will not take children (it will take children for one month with their parents)"[82] and relief rates were considered totally inadequate. The social workers who authored the brief were especially concerned with the plight of a non-resident, who couldn't return to his legal residence because it had been many years since he and his family had lived there, and he had no friends or family to help him out. A family in this situation received only a "pittance." The service that the municipal home provided was considered long outdated.[83] Using a brief to voice their concerns and frustrations indicates that the social workers had a critical understanding of the situation and were prepared to use this venue to try to advocate for change.

In November 1959 concerned citizens pressed for new legislation to address relief through the report of the Joint Committee on Public Assistance in the municipality of Saint John and called for new social assistance legislation; that provincial residence rather than payment of taxes suffice for social assistance purposes; that financing direct relief be a program shared by the municipality, province and federal government; that under the Chief Welfare Office of Deputy Minister of Welfare there be created a strong Social Service Branch with trained personnel; and that advisory and appeal boards be established at the municipal and provincial levels. This committee was launched by board members from various social agencies: the Catholic Welfare Bureau, the Catholic Women's League, the Children's Aid Society of the County of Saint John, the Welfare Services Department of Veteran's Affairs, the Family Welfare Association, the Imperial Order of Daughters of the Empire (IODE), the Local Council of Women, the Saint John and District Ministerial Association, the Red Cross, the Salvation Army, and the Saint John Labour Council. Five discussion groups were organized, each studying a phase of public assistance.[84]

Despite clearly inadequate levels of economic assistance, the poor were believed to need advice about how to prepare their meals more economically, and circa 1959 the Department of Health and Social Services produced a pamphlet (carrying on the myth that poverty was the result of unsound financial practices):

> designed as a guide for any groups or individuals interested in the economical use of the food dollar. By giving the comparative costs for a day, a month, and a year, the consumer can observe at a glance the wide discrepancy in food costs depending on menu selections. Many persons with low incomes can be guided in the selection of nourishing and appetizing meals, when a little more care is taken in food selection.[85]

The 1960s

New Brunswick experienced its share of economic and political challenges in the early 1960s. Among them were the declining sustainability of farming (particularly with the potato industry facing lowered prices), flooding brought on by torrential rainfalls, sharp increases in hospital spending, and the imposition of changes in the higher-education environment that invoked protests (for example, St. Thomas University was moved from Chatham to Fredericton, and several sites for French-speaking post-secondary education were united to form the Université de Moncton).[86]

Even as late as the 1960s, housing conditions in many areas of the province fell below a minimum standard of quality:

> Despite the very real progress which has been made in public housing in Saint John, poor housing remains a great problem for many of the families we are helping. Overcrowding, buildings badly in need of repairs, and costly and difficult to heat, and sometimes rat-infested are some of the conditions under which they are forced to live ... large families who are most seriously affected by this problem ... More subsidized housing projects are needed with more large units to accommodate big families ... additional emergency shelter accommodation is required for those who are being evicted or forced to move.[87]

The following story provides insight into the unjust challenges faced by one family in Saint John caught in the Poor Laws residency-requirement regulation and an agency that responded in creative ways to support the family's initiative to secure housing:

> During the year we were able to rejoice with a Negro family and their six children, who finally found a satisfactory solution to their housing problem. They had been brought to our attention by the school attendance officer because of the children's irregular school attendance. A visit to the home revealed the family living in the most deplorable conditions in a house slated for demolition. When it was really cold, it was impossible to keep the place bearably warm. The father, a war veteran and a steady worker, did not have residence and was therefore ineligible for any of the projects. His search for accommodation for his family was fruitless and so in desperation, and unannounced, he moved his family into a vacant house in a rural area which offered little in the way of improved conditions. Nearby, however, was a much better property for sale at a reasonable price. Through the Army Benevolent Fund, it was possible to help this man get a grant to cover the down payment. Our Agency secured a further donation for needed improvements to the house, and from the estate of an elderly woman who had been known to us, arrangements were made for the family to receive the necessary household effects. Since last spring the father has done much to fix up the house and he and his family are delighted with their new and very own home.[88]

The area of corrections was also negatively impacted because it was left as a municipal responsibility, and provincial standards were sorely needed. County jails did exist; however, "municipalities devoted little to the development of proper facilities and staffing. Many dungeons were reported to be intolerable; unfit for human existence, both physical and mental."[89]

New Brunswick schools, particularly in rural areas, were also neglected. The province's minister of education from 1966 to 1970, W.W. Meldrum, while delivering a speech in the United States, readily admitted that "historically, French-speaking education in New Brunswick was more disadvantaged than English-speaking" and shared his perspective that "for a long time, a very long time, if the Catholic Church had not been interested in education and taken the responsibility for education in their communities without public aid, there would have been parts of New Brunswick, mostly French-speaking parts, that would have had no education facilities whatsoever."[90] He continued in the same address to describe the then-current situation in the middle 1960s: "In one county there were forty-two one-room schools, thirty-two of them had no sanitary facilities whatever, four of those forty-two were listed by the superintendent as unfit for human habitation. This is the English-speaking area, not the French-speaking."[91]

Taken together, these descriptions of challenging conditions, constraints and barriers paint a devastating portrait of life for many New Brunswickers and also of the likely discouraged and frustrated people working in social service fields. The Poor Law system and practices may have appeared unchangeable to many observers, and probably few would have predicted or anticipated that massive, sweeping reformations were possible, let alone imminent. However the 1960s, a decade characterized by social and political change throughout the world, was also a time when New Brunswick would start to see glimmers of light shine into its inequitable systems and structures through the massive changes of the Robichaud era that will be discussed in chapter 10.

Conclusion

This chapter initially focused on a consideration of the Poor Law Legislation and how it affected the day-to-day life of New Brunswickers, through its many aspects. Critical analysis of its impact was also offered. The second half of the chapter considered the governmental response to poverty, followed by content related to the poverty experience, presented in the decades from the 1920s to the early 1960s.

The portrait presented reflects the conditions of disadvantage and inequality. These were generated and reinforced by prejudice, paternalism, and colonialism. The descriptions of the day-to-day realities reflect what today are known as classism and ableism. They reflect the imposition of moralistic and judgmental codes based in individualism.

Reference to New Brunswick as "parochial" is clearly warranted, as explained by Tony Tremblay:

> My use of the term "parochial" to describe New Brunswick politics comes from P.J. Fitzpatrick, whose colourful exposé of the provincial system focuses on "gerrymandering, patronage and constituencies with hereditary political loyalties kept intact by ancient ethnic and religious antagonisms."[92]

Life in New Brunswick prior to the Equal Opportunity Act meant extreme hardship for many, but particularly for those without steady employment; people living with a disability, sometimes incurred in unsafe workplaces, including the mines or the woods; and for people left to face parenthood single-handedly. Equally hard hit were residents of poor rural areas (where many Acadians found themselves) in regions where economic policies and low levels of revenue generation thwarted the means for local government to support them. Vast variation in the rates of taxes that New Brunswickers throughout the province had to pay, and variation in access to education and services, were key problems. Fortunately, forward-thinking leaders were about to emerge – leaders who would recognize the importance of centralized services in improving access and bringing about a more equitable society. Social workers hired in this era needed determination and strong commitment to circumvent the structural hazards inherent in society during the profession's early days. Specific aspects of Equal Opportunity are discussed in chapter 10.

5

Origins and Development of Social Care Agencies and Networks

LAUREL LEWEY AND LINDA TURNER

Caring for children and families was framed within the Elizabethan Poor Laws, which represented the dominant philosophy of the day that helped shape notions of the state's responsibility in providing social and economic support to its citizens. As this chapter illustrates, there were differences and commonalities in the experiences of the anglophone, francophone, and Indigenous populations.

Until the arrival of the Equal Opportunity Program, social workers, social welfare workers, and agents of the Children's Aid Societies negotiated the parish system in each county through contacting the overseer of the poor for each parish to attempt to procure basic provisions for families.[1] The overseer of the poor system was organized by counties, some with as many as ten parishes to negotiate, as described in chapter 4.

Churches and voluntary societies and organizations comprised the mosaic of supports available to families in need. Each organization existed independently of the others, and each served a role in the patchwork of services. Many Canadian women found opportunities to engage in virtual career positions in these organizations:

> "Charitable undertakings," including the collection of money, clothing, and food to aid the poor, were undertaken by both bourgeois men and women. For women, in particular, charity offered an opportunity to participate in public life, since tradition kept "ladies" out of paid employment. Church teachings, class obligations, and personal convictions combined to influence women's social-welfare activism.[2]

Municipal homes (almshouses) served as the last resort for those who found themselves with no housing options. Orphanages provided short- and long-term care for children. The first Children's Aid Society (CAS) in New Brunswick appeared in 1914 in Saint John. Its stated purpose was "to ensure that neglected and poor children had a home and also to protect them against anything that would threaten their right to life and to grow up in a moral upright and healthy environment."[3] When the Family Allowances were implemented in 1946, CAS workers kept the Office of Family Allowances aware of changes in care status of children to ensure that payments were doled out to the appropriate adult. Industrial homes served as custodial facilities that housed children in conflict with the law or those whose behaviour was deemed out of control. In some cities, Welfare bureaus existed along religious lines to serve the social welfare needs of their group (for example, the Catholic Welfare Bureau). The Family Welfare Bureau in Saint John was non-denominational in the provision of services.

Often families were in peril because they were unable to find work, or the work they were able to secure paid a pittance. In Saint John from 1930 to 1938 the number of unemployed heads of families increased threefold. Barely able to survive on the relief allowance, many families experienced malnutrition and sickness. Any additional crisis or exceptional circumstances pushed them over the brink. Helping agencies could, for the most part, react to family circumstances only if they were so deteriorated that the sole option was to take children into protective care. Gradually, but not until the 1950s, the province developed services that supported family preservation and prioritized the housing of children in settings that most resembled ordinary homes.

While business interests, through their representatives on boards of social agencies, kept control of the purse strings, those individuals who volunteered on the front line for the various service agencies were proud helpers, especially in Saint John, where the first YWCA in Canada was established by Agnes Blizzard[4] and where citizens gave generously to fund-raising campaigns.[5]

In this chapter a history of social care is presented separately for anglophones, Acadians, and Mi'kmaq and Maliseet to reflect the different experiences and systems organized for the care of these families.

Social Care of Anglophones by Community Agencies

The first orphanage to open in New Brunswick was the Emigrant Orphan Asylum in Saint John in 1847. It initially served children whose parents had perished in an epidemic. The history and philosophy of adoption was described at an annual meeting of the New Brunswick Association of Children's Aid Societies:

> Indenture was the first form, followed by the free foster homes. In 1851 a law made it possible for adults to legally adopt a child. In 1932 practice was implemented to investigate the circumstances of the adopting family. The Child Welfare League of Canada drew up legislation which was later incorporated in an Adoption Act. This legislation was revised in 1952 and is the one under which New Brunswick operated in 1962.[6]

The New Brunswick Protestant Orphans' Home first appeared as the Saint John Protestant Orphans' Asylum and housed anglophone children from 1854 until 1976. Many of the wards of the home had no relative or guardian able to contribute any money towards their maintenance, leaving the City of Saint John to assume financial responsibility. The home regularly made appeals for financial aid to New Brunswick Protestants. An appeal in 1925 tugs at the heart with two angelic photos of children; under each the caption reads, "Suppose He (or She) was yours and you were taken."[7] The home produced much of its own food, and children were responsible for chores that contributed to the maintenance of the home. In 1945 the home possessed seventeen cows, two horses, one hundred hens, and eight hogs.[8] Only in 1950 did the New Brunswick Protestant Orphans' Home begin to receive annual grants from two counties in addition to Saint John County.[9]

Also in Saint John the Wiggins Orphanage, relying on the endowment fund of Stephen Wiggins (heir to wealthy merchant Samuel Wiggins), began in 1867 to house orphaned boys aged four to ten years and later accepted boys up to the age of eighteen, including some who suffered from poverty. In 1880 the St. Patrick's Industrial School and Farm housed Roman Catholic boys in Saint John County.

In 1873 schools for children who were either visually, speech, or hearing "impaired" opened in Saint John and Fredericton for anglophone children only. Their francophone counterparts had to travel to Québec for such services.

Funded through provincial grants, in 1893 the Saint John Boys' Industrial Home housed juvenile boys deemed delinquent. It remained open until the 1970s. The industrial home was where boys aged nine to sixteen years were sent.[10] An equivalent setting for delinquent Catholic girls, the Good Shepherd Reformatory and Industrial Refuge, was established in Saint John in 1895.[11] Charitable donations were vital to the existence of both agencies. The Maritime Home for Girls in Truro, Nova Scotia, served the region and began providing housing for "delinquent" girls on 1 September 1914, when the Cottage was opened. The facility grew quickly, with expansions including the Hall, which opened 16 January 1918; the House, which opened 3 February 1921; and the School and Residence, which opened 8 May 1924. Young women who were pregnant were not admitted. Those girls committed to the Maritime Home for Girls were often under guardianship of the province of New Brunswick until the age of twenty-one but could be in the home receiving religious and domestic training, or on parole earning a living on their own.

In 1928 the Seventh Annual Report of the Nova Scotia Home for Colored Children claimed it was Canada's only orphanage for neglected and orphaned "Colored" children. It is not known at this time if children from New Brunswick were sent there.[12]

Social worker Vilma Kurol, one of three social workers in New Brunswick interviewed as part of a national CASW project in 1984, explained that in Saint John, the Catholic Welfare Bureau had a temporary boarding facility, a foster-home program, and an adoptions program.[13] According to Flora Jean Kennedy, the Catholic Welfare Bureau provided financial assistance, offering adoption for children born to single mothers and ward-care services. The agency provided counselling to individuals either at the agency or in their own home. Kennedy recalled that "these girls would come from around the province because it was a service for the whole province."[14] It did not have the mandate to do child protection but did provide child welfare services.

The Evangeline Maternity Hospital and Home was established by the Salvation Army in Saint John in 1914 and was where pregnant but unmarried women went to birth their children and to place their infants for adoption. Women from other provinces were welcomed to the Evangeline Home.[15]

Moncton's religious community Sisters of the Good Shepherd also responded to the needs of unmarried pregnant women with the Home of the Good Shepherd, originally on Church Street. The brick and stone home, built on Massey Avenue on land belonging to Reverend Stephen Humphrey, had five stories and was completed in 1948. The institution's first administrator was Reverend Mother Marie de St. Bernedin de Sienne. Women went to the home when their pregnancies began to show and would remain there until the birth. The usual practice was to place the baby for adoption. The woman then returned to her community of origin. The Home of the Good Shepherd maintained its Catholic identity until the building became part of Université de Moncton in 1963 and was renamed the Léopold-Taillon Building.[16] Since 1973 and still today, the building has been home to l'École de travail social of Université de Moncton.[17]

Nearly four hundred unmarried mothers and babies were cared for in the three homes operating in the Maritimes during the 1950s.[18] In 1955 an increase of pregnant and increasingly younger unmarried teenagers prompted the Evangeline Home to indicate that a more diversified program was needed to meet the "greater emotional upset of these young girls, and, therefore, necessitates providing educational as well as other related activities over a longer period."[19] This marked the end of the practice of their serving as a public maternity-care facility as they had since 1914.[20]

Saint Michael's Academy in Chatham (1931–69) was a boarding school run by nuns, and as early as 1929, it took in children whose parents had died, as well as children who, for whatever reason, were unable to live at home. Also in 1929 the Social Service and Christmas Exchange was set up in the offices of the Family Welfare Association in Saint John. It served as a clearinghouse and facilitated cooperation among the various helping agencies in the city,[21] and it was still in operation in 1963.[22]

Early in the 1930s the Knights of Columbus launched the Catholic Home Finding Association (CHFA), the aim of which was to find good homes for Catholic orphans. It grew from the Saint John Council in 1929 and was modelled on a Knights of Columbus program in Illinois that helped place children made vulnerable by the Depression. A 1931 report to the state convention revealed that during the previous nineteen months, sixty-four inquiries had been handled, "forty-eight in New Brunswick; fourteen in Nova Scotia; and two from the United States."[23] The CHFA not only provided twenty cents as a scholarship created for each child, but kept careful records on visits, on where the placements were made, and on details regarding transportation and other activities related to completing an adoption. The quality of the services that the CHFA provided was considered very "professional and extensive."[24] Each year approximately twelve children were placed in Catholic foster homes. In 1935 and 1936 the CHFA ran an "Adopt a Baby Week" campaign, which resulted in twenty-one children being placed. This campaign was repeated in 1936–7, and twenty-three children were placed. Although by 1936, a total of 107 placements had been made, a challenge remained in that the children were not necessarily adopted by the host families. The CHFA had a presence in all of the Maritime provinces and continued through the Knights of Columbus until 1947.

The Catholic Youth Organization (CYO) provided a recreation facility that was accessible to all youth in the city of Saint John. Although the cost of using the facility was $5 per season, "no one is ever turned away from these classes, either because of race or creed or inability to pay."[25] The CYO appealed to the City of Saint John each year for a grant, stating that "the whole aim and object of the Centre is to provide clean, wholesome, leisure-time activities for all the youth of the city and district. It is a non-profit organization and the Director, Board of Directors, Secretary-Treasurer and Class Leaders receive no salary."[26] Meeting rooms at the centre were made available at no cost to groups such as the Young Hebrew Association, the Community Welfare Council, the Decent Literature Crusade and the Saint John District Credit Union Chapter.

The Family Welfare Association in Saint John was formed circa 1930, and all its efforts and initiatives were devoted to improving the lives of families. Key issues for the agency in 1953 were unemployment, seasonal employment, Family Allowance investigations, illness of breadwinner, and acute illness.[27]

Social Care of Acadians

The Récollets and Jesuits were the first of the religious orders to arrive in New Brunswick. They arrived ahead of the most intense waves of settlers and focused their proselytizing efforts on the Indigenous people. However, Roman Catholic Church orders also became the first providers of social care to the Acadians and for more than a century were the only providers:

> From the beginnings of colonial settlement in Canada and Acadia, members of Roman Catholic orders, both cloistered and non-cloistered, were the providers of social services. Both women and men were involved in educating colonists and Aboriginals alike in Christian and French ways, while women were leaders in providing health care services to colonists. Eventually both female and male religious orders also provided shelters for the poor, while the women's orders looked after foundlings, prostitutes, the insane, and the aged.[28]

The Society of Saint Vincent de Paul, also called the Conférence de la Société Saint-Vincent de Paul, was created in 1846 and was modelled on institutions in France by Dr Joseph-Louis Painchaud from Québec. In 1868 a facility was established in Tracadie by the parish priest to care for the poor. Similar facilities were opened in the northern part of the province, presumably to serve the francophone population.[29] In 1931 the Orphelinat Saint-Antoine opened in Campbellton.[30]

Orphanages and daycare centres for poor francophone children were established first in Moncton. These centres helped impoverished women and children and also helped those who were homeless. By 1914 groups emerged with similar models to those in Moncton: for example, St-Jean-Bosco in Moncton, Notre-Dame-de-Grace in Georgetown; Ste-Thérèse-de-l'enfant-Jésus in Dieppe; and St-Jean-Baptiste in Buctouche. Les Dames de St-Vincent-de-Paul was established in 1941 and helped set up daycare centres and summer camps, placed illegitimate infants in foster homes, provided clothes to poor children, and helped women by supplying milk to their children. The society also searched out children who were then classified as "deaf mutes" and placed them in institutions.

The Catholic Church ran orphanages for francophone children in the Saint John Diocese through the Sisters of Charity, an order that included both Irish Catholics and Acadians. One was St. Vincent de Paul's orphanage, which housed girls from the ages of four to sixteen, while St. Patrick's housed boys. Many boys and girls were funnelled through the St. Vincent's Infants Home for adoption. Saint Vincent de Paul provided care for unmarried Catholic mothers and their children. Unmarried mothers were provided confinement, often for many months before the birth, as well as assistance in re-establishing themselves after the birth. Because only a few girls were able to pay for their own expenses at the home, it periodically requested grants from Saint John County to help with operating expenses. In the 1950s, seven of those working at the home were nuns with the Sisters of Charity, who were provided with basic maintenance. Until St. Joseph's Hospital decided to expand in 1954, Saint Vincent's operated as a rent-free facility.[31]

A second orphanage was located near Shediac. Les Soeurs de la Providence administered the Foyer Providence Saint-Joseph for the care of children placed there by parents, nuns, or members of the clergy. In Saint-Basile, the Académie des Soeurs Hospitalières de Saint-Joseph operated as a boarding school for girls, who entered at six years of age, while boys entered at seven. Generally, mentally challenged children were not admitted; however, younger children could be accepted if they were disabled, illegitimate, abandoned, orphaned, or if their parents were mentally ill.[32] L'Académie Ste-Famille, a boarding school for orphans and for children whose fees were paid by their parents, was established in Tracadie.[33]

The third, Orphelinat Mont Ste-Marie, opened in Edmundston in 1952 and although it initially housed children from the ages of five to twelve, it later admitted children as old as fifteen. This orphanage was unique in that children were grouped for education according to their age.[34] CAS workers from Victoria County placed children in this orphanage, called Mount St. Mary's by the anglophone population.[35]

Few of the documents found in the provincial archives relating to child welfare in predominantly francophone counties were written in French, and little service was provided to francophone people in their own language. Forms for Poor Assistance Funds were available in French in 1960, and it is not known if they were available before this.[36] The CAS agent in Northumberland County from 1948 to 1961 was bilingual although his handwritten commentary on various letters was in English. Much of the written communication between the CAS agent and other agencies in Madawaska County was recorded in French; however, family court judges may still have conducted the proceedings in English. For example, in 1958, included in a child protection file was a letter written in English by a child whose first language was probably French, as the structural errors suggest.[37] One exception was the 1955 to 1956 annual agent's report for the Children's Aid Society of Gloucester County. This report, written in French, showed that there were 371 wards in that county in that year. Yet the annual report of the child welfare officer for the Department of Health and Welfare published in 1955 reported 748 wards for the whole province. The high numbers of children taken into care may be related to the fact that historically Gloucester, in the north of the province, ranked high among the predominantly francophone counties in which poverty had been prevalent for many decades.[38]

Social Care of Indigenous Children

A brief history of Mi'kmaq, Maliseet,[39] and Passamaquoddy people in the region was provided in the introduction to this book. Previously in this chapter we discussed the mosaic of support for families in need provided by churches and voluntary organizations, as well as that provided by municipal, provincial, and federal governments. Earlier chapters have shown how the New Brunswick Poor Law of 1786 brought the Elizabethan Poor Law (1601) mentality to the province, resulting in a weak safety net with the barest of provisions available for needy families only once it was determined that they were deserving of it. Having to bring one's family to the almshouse would have been an inherently humiliating experience. While the anglophone and francophone populations of New Brunswick received the bare minimal of provisions from a variety of organizations in addition to the churches, the Mi'kmaq and Maliseet people received relief from the government of the day grudgingly and belatedly in response to desperate conditions,[40] and then upon Confederation in 1867, would have received relief from the federal government as wards of the Crown. Welfare provision was an area that the government wandered into rather than planned for.[41]

It has been shown that the francophone population of the province, living mostly in rural areas, experienced less access in their language to education, health care, employment, and justice than their anglophone neighbours. Similarly, but even more thoroughly, the Mi'kmaq, Maliseet, and Passamaquoddy people missed out on the "expanding institutional structure that assured at least some help for European-origin indigents."[42] For these Indigenous peoples, a sketchy education with assimilationist intentions provided in English was offered in the day schools more uniformly after Confederation than before, when virtually no education was offered. It should be noted that after Confederation the Passamaquoddy people were not recognized by the Canadian government. Nor were they recognized by the New Brunswick government, even though two lots of land were reserved for them early in the 1880s. The opening of the Shubenacadie Residential School in Nova Scotia in 1929 provided a significant vehicle through which their language could be destroyed and their culture disassembled, and many children were abused and died of disease there. The paucity of social care and emphasis on the destruction of cultures will become apparent in the discussion that follows. In this way, the experience of the Mi'kmaq, Maliseet, and Passamaquoddy peoples in New Brunswick is similar to First Peoples throughout Canada who were classified as wards of the Crown.

Before Confederation, as the settlers developed the land given to them by King George III, the land available to the Mi'kmaq, Maliseet, and Passamaquoddy peoples was increasingly diminished, making survival precarious. An experimental school targeting Aboriginal people in New Brunswick existed first in several locations but only at Sussex Vale from the mid-1790s until 1826. It was established by the New England Company of London, England;[43] however, the American Revolution loyalists brought it to New Brunswick, setting up a new board of directors in 1787, with the aim to "'civilize' the Indians, teach them English, convert them to Protestantism, and train them to be skilled tradesmen."[44] The "Indians" in New Brunswick, however, received harsher treatment than their U.S. counterparts: "In Puritan New England, founded by religious refugees, the colonists had confronted heathen natives whom they tried to convert; in Loyalist territory, founded by political refugees, the colonists confronted Catholic Indians whom they proceeded to exploit."[45]

The plan was for Indians to move onto the company's land and voluntarily send their children to a house built there that would serve as a school. Children would be apprenticed locally and settle in the area as tradesmen to encourage other Indians to stop their "wandering" lifestyle. Between 1804 and 1807 some commissioners pursued a plan of bribing Indigenous parents to leave their offspring as infants, purposely isolating children from their parents and not allowing parents to live near their children: "The adherence of these Christianized Indians to the Protestant faith could be assured only by depriving the aggressive, well established Roman Catholic priests of all contact with the young, impressionable natives."[46]

The "Indians" weren't interested in living on that land. Children were sent to this place likely because parents were suffering so severely from starvation and disease following the invasion of their lands by as many as 15,000 loyalists who immediately dispossessed the Maliseets of most of their village and garden sites and began destroying their waters and hunting territories. As it turned out, little or no education was provided to the children, nor is there evidence that as much land was parcelled out as was promised to apprentices upon turning twenty-one years of age. Records show that only two or three young men actually received their allotment, but the majority did not, allegedly because most apprenticeships were not completed or not completed to the satisfaction of the company. There were many issues with the company's plan. Monies given to run the operation often did not reach the children. By 1813, "more than two-thirds of the children listed as apprentice shoemakers, farmers or domestic servants were under ten years of age, and many were two years old or younger."[47] In one known case a girl had attended the school for five days before being seduced by the son of the family, resulting in the birth of a child who was kept in the care of the company.[48] In 1811 Lieutenant Colonel Gubbins, sent to New Brunswick to inspect the British troops, noted that the funds for the school were being misused and female apprentices were placed with degenerate people.[49] The New England Company's school in Sussex was investigated in the early 1820s, confirming Gubbins's observations a decade earlier:

> This time the names of children who had been sexually exploited were listed, together with the names of the abusers and families with whom they had

> been apprenticed, including the family of one minister of the Church of England. The fact that nothing had been done about this abuse, although it had been known for more than a decade, is appalling, but what seems to have been more disturbing to authorities was that the project had completely failed to achieve what it had set out to do.[50]

In the case of the New England Company's record in New Brunswick,

> it must be admitted that English benevolence came to the colonies as unconditional aid and the temptation to accept it, and use it selfishly, proved irresistible to acquisitive, individualistic colonists.[51]

The pre-Confederation colonial system appeared pervasively indifferent to education for Indigenous children. A day school was opened at Kingsclear for a short while in the 1850s, and in 1871, two more were opened at other locations but closed within six years.[52] In Esgenoôpetitj (Burnt Church) the day school closed in December 1906 and was still not open in April 1907, due to lack of fuel to heat the building.[53] Some communities had no school house at all. Such was the case in 1908 in Eel Ground where classes were held at the chief's home.[54] In 1910 Red Bank petitioned the federal government to have a school built because their children "were not used right ... at the 'White' school."[55] In 1915 members of Elsipogtog (Big Cove) wanted to have their children taught in Mi'kmaq rather than in English, because English was unfamiliar to them. They appealed to have Alma Isaacs hired to teach them. Her sisters, Rebecca, Mary, and Margaret were also available to teach the children in Mi'kmaq. According to Martha Walls,[56] that day school was closed for eight years, so it appears that their request fell on deaf ears. This was likely because the federal government was set on extinguishing Indigenous languages in order to promote assimilation. Day schools followed the pattern of public schools and ran from September to June. This schedule was problematic for people who needed to fish, plant their gardens and follow seasonal work. There were a great many problems with the day schools. Classes were taught in English, even though Mi'kmaq or Maliseet were the first languages. The school buildings were in poor condition; the education provided didn't exceed grade six; there was a lack of basic supplies, such as maps, blackboards, and lesson cards; the education was inferior to that offered at public schools; at times, when wood supplies were depleted, schools were closed because of lack of fuel, as occurred in Esgenoôpetitj in 1907. It would have been hard for children to experience consistency owing to a high turnover rate for teachers, who were paid less than their counterparts at public schools and were expected to also serve as nurses and truant officers. The administrative structure of day schools was neglected as well, meaning that the schools were seldom, if ever, inspected. In 1918 less than half of the children went to school on a regular basis.[57] Indigenous children were not allowed to attend public schools since their parents did not pay taxes, and since the federal government already funded schools in most of their communities. As well, most of the Catholic priests were opposed to allowing Indigenous children to attend public schools. And, given the intense racism of the time, there was little interest in changing the status quo.

At the time of Confederation in 1867, the federal government asserted fiduciary responsibility for Aboriginal people – that is, for "Indians" and "Indian lands," terminology used in the Indian Act. It took until 1876 to enact the legislation that the government needed to do this. As "wards of the Crown," the Indian Act, "denied First Peoples even the most basic of civil and human rights. We were paternalistically treated as 'non-citizens.'"[58] Amendments made to the Indian Act in 1886 made education compulsory and provided a rationale for forcible attendance at residential schools. Poor Law ideology shaped the government's approach to "Indian relief" as it did for all New Brunswick residents. Beginning in the 1880s, "Indian relief" meant the provision of basic rations to the elderly, sick, and widowed women with children. Able-bodied men were not eligible, even if they could not find work. The Department of Indian Affairs authorized certain agents, church missions, and the Hudson Bay trading company in Western Canada to distribute these rations to keep Aboriginal people from starvation. Ammunition, blankets, and clothing were distributed to those most destitute status Indians who were determined to be deserving of the rations.[59] Metis and Inuit persons were not eligible, because they had not been made wards of the Crown.

A federal order-in-council in 1872 created two Indian Affairs agencies in New Brunswick, one for western bands and one for southern bands, and in 1909 two other agencies were created for the northwest and southwest bands. In 1949 the northwest agency was renamed the Tobique agency and served the Edmundston and Tobique areas; the southwest agency was renamed the Kingsclear Agency and it served the Woodstock, Kingsclear, St. Mary's, and Oromocto reserves. The Kingsclear and Tobique agencies became the Saint John River Agency in 1958. It is not known at this time when the Miramichi Agency was formed; however, it was in operation in 1919.[60] Until 1968 the Indian agent, and as time went on, the superintendent, was the link between families and services. Rarely, if ever, was the Indian agent an Aboriginal person.

When the Shubenacadie Residential School in Nova Scotia was opened in 1929 in the town of Shubenacadie – not on the Shubenacadie reserve – it was the only residential school east of Québec. Isabelle Knockwood tells that the elders knew of this place not as Shubenacadie but as Sipekne'katik, or the land of the wild potatoes.[61] The Roman Catholic Sisters of Charity served as the teachers while a priest served as the principal at the school until it was closed in 1967. Walls argues that in the immediate years following the opening of Shubenacadie Residential School, the trend of pouring most of the financial resources into Shubenacadie, while cutting back resources for day schools, became apparent. She asserts that

> by allowing day schools to languish, Ottawa not only found justification to compel students' attendance at the more assimilative residential facility, but, in offering abysmal day school conditions, coercively "encouraged" Mi'kmaw and Maliseet families to enrol children at the residential school.[62]

Some refer to Indian residential schooling as "an ongoing reduction of the roster of those who had a legal claim to aboriginal title or to a Canadian obligation for service and compensation ... genocide by assimilation,"[63] and conclude that, "destroying Indian cultures is exactly what residential schools were designed to do."[64]

When Shubenacadie first opened, its stated design was for the "education and care of orphans and neglected children," criteria that almost immediately expanded to include children who lived too far away from public schools[65] – public schools that children were not welcome to attend.

In her book, *Out of the Depths: The Experiences of Mi'kmaw Children at the Indian Residential School at Shubenacadie, Nova Scotia*, Isabelle Knockwood wrote about experiences children had while at the school and how these contrasted with the way Mi'kmaq children had been raised. Upon arrival the children's hair was cut. Shaving hair was used as a punishment. Mi'kmaq and Maliseet children were confronted with what Indigenous peoples who attended residential schools across Canada were typically confronted with, which was that "all we had learned from our parents and grandparents [was regarded] with contempt and hatred."[66] As Knockwood has said, "It was profoundly confusing for us that Father Mackey and the nuns directly in charge of both girls and boys, far from being examples of Christian love and forgiveness, were for us objects of terror."[67] Once, Isabelle's mother had spoken to a girl in Mi'kmaw in front of the nun who was admitting Isabelle and her siblings. Her mother was told right away that children would not be allowed to speak Mi'kmaw, because it interfered with English pronunciation and with learning how to read and write in that language. While Isabelle was being shown around the school, her parents were ushered away before she had a chance to say goodbye to them.[68] For most children, coming to the residential school was the first time they had been away from their parents. Boys and girls were segregated from each other, and so sisters and brothers were not able to provide support for each other, and "being unable to protect their younger brothers or sisters became a source of life-long pain."[69] Children weren't given enough food to keep them from feeling hungry and were often fed rotting potatoes or rancid meat.[70] Children could be made to go hungry as punishment, sometimes for as long as two days.[71] They were always cold at the school, never had enough blankets, and were not allowed to sleep with their siblings, as they were used to doing. Children caught at night getting a drink of water in the latrines were dragged out by the hair.[72] They were punished for not looking directly into the eyes of the priests or nuns, yet in the Mi'kmaq culture direct eye contact could be seen as "challenging authority, arrogance, hostility, belligerence or sexual invitation."[73] Children grew sick at the school, and an undetermined number died there. Some were kept away from their families and communities for years, sometimes because their families lived too far away to visit them. However, even if their families lived nearby, they weren't allowed to go home for Christmas, and the toys their parents had brought could disappear afterwards. It was harder, however, for the priests or nuns to take sleds and skates away to give to their "pets" if the students carved their initials onto them.[74] What many families did not realize, and what may not have been communicated to them by the Indian agent, was that in admitting their children to the school, they were giving legal guardianship to the priest, even during summer vacations. Knockwood[75] wrote that while most children were able to spend summers at home, some children had to stay at the school year round. Getting children released from the school was not an easy process, and in some cases children weren't released until two-and-a-half years after the initial application was made. Complaints made by parents against the school were considered unfounded, even when children received brutal beatings.[76] All children were emotionally abused by being punished for speaking their language at the school. Sadly, many children were also physically or sexually abused, or both, by the people entrusted with their care and education. The policy intention for students at the residential school at Shubenacadie was that they be trained to be unskilled workers, and so no education was offered until their assigned work of the day was completed.[77] It was observed that "bright and sharp" children of fourteen years of age were working at a grade-five level.[78]

The actual number of children who were sent to Shubenacadie from New Brunswick is undetermined at this point. The damage done to generations of Mi'kmaq and Maliseet peoples by these linguicidal[79] and genocidal policies[80] directed at First Peoples in New Brunswick and throughout Canada is deep and pervasive. At this writing, of the sixty-three languages of Indigenous peoples, most are severely endangered and only three are expected to survive this century. While many Mi'kmaq and Maliseet people in New Brunswick have been working for decades to retain their languages, the prognosis for them is not good, due not only to the consequences of instruction only in English, but also, ironically, to the integration of Indigenous children in public schools.[81]

Maliseet activist and elder Carolyn Ennis from Nekotkok (Tobique) described her knowledge of the caring structure:

> I think that whatever systems were in place and what I remember in my limited memory would be family that would be the one that would look after the children. For example, I think the only ones who went off to Shubie in this community were ones whose parents, even if there was one parent left, that one parent was unable to take care of the children, then they were sent off. But for most of the other people, for example, my mother brought us up alone and when she went away to work, she just placed us with other people and she paid them, out of what little money she made, she paid them to take care of us because at that time, when I was growing up, I think what they referred to as relief was like $2 per week. There was five of us in the family, and I think the relief the Indian agent provided was $2 per week, so it was incredibly small, and so they had to rely on people in the community.[82]

The federal government determined that Indigenous peoples would not receive the benefits available to other Canadians referred to earlier by Alvin Finkel,[83] such as the old-age pension (1927) and later Unemployment Insurance (1940). Consistent with the intention to assimilate them, keeping First peoples lean on relief might force them to find their own solutions and not rely on the federal government. However, during the Depression, "Blacks and Native People were traditionally the last hired and first fired."[84] Indigenous people were eligible for Family Allowances (the "baby bonus," 1944); however, these benefits were not given directly to Aboriginal mothers but were diverted to the coffers of Indian Affairs. According to Hugh Shewell, "Family Allowances for registered Indians were used as a form of relief rather than for their intended purpose (i.e., to supplement wages to assist in providing minimum requirements to children)."[85] The federal government, "had never assumed statutory responsibility for Indian welfare; rather, it had 'wandered' into the provision of relief from band funds, who administered it by default because none of the other jurisdictions, provincial or municipal, had been willing."[86]

In 1946, Nora Lea, executive director of the Canadian Welfare Council, contacted each province regarding its policy on the adoption of "Indian" children. Richard H. Scott, provincial welfare officer for the Department of Health and Social Services working out of Fredericton, told Lea that there was

> no special relationship or understanding between the Provincial Department responsible for adoption and the Department of Indian Affairs in Ottawa. I called the Indian agent here in Fredericton, Mr. Edward Whalen, who states, "as far as adoption is concerned it is the same as with white children, that the Dept. of Indian Affairs at Ottawa does not interfere."[87]

Mr Whalen also advised that

> when the war started there were a number of children in foster homes or in homes other than their own, and the heads of families put in for Dependents' Allowance. The cases were investigated by the Dependents' Allowance Board and it was found that the children were not legally adopted and before any allowance could be paid, legal adoption was required, so the same order applied under the rules of the Supreme Court of this Province. You understand, adoption is outside of our jurisdiction and that of the Government as it is handled altogether by the Supreme Court of the Province, when a petition is made for adoption, the Court has all power.[88]

Since family members practising customary adoption were unlikely to legally adopt their family members, they wouldn't be receiving Dependents' Allowances but rather only extra food relief. The following explains customary adoption:

> Traditionally, when Aboriginal parents were unable to care for their children, those children were taken in and cared for by relatives or others in their communities. One aspect of Aboriginal customary adoption is that there is no secrecy. If the biological parents are alive, the children will usually have contact with them.[89]

In the post–Second World War period, the federal government was very receptive to consultation with the Canadian Welfare Council (CWC) and the Canadian Association of Social Workers (CASW)[90] about various issues and particularly First peoples. A 1947 brief entitled "Indian Affairs" was jointly prepared by the CASW and the CWC. In it, they claim to be "their [the 'Indians'] recognized spokesman." This brief influenced amendments to the Indian Act in 1951.[91] Although the brief cited deplorable living conditions, troubling high rates of tuberculosis, high infant death rates, widespread malnutrition, and a wide array of social problems, the brief did not find "the existence of residential schools as undesirable," particularly as part of a larger educational plan for children of migratory families. In the CASW brief they did, however, find fault with the government for not paying institutions the full cost of the service that they provided. Highlighted recommendations included acceptance of the full assimilation of Indians into Canadian life as the goal of the government's Indian program; extension to the Indian population the services of provincial departments of education, health and welfare; appraisal of all present staff members in the Indian service, to ensure that persons so engaged were qualified by training, experience, and personality; hiring of qualified Indian personnel and to recruit potential Indian personnel; modernization of the educational systems on reserves and to stop the practice of sending children with child welfare needs to residential schools; and placement of a social worker in each of the Indian agencies. This consultation with Indian Affairs in 1947 was the first time that Aboriginal witnesses had been invited to speak, and "delegates forcibly asserted their status as distinct people, raising complaints about unfulfilled treaty obligations and requesting self-government."[92] These concerns remain unresolved at this writing.

In 1949 the Indian Affairs Branch was moved from Mines and Resources to the Citizenship and Immigration portfolio. Prime Minister Louis St Laurent declared that the reason for doing this was "to make Canadian citizens of those who come here as immigrants and to make Canadian citizens of as many as possible of the descendants of the original inhabitants of this country."[93] The portfolio may have shifted, but the century-long obsession with assimilating Aboriginal people had not. Again, the vision of the elimination of the Indian Affairs Branch was seen as within reach once First peoples were turned into Canadian citizens. The vocational training programs that were trotted out were a continuation on the theme of preparing Aboriginal girls to be homemakers or domestics and Aboriginal boys to be farm workers, or both girls and boys could be trained as unskilled workers in hospitals or institutions.[94] The wrinkle in this plan was that

> Aboriginal peoples had continuously articulated their own visions of the relationships between their nations and settler societies. They have rejected assimilation and continued to assert their distinct identity.[95]

The Diefenbaker government granted Indigenous peoples the right to vote in federal elections in 1960, without consequences such as losing status or challenging treaty rights, thus putting to rest the prevailing view that paying taxes defined citizenship rights. Dickason described how elections were made mandatory as early as the 1890s for seven bands in New Brunswick, as well as bands in Ontario and Québec.[96] By 1899 all bands in New Brunswick, Nova Scotia, Québec, and Ontario were forced to use this form of government. Amendments to the Indian Act in 1951 stipulated that bands could incorporate as municipalities and women could vote. According to Dickason, on a national level, "within two years 263 bands were holding elections; by 1980 the number had risen to 349."[97]

In the amended Indian Act of 1951, the federal government was made financially responsible for the child welfare policy and services that had been delegated to provincial and territorial governments. It appears that only in the 1960s did New Brunswick begin to intervene in crisis situations in First Nation communities, mostly at the request of a relative, a chief, the public health nurse where one existed, or the RCMP. At this point, the province might take children into temporary care and place them with another family in the community; however, children were also placed off reserve and taken into permanent guardianship. The cost of these services provided by the province was billed to Indian Affairs. In 1979 the chiefs of Big Cove, Burnt Church, Eel Ground, and Tobique began a three-year pilot project to offer child welfare services in their own communities. What happened between 1967, when the Shubenacadie Residential School closed, and 1986, when the tripartite agreements were finalized between the province, Indian Affairs, and the agencies, is considered the New Brunswick equivalent of the Sixties Scoop (journalist Patrick Johnson coined this term in 1983 to refer to the period between the 1960s and the 1980s when large numbers of Aboriginal children were taken into care by child-protection agencies across Canada).[98] The actions of the chiefs in 1979 effectively stopped the continued removal of children from these communities, and children in permanent wardship were brought back to the communities when the agencies applied for a reversal of guardianship orders.[99] The last communities entered into this agreement in 1995, when the Four Directions Child and Family Service agency was formed to include Indian Island, Fort Folly, Pabineau, and Buctouche.

In 1955 Indigenous people were eligible for Disabled Persons Allowances.[100] As late as 1963, universal provincial benefits, such as those provided through the Mentally Retarded Children's Act, were unavailable to Mi'kmaq and Maliseet children; however "deliberations at this ministry are still underway concerning universal welfare benefits to the Indian population in the province."[101] In 1963 it is known that the chief and council of one particular community contacted a Children's Aid Society, concerned about an abandoned child.[102]

A press release on 7 July 1964 from the Department of Citizenship and Immigration announced that "Indian communities will be assisted in raising their living standards by means of an intensified community development program which will supplement present government assistance." The press release went on to state,

> While this latest self-help program of the Department will not solve every Indian problem, its success is expected to bring reserves closer to being self-sufficient communities and thus reduce the need for reliance on relief and other welfare assistance. This will depend in large measure on the participation of the Indians themselves in efforts to improve their level of living with as much reliance as possible on their own initiative. This program makes provision for technology and other services which will help them to establish self-sufficiency.[103]

However, late in 1963 community-development workers were already hired and working in the Adult Education Pilot Project located in Chatham, New Brunswick. Social workers Mary Gillis and Nelson Hall were community-development education officers who conducted home visits early in 1964 in Esgenoôpetitj and also met with Chief Sommerville, the superintendent, Father Gratton, and another reverend. Frank Paul joined the community development council established there, and the next year Paul was elected chief. It was noted that he was interested in Christmas-tree production. It was also mentioned that there was interest in community development in Eel River Bar.[104]

In October 1964, Superintendent H.S. MacNeill was pressed to respond to a situation by an official with the Department of National Health and Welfare, stating,

> I agree that action needs to be taken in cases similar to this, but I wonder if he [the concerned citizen] is aware of the difficulty of apprehending children on an Indian reserve. Indian Affairs Branch employees by themselves can only attempt to persuade the parents to allow us to place their children in foster homes or residential school. Unless there is entire cooperation on the part of the parents, it is extremely difficult to accomplish anything.[105]

At this point only officers of the Children's Aid Societies were given the power under the Child Protection Act to apprehend children.[106] Still, in 1964, Aboriginal grandparents raising their grandchildren were not treated by the province as foster parents; instead, they were given extra "relief food and relief assistance at the provincial rate." In one particular situation, the grandparents had been paid extra relief since 1959 and provided with clothing "periodically on request."[107]

It was in 1968 that the Indian Affairs Branch released guidelines for band administration of welfare services, maintenance of school facilities, and the transportation of pupils. Specific guidelines for child welfare were to develop a system of referral of neglect and/or potential neglect situations to the appropriate child welfare authorities, when these were available; to establish the conditions under which financial responsibility could be assumed for maintaining children in foster homes or institutions; establish rates of maintenance for children placed in foster homes by band employees, which, it was assumed, would be similar to the rates for children placed by authorized child-care agencies; and to specify the measures that band employees might take to protect neglected, abandoned, and dependent children. Placements in foster homes and institutions were to be arranged with the written consent of parents or guardians.[108] At a regional welfare workshop on child welfare services held in February 1968, the welfare consultant explained the Indian Affairs Branch was entering the field of child welfare services because "Indian Affairs has come directly under the jurisdiction of the federal government and provinces have been reluctant to date to assume its responsibility even if the Indian people themselves would favor such a move." He expressed the current emerging philosophy that

> child welfare services should begin with children in their own homes, not after the child has been removed from the home. It would appear that much of the child welfare provisions under the Child Welfare Act are to provide services after removal. However, there appears to be emerging at the present time a real concern for family services both on the part of Public Welfare Department as well as child caring agencies.[109]

With respect to removing Aboriginal children from their homes, the welfare consultant explained that the policy of the branch allowed branch officials to make temporary arrangements with parental consent when child-care agencies are not available. He clarified that temporary arrangements were not necessarily made with what the Child Welfare Act termed "foster homes," which he believed should be referred to as "boarding homes." He went on to say that "since these children have been placed, we do not have any periodic reviews or reports on conditions prevailing in the home, we do not know really what services are required or being received. We only know that payments are going out to the home."[110] This last statement shows that children who had been taken away from their families, even on a temporary basis, were not necessarily less vulnerable than they had been in their own homes.

The history of social care differed among the anglophone, francophone, and First Nation populations. Anglophones experienced a system shaped by British Poor Law ideology, in which people who had been ascertained to be deserving of it were provided with meagre and demeaning support, which involved workfare if placed in an almshouse or orphanage. Poor counties typically had a smaller range of provisions to disperse and ran out of these provisions more quickly than richer counties. The francophone population was largely served through the Catholic Church or affiliated organizations. It appears that before Equal Opportunity was implemented, child welfare services offered through CASs were seldom provided in French. Overall, the francophone population had less access to education, employment, health, and justice, and much less in their own language. The largely Acadian counties were located in rural areas, rendering access to services less likely.

Once determined to be deserving of it, relief for Indigenous New Brunswickers consisted of basic rations. A non-Aboriginal Indian agent, and later the superintendent, made the decisions related to relief.

Mi'kmaq and Maliseet people did not receive the benefits available to other Canadians, such as the Old Age Pension (1927), Unemployment Insurance (1940), the baby bonus (1944), the Dependents' Allowance, which began to be offered when the Second World War started, nor did they receive the Disabled Persons Allowance until 1955. For Mi'kmaq and Maliseet people, a sketchy education was available in English after Confederation – initially in day schools with an assimilationist educational agenda, if available at all. Attendance in public schools was not an option because First Nations people did not pay taxes. Day schools were allowed to languish until the Shubenacadie Residential School was opened in 1929, initially taking students who were considered abused, neglected, or orphaned, but soon expanded to include children who lived a considerable distance from a public school. Isabelle Knockwood chronicled the abuses that children experienced at Shubenacadie.

When amendments were being made to the Indian Act in 1951, the provinces were encouraged to take responsibility for the provision of health and education. After this time, public-health nurses began to appear in New Brunswick. It appears that the province did not become involved in the provision of child welfare to the Aboriginal population until the 1960s, and then only for crises because welfare provision was an area that the federal government had wandered into rather than planned for.[111] In 1979 the chiefs of four of the largest bands in New Brunswick initiated a three-year pilot project to establish child welfare services. Their action effectively stopped the Sixties Scoop occurring in New Brunswick between the 1960s and the 1980s, when the tripartite agreements were established among the bands, the Province, and the federal government.

We now turn, in the next chapter, to the evolution of child welfare in New Brunswick.

6

The Evolution of Child Welfare

LAUREL LEWEY

With the exception of the Province of Québec, where church-driven agencies were the norm, Children's Aid Societies were the common vehicle for addressing the protection of non-Aboriginal children in Canada. A variety of voluntary agencies provided the patchwork of support services available to child welfare workers.

As described in the previous chapter, the first Children's Aid Society (CAS) in New Brunswick appeared in 1914 in Saint John.[1] The Fredericton CAS was incorporated in May 1916 and included York County. The society maintained its own shelter, run by a matron assisted by necessary household help and was able to accommodate fifteen children up to the age of fourteen years, of any "race, creed, nationality, or colour"; however, "defective children were not admitted."[2] The Fredericton CAS also provided detention facilities for children awaiting a hearing in the regular court since there was no juvenile court at that time. The CAS agent was responsible for finding homes for children, placing children, and supervising the homes. The CAS agent worked closely with the Victorian Order of Nurses[3] and the Poor Law commissioners. A CAS was formed in Nova Scotia in 1909.

By comparison in Ontario, the first CAS was formed in 1891 in Toronto inspired in large part by the efforts of reformer J.J. Kelso. The child protection legislation that was passed in 1893 included provision that shelters specifically for children were required in communities of 10,000 or more. The opening of foster homes as early as the 1920s led to closures of some orphanages. Institutionalized shelters for placement of children other than those with special needs had, by 1945, been replaced by smaller group homes.[4] There was a Catholic CAS in Ontario in 1930. Meanwhile Québec's 1977 Loi sur la protection de la jeunesse was the culmination of many decades of developments in legislation, including a law related to reform schools in 1869, a 1909 law on juvenile delinquents, adoption laws in 1924 and in 1937 creation of the Société d'adoption et de protection de l'enfance de Montreal. Between 1943 and 1945 the society registered 2,796 legal adoptions.[5]

In Fredericton in the 1930s the municipality and county provided lump-sum grants to the agency, and the CAS shouldered the costs, through its charitable donations for children who became wards of the state. Some believed that the responsibility for the maintenance of wards should devolve to public authority.[6] The municipal home in Fredericton referred all cases to the CAS and so was commended because it did not admit children, "contrary to the deplorable practice in the province."[7] The county almshouse, however, was located near Fredericton and did house children in care.[8]

The constitution of the Children's Aid Society of the city and parish of Moncton defined a member as any person who paid the sum of $1 annually. For $25, a lifetime membership could be secured. The constitution also stipulated that the board of management could appoint an agent to perform the duties authorized by the act.[9] A CAS appeared in Moncton in 1917, and then in Sackville in 1924. The Children's Protection Act in 1913 represents the first child-protection legislation in New Brunswick.[10] This act was revised in 1919 and 1927.[11] These CASs were formed independently without the province delegating a person responsible for child-protection services, as had occurred in other provinces. CASs in the various counties were operated by boards of directors composed of volunteers, who were often prominent citizens in the community. Their responsibility was to hire a person, who in turn reported to the board annually regarding their responsibility for all child-protection matters. The CASs functioned because of funding provided by municipalities and donations earned through their annual campaigns. Only in 1953 did the societies no longer have to submit grant applications on an annual basis when they were seen as a permanent expenditure for municipalities.[12] This was later than what evolved in other parts of Canada.[13] CASs were responsible for enforcing the Child Protection Act (1927), the Children of Unmarried Parents Act (1956) – changed from the Illegitimate Children's Act of 1926 – and the Adoption Act of 1947.

Discussed subsequently will be the timing of the spread of CAS agencies to the remaining counties in New Brunswick, which was not embarked upon until 1941. Since a CAS provided services only to the county in which the agency was located, it becomes apparent that the few CASs served York County, where Fredericton is located; Saint John County, where Saint John is located; and Westmorland County, where Moncton and Sackville are located. These counties represented the anglophone population. Agencies became available for the francophone population beginning only in 1941, a process that continued over the next decade. The previous chapter discussed the practice of sending Mi'kmaq and Maliseet children for education and child-care issues to the Shubenacadie Residential School in Nova Scotia beginning in 1929. "Shubie" closed in 1967 and child-protection emergencies were assumed by the province in the 1960s.

In 1927, social worker Charlotte Whitton, the executive director of the Canadian Council on Child Welfare (CCCW) in Ottawa, was commissioned by the Department of Public Health in New Brunswick to chair the study group on child welfare services, the first major study conducted by the CCCW. This evaluation of the health and protection services for children was published in 1929. Whitton's experience in other provinces across Canada[14] led her to conclude that child welfare in New Brunswick needed to be modernized. She went about this task by suggesting the introduction of legislation and a template of administrative services successfully adopted in other provinces. To that end, one of Whitton's recommendations was to establish a CAS in every county, along with an administrative structure for the future. It took many years for her recommendations to be implemented, partly because of lack of political will and partly because of lack of endorsement by some of the key players, who were loath to endorse Whitton's goals. For example, it was not until 1941 that the province began to establish a plan for a CAS agency in every county.

Whitton's study identified a lack of adequate legislation, which she attributed to the uneven development of welfare services in each of the city centres. Whitton also identified New Brunswick as the only province "without an official delegate responsible for child protection services, and without an Act requiring that any be put in place."[15] New Brunswick was unique in that the power to take children into guardianship was vested in the province rather than with the individual CASs, which Whitton deemed backward. Taking children into guardianship was not uncommon in some states in the U.S.: for example, Massachusetts chose state guardianship.[16]

Whitton's plan to modernize the child welfare system entailed replacing informally trained and voluntary staff with professional social workers in all organizations that provided child welfare services. Whitton sensationalized "shocking" conditions in the press, and so "the [Canadian Council on Child Welfare] constructed an image of the province as lagging behind national standards of child welfare development, with high illiteracy rates, dangerous family contexts, archaic institutional settings, [and] problematic legal devices."[17] At that time children were not segregated from adults in the almshouses or municipal homes. Whitton and Elizabeth King (a New Brunswicker whom Whitton hoped to advance to oversee the reorganization of child welfare services in Saint John by establishing a social service exchange and a family welfare bureau)[18] were both critical of the fact that children were housed in institutions along with adults.[19]

Research suggests that Whitton took a dim view of people employed in social service positions who were not professionally qualified social workers. She got in a particular lather about the first agent of the CAS, Reverend George Scott, charging that he "will simply not do things. He will take the papers from you, fold them up and put them away. He will refuse to take action for days, and object sharply and bitterly if the agencies press him." Whitton went on to suggest that Scott "might be better employed by the Bible Society or the Society for the Prevention of Cruelty to Animals,"[20] clearly favouring the presumed competence of a professional social worker instead. Whitton lamented that Reverend Scott relied on the 1919 legislation rather than on the revised legislation of 1927 and that his "inefficiency was well known in Saint John."[21] Furthermore, he placed Catholic children in Protestant homes without consulting the "local Catholic hierarchy."[22] Whitton had also pushed for the municipality to shoulder the financial costs of a child being placed in care. This may have been seen as a way to contravene the practice of the Protestant Orphan's Home receiving payment from a family whose child was boarded out as an apprentice.

Whitton maintained that the archaic system that operated in New Brunswick "compromised Canada's claim to be a modern and efficient nation."[23] Her views flew in the face of the Maritime Rights Movement, which asserted that New Brunswickers should retain local control of their own social development, a position that was considered "reflective of a thoroughly modern, communitarian sensibility."[24] For example, in 1918 New Brunswick passed the Vocational Education Act and established two anglophone vocational schools, which was a first in the region prior to the Second World War. In 1928 the province implemented the policy of paying for new textbooks for students from grades one to eight.[25] Citizens from Saint John gave generously to fundraising campaigns: "the tags of Vimy Ridge Day, Lest we forget day, Rosebud day, tag days for the milk funds, and the like." As well, the Local Council of Women, the Woman's Christian Temperance Union, the Imperial Order of the Daughters of the Empire and the Women's Institute all flourished in Saint John as did fraternal organizations and other voluntary organizations that provided services for men.

According to Sharon Myers, the controversy that surrounded the Whitton survey highlighted some dynamics particular to New Brunswick that helped to defeat Whitton's purposes.[26] First, as was previously discussed, New Brunswickers, and particularly those in Saint John who considered themselves progressive, were offended by her portrayal of their city as backward. Second, the Protestant Orphan's Home feared losing the income gained from families when their children were boarded out as apprentices, revealing the potential loss to such a voluntary agency if social workers replaced them. Third, voluntary agencies feared a loss of control if the profession of social work successfully positioned itself as the best way to address poverty and social issues. The assertion by social work as the profession best able to understand the issues that the poor faced was common during the years that helping transitioned from volunteerism to professionalism. In the end, Whitton "won neither the revisions that she sought to the Children's Protection Act or the immediate appointment of a Superintendent of Child Protection."[27] She was later to lament in the *Calgary Herald* in 1944, "It is regrettable that Alberta should continue to have the lowest standards of any province but New Brunswick in child welfare."[28]

The federal pension program that was introduced in 1927 was cost-shared with the provinces. New Brunswick, however, did not sign on until 1936, almost ten years after British Columbia had signed on.[29]

In 1941, responsibility for the Act Respecting the Protection of children and War Time Guardianship shifted from the Department of the Auditor General to the Department of Health. Thereafter, the Department of Health was responsible for the CAS in all fifteen counties in New Brunswick. Those agencies already formed in Saint John, Fredericton, Moncton, and Sackville served their own counties. The remaining counties of Carleton, Charlotte, Gloucester, Kent, Kings, Madawaska, Northumberland, Queen, Restigouche, Sunbury, and Victoria would wait for agencies to be established over a ten-year period beginning in 1941.[30] Robert Scott was the first director of the newly created New Brunswick

Child Welfare Division and was initially the sole employee. His task was to create a CAS in every county in the province and oversee all CASs. In 1944 the Department of Health was renamed Department of Health and Social Services, and the Child Welfare Bureau came under the responsibility of child welfare agents. The Child Welfare Bureau was not a ministerial branch and so operated at the same administrative level as the other eight branches and three offices of this department. In addition to supervision of all CASs, this department was responsible for the mandates of the various pieces of legislation that pertained to child welfare, which at that time were the provincial Child Protection Act (1913, Revised Statutes, 1927); the Illegitimate Children's Act (1926); and the Deaf-Mute and Blind Act (1927).

The Second World War and the expansion of the welfare state provided new arenas for social work practice in Canada. During the war, the United Nations Relief and Rehabilitation Administration (UNRRA) was created in 1943, as were various branches of the Armed Services. Some social workers moved to Ottawa to find work at newly created jobs at the Dependent's Allowance Board, the Dependent's Board of Trustees, War-time Housing, and Women's Voluntary Services. The Department of National Health and Welfare housed Family Allowances and Old Age Security. Social-service departments were created in veteran's hospitals, and caseworkers were needed in wartime nurseries.[31] According to Joy Maines, long-serving executive secretary of the CASW from 1945 to 1964, pioneering jobs were available for social workers "in the Department of Citizenship and Immigration, Indian Affairs Branch; Civil Defence; Royal Canadian Air Force; Mental health; Rehabilitation Services; and, the Department of Northern Affairs."[32] Also, medical social work had been a rapidly developing field since 1944. Social workers were in great demand during this period but were not in great supply. Universal Family Allowances, commonly referred to as the "baby bonus," were introduced in 1944 during the MacKenzie King government. Although the program that was implemented was not what was proposed by Leonard Marsh and his supporters in the *Report on Social Security for Canada* (1943), it did reflect responsibility at the federal level for the welfare of all citizens. Dennis Guest reports that: "By May, 1946, 92 per cent of all children under the ages of 16 years of age, numbering 3,333,763 were in receipt of benefits. The average monthly payment per family was $14.18 and $5.94 per child," less than the $7.50 per child recommended by Marsh. By 1949 the Family Allowances Act was amended to reduce the allowance on the addition of the fifth child in a family.[33] The baby bonus must have made a significant improvement to the quality of life for those families receiving it. In the previous chapter we learned that Mi'kmaq and Maliseet mothers, however, did not receive the baby bonus cheques directly, but rather that precious source of income was diverted to the coffers of the federal government.

The New Brunswick Association of Children's Aid Societies was formed in 1947 largely to decrease the isolation of those working with children and families. Professional conferences were held between 1946 and 1952 in Halifax, Saint John, and Fredericton, and keynote speakers were often provided by the Canadian Council of Child and Family Welfare in Ottawa.[34] With the passing of the Adoption Act in 1947 during John Babbitt McNair's tenure as premier, child welfare legislation was rendered more comprehensive. Societies had responsibility for children while they awaited adoption, and so the CAS extended its responsibility to the supervision of homes that provided foster care in the province.[35] Flora Jean Kennedy was one of those social workers and believed that the only program that was well developed in the province at that time was the adoption service. She credited McNair, for the development of a new adoption act that clearly stated what the legal requirements were.[36] This clarity made it easier for social workers to know the steps that had to be taken. Children who were not adopted remained in the homes or orphanages and also became the responsibility of the CASs. The development of legislation geared towards children was a trend occurring across Canada after the Second World War. Steven Hick and Jackie Stokes note overall trends in the child welfare field: that is, a shift away from volunteerism to professionalism; and, the delivery of child welfare services in particular becoming a responsibility of provincial governments.[37]

Flora Jean Kennedy recalled that "the kids who were disabled wouldn't be adopted."[38] Although the CAS was responsible for adoptions in the province, the only agency that kept track of children in care was Family Allowances. Kathleen (Tally) Morrissy was said to be the only social worker hired by the federal government to service the whole province of New Brunswick with respect to Family Allowances.

Morrissy responded to complaints of children not going to school, and also to changes in guardianship due to children being adopted entering the care of the CAS, all of which would affect eligibility for Family Allowances. She was also responsible for auditing CAS books annually to ensure the funds were received and dispensed for the children. Although the tendency of many agents was to save this money so that the children would have a lump sum when they left care, Tally's role was to encourage them to spend it on the children to help them at that time, to purchase a bicycle or a musical instrument, for example. She also promoted the importance of planning for children.[39] Carol Proctor thought very highly of Tally Morrissy, stating that, "she made every referral she ever made to us a matter of great importance. She gave us a lot of support to follow through, worked closely with our agencies."[40]

Some of the social workers interviewed referred to a "grey market" in adoptions. Placements were done in the United States – about the same time as the "butterbox babies" scandal – and babies were sold for as much as $5,000 each. "Butter boxes" were dairy boxes. Babies who were deemed unadoptable due to health or skin colour, and who were abandoned to die, were buried in butter boxes at the Ideal Maternity Home in East Chester, Nova Scotia (1928–45).[41] The home, operated by William Young, where unmarried mothers came to birth their babies, became known for the death and black market sale of babies:

> From the perspective of government officials and professional social workers inside and outside of Nova Scotia, the Youngs moved babies across borders in a deliberate effort to avoid government regulations and professional oversight. The result, they argued, was the dangerous exploitation of birth mothers, adoptive parents, and, above all, innocent children.[42]

As Nova Scotia scrambled to put through legislation to bring in greater control of adoptions and to protect babies and their mothers from exploitation with its 1943 Adoption Act, New Brunswick's lack of controls thwarted those efforts, since New Brunswick did not acquire such legislation until 1947. Karen Balcom's research reveals that the owners of the Ideal Maternity Home advised potential American adoptive parents that they could undertake court procedures and complete the necessary paperwork in New Brunswick without facing the hindrance of the residency requirements or the probationary periods that the new Nova Scotia legislation presented.[43] The RCMP became involved, and the operation was eventually closed down.[44]

By 1962 the philosophy with respect to adoption reflected the belief that children possessed rights that should be protected; that compatibility should be sought in the backgrounds of both parents and children; that proceedings should be confidential; that adoptive parents should be chosen carefully to respect adoption as a sacred trust; and that private placements were discouraged and the black marketing of babies abolished.[45]

Shifting Philosophy towards Child Welfare in New Brunswick

Although Whitton had studied the child welfare situation in the 1920s and recommended changes, the practices she was critical of were slow to be abandoned and in some communities continued well into the 1940s: "In 1943 Whitton felt confident in claiming that among English-speaking provinces, New Brunswick shared with Alberta the worst record in caring for its dependent children."[46]

Things began to look up when in 1948 Ruth Cook Wilson was appointed by the federal government to study child welfare issues in New Brunswick under the auspices of the Health Survey Committee. These issues included orphanages and other institutions; difficulties experienced by school children in New Brunswick; and the CAS. The results of her study were released in 1951, and among the recommendations was that single mothers be included in the legislation; that children in care be released from institutions whenever possible; and that all children's services be integrated under the CAS. In 1951 the CAS in Queen's County pleaded that the federal and provincial governments provide financial recognition for CAS volunteers; that a drive to obtain more volunteers be made; that uniform regulations be created for settlement of children outside of New Brunswick; and that uniform standards be established regarding the hospitalization of wards of the CAS.

The first minister of health and welfare in New Brunswick was appointed in 1953, and the Social Services Branch of Health and Welfare was created in 1954. This was followed by the appointment in 1954 of the first child welfare officer for the province. The first annual report of the child welfare officer was completed on 31 March 1955. This report specified standards for child welfare workers with respect to children requiring protection:

> When an agent of the Children's Aid Society finds a neglected and underprivileged child in a certain area of the Province, it is the duty of the agency to apprehend this child and bring it before a Judge within ten days. If in the Judge's opinion, from the evidence submitted, the child should be committed temporarily or permanently to the Children's Aid Society or to a Place of Safety, the Judge is authorized to make the commitment by the

> Children's Protection Act. The children must remain in the home and only as a last resort are they removed from the family.[47]

New Brunswick social workers worked doggedly to entrench professional social workers in the bureaucracy. In March 1953 the Social Service Council of Fredericton appealed to the mayor and city aldermen to create a central welfare bureau with a trained social worker, as was done for every municipality with a population of 10,000 in British Columbia. They stressed that the Canadian Welfare Council in Ottawa could provide any assistance needed to work out such a program as well as an outline of the duties for a worker in a city welfare department. For example, duties would include helping to preserve a family unit through the following: marital or financial counseling; referral to community resources or assistance with housing; providing financial assistance to families in need; assisting in the development of a workable scale of financial assistance; and helping coordinate all agencies and welfare groups in the city. The New Brunswick–Prince Edward Island Branch of CASW and the Association of Children's Aid Societies united in 1955 in their mission to establish a social worker in the position of chief welfare officer for the province by meeting with the cabinet of the province of New Brunswick.[48]

The 1955 fact-finding study undertaken by the Canadian Welfare Council (CWC) reinforced the 1951 findings of Cook Wilson and stressed the provision of more comprehensive services by the CAS agencies to recognize the mental, emotional, physical, and spiritual development of a child.[49] The study also promoted improving public awareness of CAS, expanding the responsibility for the agencies and securing funding for them.[50] The New Brunswick Association of Children's Aid Societies agreed with the direction the Canadian Welfare Council was taking, which stressed the psychological importance of suitable clothing to children in order for them to grow and develop in a healthy way.[51]

The Children's Protection Act was passed in 1957. During the 1950s, orphanages were gradually replaced by foster homes, although municipal homes were still in use, especially in cities where there were shortages of foster homes.

At the 1962 annual meeting of the New Brunswick Association of Children's Aid Societies, numerous resolutions were passed that were intended to pressure policymakers in the provincial government, supported by the research of the New Brunswick's Association's various committees with respect to the following: non-ward care service; Deserted

Wives and Children's Maintenance Act; and the Adoption Act.[52] An annual report of the Children's Aid Society for Carleton County in 1963 echoed the CWC report of 1955 that it was important for social workers to spend time with families and strengthen the family unit because children belonged with their families and so wardship was sought as a last resort. The lack of proper housing available to families was also noted.[53]

The Report of the Committee of the Unmarried Mother was presented to the New Brunswick Association of Children's Aid Societies in October of 1955. This committee compared rates of illegitimacy in New Brunswick with the rest of Canada; provided statistics on illegitimate births in New Brunswick by county; critiqued current services provided to unmarried mothers and recommended that the provincial government assume the entire financial responsibility for the maintenance of unmarried mothers and their children, specifically to include payment for hospitalization for the birth, payment of maintenance during the pre- and post-natal periods, and payment if the child was put into care. The committee also recommended that religious and social agencies that meet necessary standards of service and care be used; that the province ensure that any care provided be at an acceptable standard; that mothers receive the usual sources of assistance that the community allowed wherever they wished to provide a satisfactory home in which to care for their children; and that all municipal residence requirements for unmarried mothers be abolished and that the provincial government assume full responsibility for unmarried mothers as residents of the province.[54] In 1956 the Illegitimate Children's Act was still in force, and the Children's Aid Society of Fredericton recommended that the word "illegitimate" be taken out and the act be renamed the Child Welfare Act.[55] However, as of 1 April 1956, the Illegitimate Children's Act became the Children of Unmarried Parents Act. This new act did not alter the responsibility, specified in the Poor Law, for the illegitimate child and his or her mother. The act also designated agents of Children's Aid Societies with the authority to construct affidavits for court purposes – a shift from the designation previously given to the overseer of the poor.[56] The minimum amount payable by the father was increased to $600 on a one-time basis. Changes were made to the Vital Statistics Act as well, which enabled a child born out of wedlock to have the name of the father put on the birth certificate provided he gave permission or an affiliation order was made. Recognition was also given to the changing nature of society and so changes to the Settlement Act reduced the residence requirement from three years to one.[57]

The Mothers' Allowances Act was repealed effective 1 April 1960 and was replaced by Part I, Provincial Assistance of the Social Assistance Act.[58]

In 1965 the province took over the administration of all social assistance and child welfare in the province.[59] In that year there was a total of thirty-seven field staff working in the CAS, seven of whom had master's degrees. The rest had varied educational backgrounds in business, education, and nursing. George Caldwell from the Canadian Welfare Council, commissioned in 1965 to study the recommendations from the Byrne Report, estimated that 105 social workers would be needed to carry out the child welfare mandate.[60] The Child Welfare Act of 1966 replaced the Children's Protection Act, the Adoption Act and the Mentally Retarded Children Act. It outlined its purpose as the protection of children, as well as its preventive approach to child welfare; defined wardship and placement for child care; outlined fifteen conditions upon which employees of the Department of Health and Welfare or the police could apprehend a child; and outlined what actions were available to the courts, based on the act. By 1 January 1967, the provincial department assumed most of the functions previously administered by the Children's Aid Societies. There was a clear need to remedy the uneven services that were experienced in the province and to address the work load that was created with the introduction of the Non-Ward Program in 1964–5, a program in which families voluntarily placed children in the care of the department because of illness, extreme family poverty, temporary abandonment, or death of a caregiver. From 1968 to 1969, Social Welfare and the Child Welfare Divisions were integrated with the Department of Health and Welfare.[61]

Specific Issues Affecting Child Welfare in New Brunswick

The discussion in this section of specific child welfare issues in New Brunswick will include the terminology reflective of the time; the lack of legislation to address the treatment of crippled children; the arrival of British refugee children; morality and Mothers' Allowances; the frustrating rules regarding veterans' benefits and Old Age Pensions; the lack of services for the francophone population; the lack of services in rural areas; jurisdictional limitations; the lack of professional social workers; and issues around race and religion.

Terminology reflective of the time and historical context

In New Brunswick, as in the rest of Canada and industrialized countries, categories of "feeble-mindedness" were used as guides to determine a person's mental level of functioning. This categorization was reflective of the eugenics movement. Eugenics was "a type of scientific racism that flourished between 1865 and 1945. Allegedly based on science, eugenics held that unfit parents passed their inferior traits to their offspring, weakening the gene pool."[62]

Gerald O'Brien provides insight into the societal context where eugenics arose to quell fears related to perceived affects and characteristics of "feeblemindedness."[63] He points to the long historical trajectory of the movement that many are unaware of. Its origins were in the realm of animal and plant science, in which "good stock" for breeding was important. The practice migrated into human life, where "eugenic policies can include any measures designed to ensure that the 'best' members of a society reproduce in greater numbers, or that the reproductive opportunities of the 'worst' members are limited, either voluntarily or, more often, by force." Intelligence tests and birth control are the result of the eugenics movement. The Binet Intelligence Test, which emerged in the first decade of the 1900s, was a tool that normalized classification based on assessment of intelligence – albeit a highly biased tool when cultural differences are recognized. In 1918 social worker Jessie Taft noted that "[t]here is no question that the swift rise of the mental test as a center of interest and experiment in applied psychology has had much to do with the growth of popular recognition of feeblemindness as a social problem."[64] Fears about transmission of "moronic" capacity flourished.

Angus McLaren asserts that "for all their talk of protecting the 'race', eugenicists did not see themselves as racists or nativists. Eugenics was, its followers claimed, both an international movement and a science."[65] Helen MacMurchy was Canada's expert on eugenics and in her 1915 annual report for the Ontario Legislative Assembly, entitled simply "Feeble-Minded in Ontario: 10th Report," she claimed that "feeble-mindedness was in turn responsible for poverty, unemployment, alcoholism, and prostitution."[66]

Some early feminist activists, admired as advocates in the Women as Persons Case, moved with comfort in the eugenics movement. Alberta was the only province in Canada other than British Columbia to legislate sexual sterilization in 1928. According to author Erika Dyck,

> The Famous Five were vocal proponents of eugenics, sexual sterilization, and restrictive marriage laws – indeed, they were the key motivators of Alberta's original Sexual Sterilization bill. Their unwavering support for women's rights was based in some measure on emphasizing the inferior qualities of non-Anglo-Saxons. With the complicated mixture of feminism

and racism, more commonplace during the early twentieth century, these women are now remembered as difficult heroes and curious villains.[67]

The League for the Care and Protection of Feeble-Minded Persons was formed in Nova Scotia in 1908.[68] No such organization appears to have been formed in New Brunswick. However, Leslie Baker's doctoral research reveals that a leading physician in the Maritime provinces from Saint John, O.J. McCully, delivered his 1905 address as president of the regional medical society. It was published and distributed to the medical community, thus contributing to the eugenics movement. Baker writes that

> McCully used foreign sources to establish correlations between the "constitutional" criminal and heritable traits of laziness and alcoholism, bringing the larger eugenic discourse to bear on Nova Scotian communities. These ideas gathered momentum in the province during the early decades of the twentieth century and contributed to a thriving network.[69]

Eugenics is also evident in the New Brunswick Child Welfare Survey conducted in 1927 by Charlotte Whitton. The survey, undertaken by the provincial Department of Health, engaged in a special analysis of the statistics obtained from the 1927 census regarding categories of persons defined as "feebleminded." It identified a total of 526 persons distinguished in the following three categories: idiots, imbeciles, and low-grade morons; with a total of 435 in a fourth category, that of high-grade morons. These categories were applied in children's institutions, almshouses, in the provincial hospital for the insane, and in the community.[70] It was believed that feeblemindedness affected all problems in the child welfare field and to ignore it would increase social costs in terms of widespread dissemination of conditions of filth, disease, criminality, immorality, and "vice," which Whitton noted resulted in the obvious and marked physical and mental degeneracy especially in numerous small pockets in New Brunswick.

Lack of legislation to address children with special needs

The Deaf-Mute and Blind Act became law in 1927 in New Brunswick. Two schools for the deaf were established in New Brunswick: in Saint John in 1873, and in Fredericton in 1882. Blind children had to attend school in Halifax at the Halifax Asylum for the Blind, established in 1871 and renamed Halifax School for the Blind, in 1884.[71] In 1928 in New Brunswick there was no legislation that specifically addressed treatment for "crippled children." With respect to liability for these children whose parents could not pay for medical treatment, the 1923 amendments to the Public Hospitals Act indicated that except in cases of accident or emergency, no hospital receiving government grants would take for treatment cases unable to pay for their own treatment, unless a signed order for treatment was received from the mayor, councillors, aldermen, or overseer of the poor from the city or town parish where the person had legal residence.[72]

At some point in 1956 an executive secretary was appointed to the newly created Coordinating Council for the Handicapped. Forty-one percent of children were not able to be cared for unless funds were made available through sources other than the Department of Health and Social Services.[73] Parents of handicapped children navigated a maze to obtain corrective services. The Maternal and Child Health Division of the Department of Health and Social Services maintained the central registry to hold information on crippling conditions among children in New Brunswick and administered the federal Crippled Children Grant. The Department of Health and Social Services allotted beds in the polio wing for non-orthopedic cases, if available. Children classified in the non-orthopedic group, which consisted of plastic surgery, heart, eye, neurological, and other cases were referred to the council's registry. These conditions were not deemed eligible for the federal grant, and so if financial assistance for corrective surgery was required, for example, a public health nurse was contacted. To ascertain eligibility for service benevolent funds, the nurse investigated each case and determined if the family had any kind of hospital or group insurance and whether the mother or father was a veteran. If it was determined that no assistance could be provided through that source, the family was referred to a service club in the area, and if one didn't exist, assistance was requested from the New Brunswick Society for Crippled Children. This was considered supplemented assistance and could only be authorized by the four Rotary Clubs in the province.[74] In 1958 the Mentally Retarded Children Act was passed, which allowed for lump-sum payments to foster homes for disabled children. Children with behavioural and intellectual disabilities were usually placed in the provincial hospital in Lancaster, later called Centracare. A blind child could not receive any assistance from the Canadian National Institute for the Blind until the age of six.[75] The "School for Mentally Retarded Children" opened in September 1963 in Lancaster, New Brunswick. Those who worked with "mentally retarded" children made plans in the fall of 1963 to petition the government to pay the full cost of education and special care for these children, rather than continuing to rely on service clubs.[76]

British refugee children

The war necessitated special action for New Brunswickers. The City and County of Saint John responded to the wartime need to provide safety for British refugee children in 1940 by receiving one hundred children. Extra staff were hired to help respond to the need.[77] The Children's Aid Societies in the counties of Albert and Westmorland also responded to this exceptional circumstance. Albert County provided $45, and Westmorland County earmarked $270 to respond to the need.[78] University Women's Clubs provided additional support in the form of home placements for children. The Moncton chapter of the University Women's Club offered to place approximately eight children and noted that "over 60% of our members are single women living in rooms. Four of these will take in a girl if the need is urgent and practically all will help with clothing, vacations, education, etc."[79]

Morality and Mothers' Allowances

Issues surrounding the Mothers' Allowances represented a constant frustration to social workers in the province. Although all the provinces eventually called the supplement to women in financial need the Mothers' Allowances, it first appeared in British Columbia in 1920. The term "pension" was used to describe the benefits of what was really a public-assistance measure. Women in need of financial assistance were encouraged to apply. This was one of the goals of the Mothers' Pension Movement – the lessening of charity stigma that was part-and-parcel of relief up until this time[80] – and reflected a "significant departure from traditional poor relief practices which had existed from colonial times."[81]

In New Brunswick, the statute passed in 1938 became effective only in 1943, thirteen years after Nova Scotia, six years after Québec, and six years before neighbouring Prince Edward Island.[82] Thus New Brunswick mothers were provided cash allowances only in 1943. In 1939, in British Columbia, and similarly in Ontario, a woman was eligible to receive financial help if her husband was housed in a sanitarium for tuberculosis, a mental hospital, in prison, or "totally incapacitated";[83] however, the Mothers' Allowance program in Nova Scotia did not allow for any of these sets of circumstances. There was a residency requirement of three years in New Brunswick, Nova Scotia, Prince Edward Island, and British Columbia, compared to no residency requirement in Alberta and one year in Saskatchewan, while in Manitoba and Ontario a two-year requirement existed. Women in Québec had to wait five years before becoming eligible,[84] which speaks to the lack of uniformity across provinces.[85]

Citizenship requirements for Mothers' Allowances stipulated that the child and mother must be British subjects and that the applicant must not be an Indian as defined by the Indian Act of Canada.[86] Women who had been deserted by their husbands were required to charge for non-support under the Deserted Wives and Children's Maintenance Act to secure financial support for the children. Only if it could be proven that the husband's whereabouts could not be determined and, therefore, no support would likely be forthcoming, would the woman receive food or donations of clothing for her children. At times a CAS agent would be engaged to put pressure on the "deadbeat dad" as the following 1953 letter indicates:

> I am writing to advise you to pay up all you owe your wife for the support of the family. Do this at once or you may find yourself in jail. If she takes this matter up with the magistrate, a warrant will be out for your arrest and you will be sent home to stand trial. So take my advice and do not delay to settle this matter at once.[87]

Women were scrutinized and had to be "in every aspect a fit, proper and suitable person to have the custody and care of her children."[88] The Schools Act (1941, 1943) required mothers to ensure that their children attended school or the consequences would render them ineligible to receive the "scarce bits of lard, flour and molasses" they might receive on relief.[89]

The Illegitimate Children's Act became legislation in 1926 and was renamed the Children of Unmarried Parents Act in 1956. Women must have felt pressure from the province determined to shift responsibility for them to a real or imagined male breadwinner. Indeed, conservative social worker Whitton, director of the Canadian Council for Child Welfare in Ottawa since 1920, promoted the belief that "unmarried parenthood [was] the chief factor contributing to dependency." Margaret Anstey, one of New Brunswick's earliest professionally qualified social workers, seemed to be the exception as she tried to work with unmarried mothers to assist them in keeping their children. An unmarried mother faced many judgments and even more hurdles if she wished to keep and raise her child, for not until 1961 were women eligible to receive Mothers' Allowances for an illegitimate child, and then only in certain circumstances.[90] At times a CAS agent was called on to investigate situations to gauge if the mother was sufficiently contrite to receive any kind of assistance at all, as the following 1948 letter indicates:

> The above was receiving Mothers' Allowance, but because of giving birth to an illegitimate child in the latter part of March, her cheque was cancelled. I would ask you to visit the home of ______ to impress upon her the necessity of being a proper example to her children, and ask her what she intends doing about her future behavior. It does seem to me that a woman who was receiving an allowance for her children, should behave herself and be a proper example to her children. If you call and find that she is sorry for this happening, and that she promises it will not happen again, please report same to me and I shall be glad to refer the report to the Commission of the Mothers' Allowances.[91]

The CAS worker was able to report back that neighbours were sympathetic towards the woman and her children because the man had left and had not returned to marry her. Another similar visit by the CAS worker was requested in a letter written in 1949:

> The above's allowance has been cancelled. The fact that she had this child disqualified her for Mothers' Allowance. Would you kindly call her at home to get the story, and report your findings in duplicate to me.[92]

The CAS worker did as was requested and reported back that, according to neighbours, "no men had ever visited her in her home." He reported that because she was not intelligent, she could do only certain kinds of work, and that she had no intention of getting married to the father of the child because he seldom ever worked. The CAS worker asked if the child welfare officer might help her out after all.[93]

By 1954 it seems that the opinion tide had turned more kindly towards unmarried mothers as evidenced in a letter to the CAS worker of Northumberland County on behalf of the regional director of Family Allowances:

> Thank you for your report on the ______ case. We are definitely in agreement with you that nothing should be done to jeopardize this home situation since it has been established that the care which the mother and

> grandfather are giving the children is satisfactory. We have found that unmarried motherhood is something that can happen in any family situation and there must have been a great deal of affection and security on the part of ______ that she had to seek this through her many children. She will continue to receive family allowances on their behalf.[94]

It was still critical that the father's name appear on the baptismal certificate in 1953 or the child would not be classified as legitimate.[95] A putative father was expected to pay any medical costs related to the mother's confinement as well as provide financial support for the child if the mother kept the child. At times, little cooperation was forthcoming to locate a putative father, as this letter written in 1958 reveals:

> Re the above, I called the Orderly room of the RCAF (Royal Canadian Air Force) station, a couple of times in order to find out if _____ was on the Station. At that time he was not there and nothing further was done on the matter. There is little or nothing that can be done on a case of this type as we do not receive the cooperation of the RCAF staff that we did in the past. They have been bothered with too many cases of this type.[96]

Sometimes mothers with children born out of wedlock had to adopt their own children and "legitimize" them in order to receive benefits,[97] and a seal of approval from a CAS agent was influential with Family Allowances.[98]

When families receiving Mothers' Allowances had medical expenses they had to turn to a limited range of agencies to determine one that might be able to help depending on their circumstances – agencies such as the Catholic Welfare Bureau,[99] the Canadian Legion, the Women's Institute, the Ladies Auxiliary, the Red Cross or the Shriners. Often, families were referred to municipal authorities since the CAS also did not pay hospital and doctors' bills.[100] In some cases the CAS agent advocated for a municipality to provide financial support when an agency provided only partial support.[101] Mothers' Allowances came under the welfare department when the province centralized programs in 1966 and health cards were provided.

In December 1951 the New Brunswick Association of Children's Aid Societies passed a motion recommending to the minister of health and social services and to the director of Mothers' Allowances in Fredericton that the monthly payments to mothers be increased.[102] By 1956 changes were made to the Mothers' Allowances Act that extended the child's maximum age to receive benefits to seventeen, providing the child was in school and adopted by the child's unmarried mother.[103] In 1953 widows returning to New Brunswick were required to reside in the province for three years before their children could qualify, which "caused unnecessary hardship on very deserving cases."[104] Although no maximum amount for receiving income in addition to Mothers' Allowance was outlined,[105] in 1953 the amount was reduced by an average of $15 per month when a husband became eligible for an allowance under the Disabled Persons Allowance Act.[106] In 1958 the annual report of the Family Welfare Association reflects that Mothers' Allowance payments were still too low to meet the cost of living.[107]

The process of bringing a family to the county home was an ordeal. The following notation from the CAS worker in Northumberland County provides some insight into the process:

> On February 13th I had a phone call from Mr. ______ about the above mentioned family. I did not manage to go to ______ until the 19th. On finding the conditions in the home had not improved the only thing to do with the family was to move them to the county home. I contacted ______ (the alms commissioner) but could not move the children as they had no clean clothes and little or no dirty ones, I advised all parties that I would be back on Wednesday of the following week. I contacted ______ and asked her for clothing for the children. On Wednesday the 23rd I called for the clothes at the Red Cross rooms and Mrs. ______ gave me a box of clothing for the children and a coat for their mother. I did not lose any time going to ______, I contacted councillor ______. Mrs. ______ went with me to get the children ready, Mrs. ______ came over to help get them ready, by the time the children were ready Mrs. ______ was ready and seemed anxious to get to the county home. After I was there on Saturday some of the neighbors gave them some clothes for the children. All the food in the house was bread, molasses and beans. We arrived at the county home just after dinner, but they were given dinner.[108]

Frustrating rules for Veterans' Benefits

CAS workers experienced double binds when trying to assist people manoeuvring their way through eligibility rules. Howard Young sought advice from the director of Mothers' Allowance in Fredericton on behalf of a woman who lived only on Mothers' Allowance because she did not meet the requirement of the Department of Veterans' Affairs (DVA) widow's allowance: that is, to be either mentally or physically disabled or over fifty-five years of age. The woman had four children to raise and had received a payment of $90 per month for one year only after her husband had died.[109]

A particularly frustrating situation was when the CAS worker tried to find funding for a veteran who required frequent hospitalization and was unable to work. He had no pension and no money. His classification as a veteran allowed for free hospital care, but no allowance for the family. His application for War Veterans Allowance was declined because he was less than sixty years of age and not considered permanently unemployable or incapable of maintenance. If help was not found for the family, the children would have been placed in foster homes.[110]

Lack of services for Francophones

It appears that the process of extending CAS services in francophone counties occurred from 1941 to 1951. Historically, the francophone population was unable to receive services in their own language. Anglophone social workers did not necessarily recognize the importance of services being available in one's first language, as the following situations attest: "I did not speak French so it was not easy to talk with all these people. I thought Mr. _______ spoke English quite well, but he seemed not to follow me, or would not trust his understanding of English."[111]

Mary Bishop, who was administrator at the CAS in Saint John from 1949 to 1959, expressed frustration with the language barrier when she wrote to Howard Young, "it was explained to her the necessity of taking immediate action in regards to her child. Being French it was hard to explain to Miss _____ the circumstances but she assured [the CAS] worker [in Saint John] that she would look into the matter."[112] It was a sign of progress when in 1955 the director of welfare for New Brunswick, Mr LeBlanc, led the round table discussion of a meeting of the Association of Children's Aid Societies in French. It was reported that "those who speak little or no French were welcomed and, with a little interpretation, were able to participate in spirit if not verbally. It was the general consensus of opinion that one session each year should be conducted in the French language."[113]

Several decades with an official languages act in New Brunswick have led to greater awareness and sensitivity for linguistic rights and respect. Comments above reflect an inability of early anglophone social workers to view their own language limitations as part of the equation or to comprehend the formidable challenge inherent in addressing others in a second language, particularly those with authority and power over one's life. Because language reflects culture and context, an assumed expectation to speak the dominant language or language of a dominant culture with ease and confidence can be experienced as oppression.

Lack of services in rural areas

Social workers discussed barriers to basic services because of living in a rural area. Access to health facilities was identified as a problem due to the long-distance transportation. According to Mary Burns, in the County of Restigouche in 1956, some school districts were without teachers. Eighty percent of the children in rural schools were taught by teachers with local licenses, and two inexperienced teachers were responsible for 126 students. Of concern as well was that fifty children were not even registered and nothing was being done about it as there was no place for them in the school.[114] However, in 1962, a Dr Chiasson "made some observations regarding the work of the agencies in rural areas and the appreciation of the municipal authorities of the services rendered these communities."[115]

Jurisdictional limitations

Jurisdictional restrictions of a Children's Aid Society had implications for the protection of children. In 1958 a representative of the Sussex Women's Institute wrote to the CAS in Saint John, concerned about a family of children "in desperate circumstances" in Sussex. The response she received was to try to have the children admitted to the New Brunswick Protestant Orphans' Home if the children were of average intelligence and in good health because the Saint John CAS did not have jurisdiction in Sussex.[116]

Lack of professional social workers

The lack of professional social workers has been a perennial concern in the province and nationally. Previously discussed was the great need for social workers in Canada in the post–Second World War period. In 1957 the CASW stated that Canadian schools of social work were not graduating sufficient numbers of trained social workers.[117] In 1965 the minister of youth and welfare acknowledged a request by the county secretary of

Saint John for more qualified personnel and responded favourably by noting the possibility of bursaries for qualified candidates at Memorial University College.[118] The county secretary wrote back to the minister on behalf of the municipal council to formally request that the provincial government institute a training course for non-professional social and welfare workers, suggesting that they be held at the University of New Brunswick Branch in Saint John, the New Brunswick Technical Training School in Simonds, or the Saint John Vocational School.[119] It was noted previously that even in 1965, out of a total of 37 field staff working in Children's Aid Societies, only seven had master of social work degrees.[120]

Issues around race and religion

CAS workers had to show caution with respect to race and religion when placing children. It was the law that a Protestant child could not be placed for adoption in other than a Protestant family.[121] Furthermore, a home in which one parent was Protestant and the other Catholic would not be deemed suitable for adoption.[122]

Conclusion

In this chapter we have seen how the agencies to protect children evolved during the first decades of the last century, first in Saint John, the largest city, followed by Fredericton, Moncton, and then Sackville in 1924. It wouldn't be until 1941 that anglophone CAS agencies began to be established in every county, which meant that the francophone population was likely not included for whatever services the CAS provided. Mi'kmaq and Maliseet children were sent to Shubenacadie under the guise of the provision of education; however, some were also sent there, from 1929 until 1967, as a solution for child-care issues. Where agencies existed, children were taken from their home at the times of a crisis. The fact that Mi'kmaq and Maliseet peoples received few services from the federal government and were eligible for few provincial programs until the 1950s was discussed in chapter 5. This chapter described how the monthly baby bonus allotments were not sent directly to Mi'kmaq and Maliseet mothers but were diverted to the federal coffers. It was shown how francophone New Brunswickers did not receive CAS services in their counties until 1941 through to the early 1950s. Francophones were also unlikely to receive services in their own language until the

1960s and Equal Opportunity. Those living in rural areas experienced further barriers in accessing basic services and an adequate education.

Until 1953 CASs had to fundraise to augment the allotment provided by the municipalities in which they were located, a step behind other jurisdictions in Canada. Following the trend across Canada, the philosophy towards children started to shift during the 1950s. In New Brunswick, these shifts were influenced by the sponsored study of child welfare services completed in 1951 by Cook Wilson, followed by a Canadian Council on Child Welfare study in 1955 when the institutional care of children was discouraged in favour of foster homes, although the municipal home in Woodstock was not closed until 1966. The importance of the mental, physical, emotional, and spiritual development of children was recognized in New Brunswick, as in other parts of Canada. In 1953 New Brunswick social workers lobbied in vain to have the province adopt a system similar to that in British Columbia which provided one social worker for every municipality with a population of 10,000 to administer services that would help families remain intact, as opposed to taking children out of their homes. During the 1950s the word "illegitimate" was taken out of parlance, and women left to raise children on their own were referred to as "unmarried mothers," marking a significant step away from the stigmatization that unmarried mothers had endured for more than one hundred years. By the mid-1950s the province was further urged to foot the medical bill for children born of unmarried mothers, as well as to provide for pre- and post-natal maintenance and the placement of children in care if adoption was pending. Also in the 1950s, services for children with special needs began to be coordinated. By 1962 children were seen to have rights, and the province's adoption process evolved to respect some of these rights, as it did in other parts of Canada.

The number of social workers in New Brunswick was small, as was the population of the province compared to large city centres such as Toronto, Montreal, Ottawa, Winnipeg, and Vancouver. There was no welfare or community council in the province where radical social workers could influence policy development. Only when Equal Opportunity placed the coordination of child welfare services with the CASs did the overseer-of-the-poor structure dissolve, removing at least one layer of frustrating rules. There is no evidence that any radical social workers practised in the province. However, when practising social workers learned of advances in child welfare, for example, they were receptive and lobbied government to affect such advances in the province.

Louis J. Robichaud was elected premier of the province of New Brunswick at the start of the Quiet Revolution in Québec and at the time of emergent social movements. It is hard to know what influence social movements occurring across Canada had on events in New Brunswick. We know that some New Brunswickers were active socialists early in the twentieth century. We also know that the CCF party was the most active during the 1940s but had little presence before or after that decade. A small leftist contingent appeared in the form of the "Waffle movement" in the provincial NDP early in the 1970s, but that is beyond the time frame of this book. There were no community welfare councils in New Brunswick as there were in more populated areas of Canada, where social workers could form coalitions with other groups and individuals to fight for causes such as daycare in the post–Second World War period, to advocate for control of consumer prices in the post-war period, to fight poverty, to fight for rights for the unemployed, or to join the trend of leftist social workers to advocate for unionization. Thus there is no evidence that social workers practising in New Brunswick were aware of these issues, which engaged their radical counterparts in other parts of Canada.

That the CCF presence could not be sustained in the largely anti-labour atmosphere, in which people feared losing their jobs if associated with even a mild form of socialism, is telling. Perhaps it is sufficient to conclude that the few social workers who practised child welfare in this province, who maintained large caseloads with few resources for the first half-century of its existence, should be given credit for their part in ending stigmatized services to the poor, to unmarried mothers and their children, and to francophones in spite of the circumstances they had to endure.

The earliest social workers and the context in which they worked are discussed in the following chapter.

7

A Portrait of New Brunswick's Earliest Social Workers

LINDA TURNER

When were New Brunswick's professionally qualified social workers first hired by private agencies and by government? What roles did they play and how did they describe their experiences and perspectives? In this chapter the lives and stories of social workers employed in the province before 1967 are shared, and in Appendix 2, readers will find names and available information on every individual who was discovered during the book's research who held social work credentials or had extensive work experience in social work positions.

Among New Brunswick–born social workers, Elizabeth King appears to be the first. After completing a BA and master's degree, she attended the American Red Cross Summer Course in Social Work in 1918. She engaged in a variety of roles in Ottawa and New York, eventually returning to New Brunswick. King was a staff person for Charlotte Whitton's 1927 New Brunswick Child Welfare Survey in Saint John, New Brunswick (1927–30).

Another early professionally qualified social worker in New Brunswick was Jennie Robinson, born in Sweetsburg, Québec, who moved from Edmonton, Alberta, after accepting the position of superintendent of the Interprovincial Home for Young Women in Coverdale, near Moncton. She was already a member of the Canadian Association of Social Workers in 1926. Besides King and Robinson, few social workers had emerged even twenty years later, reflected in the statement that "in 1942 there was not a professionally trained social worker employed by any public agency in the province."[1]

Minutes of the meetings of the committee that worked to create the Interprovincial Home for Young Women reveal a hiring process that seemed committed to ensuring that a high quality of candidate was found.

Miss Robinson, who at the time of hiring was working in an Edmonton home for girls, was successful and arrived as the home opened in 1925. Her salary was $60 per month. Excerpts from a letter she wrote thanking an overseer of the poor for a maintenance cheque provide a contextual appreciation of some of the institution's values:

> With reference to this girl, she is very bright, liking fun more than work, however, but is doing well, and I feel sure will make good. We have broken her of several very bad habits. She takes an interest in the "Home" and tries to do her best. She learns anything very quickly, had she the education, I believe she could make quite an artist; she can draw anything without the slightest effort. I shall be pleased to give you a report on her progress at any time, if you desire it.[2]

The membership approval lists of the CASW show Miss Jennie Robinson, Superintendent of the Home, listed as a new member, among the dozen that include James Shaver Woodsworth, social justice advocate and House of Commons Labour Party member in Winnipeg. In 1928 a request was approved for Miss Robinson to travel to Montreal for four days to attend the first Canadian conference on social work, a landmark event with more than 700 attending from numerous provinces.

Despite continuous positive reports about the superintendent in the minutes, late in 1928 a mysterious emergency meeting of the board members, men from protestant Maritime congregations, was called, and five female employees appeared in front of them, with the social worker appearing last. The outcome recorded in the minutes was that the first two women appearing would be asked to withdraw their letters of resignation, Miss Robinson would be going on a two-month leave, and a Miss Bearisto who had been employed would be let go. In subsequent minutes it is acknowledged that Miss Robinson left; however, it is not clear if she chose to do so. In December of the year of this crisis, Christmas presents for the residents from Miss Robinson and Miss Bearisto are mentioned. No further information could be found regarding Miss Robinson's location or activities.

A contemporary of Robinson's was Margaret Anstey who was born in London, England, and graduated with a diploma in social services from the University of Toronto. After living in Italy and working as staff at an infants' home, she was director of the Children's Aid Society in Saint John from 1930 to 1934. She had been on loan to the CAS from the

Central Welfare Council of Saint John to establish modern casework practice in the city. Sharon Myers believes that Anstey was fired from the CAS because "Anstey had successfully managed to increase donations to the CAS but at the expense of the [Protestant Children's] Orphanage, and she had managed to reduce the supply of money-making babies available to Miller by supporting unwed mothers in their efforts to keep their children."[3] Myers suggests that the director, Usher Miller, had convinced the board of the CAS to fire Anstey.

The authors of the Moncton survey report of 1939 articulated the view that hiring professionally trained social workers was essential: "You do not hope to control crime without a police force, and in this day it is about equally hopeless to control social deterioration without employing social workers to do it … if the three key points, Welfare Bureau, Children's Aid and Municipal work are manned with minimum professional service, a few years will show improvement in this very serious situation."[4] The comment clearly reflects a set of expectations that the role's focus was "controlling social deterioration," an arguably lofty and not clearly defined goal. Jennissen and Lundy devote a chapter in their book, *One Hundred Years of Social Work: A History of the Profession in English Canada, 1900–2000*, to discussing the range of perspectives that characterized how social workers imagined their roles when facing the poverty of the 1930s. Some strongly encouraged stepping up to offer leadership that could contribute to an amelioration of the social and economic conditions, while many, comfortable in the casework approach, focused on individual adaptation and functioning, and did not see social work as holding a moral or social responsibility to engage in social activism.

Miss Margaret Rowley was the first New Brunswicker to gain a master's in social work from an Atlantic school of social work, joining the Maritime School of Social Work's small graduating class of four students in 1943. By the spring of 1947 the Maritime School had a student in a field placement at the Children's Aid Society of Saint John.[5] A group of nine from the school, composed of the two paid faculty and seven voluntary field instructors, also travelled to Saint John later that year to participate in the "Maritime Conference on Social Work."

Up until 1940, the Canadian Association of Social Workers had membership branches in Ontario, British Columbia, Manitoba, Nova Scotia, and Québec. Before long New Brunswick and Prince Edward Island joined together to fulfil the branch membership requirements. In 1948 the New Brunswick–Prince Edward Island Branch was formed. Meetings alternated between the provinces. A few of the New Brunswick social workers who on occasion travelled by ferry to meet their counterparts were Freda E. Vickery, Margaret Gibson, Rosalie MacLaughlin, Kathleen (Tally) Morrissy, Lorna B. Warneford, and Carol D. Proctor. Tally Morrissy took minutes of the Branch meetings.[6]

A New Brunswick–Prince Edward Island chapter meeting on a Saturday in March of 1952, covered by the Charlottetown *Guardian*,[7] reveals several points of interest. All members attending are named and their positions identified. None appear to have been from Prince Edward Island, nor are any Francophones apparent among the individuals from Fredericton, Saint John, Moncton, and Sackville. Committee reports predominated the agenda, including "several" committees that shared their reports pertaining to "Public Assistance and the Unemployed," a study report from the Canadian Welfare Council in Ottawa. A focused discussion, led by Stan Matheson, generated topics "to be taken up at the international conference on Social Work to be held in Madras, India" which would be nine months later. Coverage of the meeting indicates commitment to organization and involvement, even at the international level.

Stanley Matheson, mentioned above, was a social worker at the provincial psychiatric hospital in Saint John, known for many years as "Centracare." The institution, first called the Provincial Lunatic Asylum, is of historical significance, as it was North America's first mental-health facility. Matheson would soon become the supervisor of numerous mental-health social workers throughout the province, including this book's co-author Louis J. Richard. Matheson recalled that during his first week, while being taken around the hospital for orientation, he was brought into an operating room where a lobotomy was being performed. He also remembered helping to advocate against admission to the psychiatric hospital of a young girl with epilepsy from a rural community near Woodstock, who was not permitted to attend school because of the condition. He credited a young female psychiatrist in the area with creating opportunities for the young girl to gain skills and to continue to develop, even though she was not permitted to go to school.[8]

The mental-health field welcomed a great number of New Brunswick's first social workers. In the north, the Clinique de santé mentale in Edmundston was one site, as was the provincial hospital in Campbellton. Meanwhile Moncton, Fredericton, and Saint John hired social workers in mental-health clinics, and the Saint John General Hospital Psychiatric

Department also offered social work services, in addition to social workers being employed at the provincial hospital.

General and veteran's hospitals also provided employment, including Moncton Hospital, a provincial hospital at River Glade, the Edmundston Regional Hospital, Lancaster DVA Hospital, and Dr. William F. Roberts Hospital School. In addition to taking positions in the child welfare field, the earliest social workers also turned up in the corrections field at the New Brunswick Central Reformatory in Kingsclear and Dorchester Penitentiary, as well as in the City of Fredericton's Welfare Department.

In 1961 CASW members from New Brunswick numbered thirty-eight, about one-third of Nova Scotia's membership, but quadruple the number of members from Newfoundland. Four years later in 1965 when the New Brunswick Association of Social Workers came into existence with an act of the legislature, the eighth province to establish a social work professional association, it had a membership of fifty.[9] Founding members of the New Brunswick branch were Carol Proctor, Marcel Arseneau, Joseph Laviolette, Norman Clavet, Stanley Matheson, Murray Manzer, and Constance Harrison. A history of the NBASW is found in Appendix 1. Before enough social workers existed to form a branch, Kathleen (Tally) Morrissy served as a non-branch representative, which required attending CASW meetings and writing a report of what was discussed at the meetings.[10]

By the time Louis J. Robichaud's Equal Opportunity legislation was implemented, more than one hundred New Brunswickers with social work qualifications, (in most cases a master of social work degree), could be found among the association's membership lists or in agency documents. There were few work locations in the northern regions. Edmundston's Clinique de santé mentale, the Provincial (Psychiatric) Hospital in Campbellton, and la Societé de l'aide á l'enfance in Caraquet had social workers on staff before 1967. In the southern half of the province, where the province's three major cities lie, the agencies employing professionally qualified social workers were far more numerous and included Moncton Hospital, mental-health clinics, the provincial hospital at River Glade, municipal welfare bureaus, child welfare services, Boys and Girls Clubs, the Interprovincial Home for Young Women, YMCA, Dorchester Penitentiary, welfare departments, the National Health and Welfare Family Allowance Program, New Brunswick Central Reformatory, Catholic Welfare Bureaus, the provincial hospital in Saint John, Lancaster DVA Hospital, New Brunswick Boys Industrial Home, and Dr. William F. Roberts Hospital School.

Names of professionally qualified social workers who surfaced during the research for this book are included in Appendix 2, along with any career related details that were found.

Some specific aspects of the experiences they faced are examined in the next section.

Challenges

Influence of the Church

The association of Christianity with social work service predominated in its early days. Three New Brunswickers were among the nine Maritime School of Social Work master of social work graduates of 1948: Miss Margaret H. Gibson, Saint Andrews; Mary Katherine O'Connell, Campbellton; and Edna Myrna Smith, Elgin. The guest speaker address by Reverend Hugh Joseph Somers, vice-president of St. Francis Xavier University, was mentioned in the *Halifax Mail* and reflects Somers's assumptions that religious conviction and Christian duty was part of the profession's ethos:

> True democracy can only be founded on a social structure based on the teachings of Christ, Rev. Hugh Joseph Somers, Ph.D. (C.U.A.), vice-president of St. Francis Xavier University, said in his address to the graduates. Work of the graduates, if they were to make their contributions in the world, should be more than a "statistical journey through the slums of our cities," Rev. Dr. Somers declared. The "Magna Carta" of social service was laid down by Christ Himself and graduates must never consider their work just a position but think of it as a vocation made holy by Christ.[11]

Three of the people interviewed for this research mentioned the significance of one's religious affiliation and of the influence of the bishop on social workers of the Catholic faith. The following story is one of two that emerged about religion influencing hiring. Archie Smith was applying for a position that had opened up temporarily because an employee had suffered a heart attack. He recounts what happened when he appeared for his interview:

> So the guy says, just a moment I have got to make a phone call before I can hire you. I said sure. So anyway, the stupid arse goes around the corner and he calls up and he says, now he is not a Catholic because his name is Smith.

> So anyway I am thinking what's this got to do with Catholics. So anyway he came back in and he said yeah, I made the right call and you can come to work tomorrow. So I went out and saw ____ _____ and I am not sure how ____ is spelt but I know one is with an e and one is with a k. I don't know which one is a Catholic version but he was a Catholic but he had a Protestant version of the spelling of his name. He called me outside and he says he knew I was a Catholic because he went to the Catholic Church, same as I did. He said, don't tell them that you're a Catholic. I said why? He said Catholics aren't hired by the government. I said how did you get in here? He said because I have got a protestant spelling of my name, the same reason you did. That would be back in 1960, possibly '61, so that shows you how bad things were.[12]

References to the power and influence of the bishop surfaced in two contexts. Two of the interviewees said that the bishop told them he wanted them to go study to become social workers, and as one summed it up, "if the Bishop told you that you were going to do it, you did it." Another spoke of the extensive decision-making powers of the bishop, who alone could determine if extra funds could be given to families at Christmas time, or to individuals at other times.

Stereotypical roles

Views about the roles of men and women fell along stereotypical lines. A welfare survey's authors shared this opinion: "as it is unlikely that the Commission could afford the full-time salary of a male social worker, and as work with families is more successfully carried out by a woman, it is advised that this worker be a woman."[13] That perspective resonates with a situation that occurred a few years earlier, two provinces away, in Ottawa, when its welfare bureau was transformed by the dismissal of forty women, to be replaced by a smaller number of men, and relief was separated from social services. Jennissen and Lundy explain the thinking of the day with a 1936 *Social Worker* article, that "men investigators did better work than women; they were not interested in social service but in seeing that those on relief gave the city the right information and reported their earnings."[14]

A predominant role for men in community social welfare provision was assumed to be leadership through membership on the boards of the proposed welfare councils:

> It cannot be too strongly stated that the Board should be selected mainly from among the best business men in the city – older and younger. The

> financial stability and good administration of the whole Council depends on drawing into this Board the best of Moncton's many socially minded business men. It is not intended to imply that it should have no women, but they too should be selected for their business capacity, and their general knowledge of the community as a whole.[15]

A staff person in the role of executive officer was expected to serve as a counsellor and play a role in ensuring service provision. The individual was presumed to be a woman who held "… the discerning mind and understanding heart which good personal service demands, [and] must possess the natural gift of arousing and encouraging the confidence of men and women, and wisdom, based on knowledge and experiences, to guide her in the counselling and directions of lives, other than her own."[16]

The notion that family and child welfare were domains for female social workers probably played an influential role in career choices of men. As quoted in our introductory chapter, in 1966, a newly appointed male case worker for a Children's Aid Society who questioned his employer regarding why he had been hired in spite of not having completed all his degree requirements said he was told he was hired because he was a man. The worker assumed that in an office with eighteen women and no men, his presence would be particularly welcome when there was a need to respond to a night call. Only one social worker interviewed mentioned a dress code, and this related to female social workers: "They made us wear brogue shoes which some people don't remember, but they were very formal footwear, and you had to wear a dark suit and you had to wear a felt hat. I didn't even own such a thing as a hat, and we thought that was pretty weird. But we had to do that and we had to present ourselves as being very prissy and formal."[17] In the next chapter, in which the experiences of the first Acadian social workers are shared, it is noteworthy that eleven of the twelve are male, in contrast to the situation relative to anglophone social workers.

Working conditions

By the mid-1950s the province began to see a rise in professionally trained social workers, a phenomenon influenced by increased educational opportunities. One pioneer provides this information about her beginnings during this time:

> I got $100 a month. I was supposed to work part time, which was two thirds of the time. Most people were working a six-day work week then so I was

> supposed to be working four days a week. But in fact I worked seven days a week, sometimes all night long. If you apprehended kids at midnight who had been neglected and left all alone, little kids left in a home, for three days you were up all night, and so I was paid the $100 and I also had to pay out of that my car expenses and on top of that if I had children, I was moving around for the day to Moncton to a doctor and I had to feed them out of that too.[18]

Salary details from one source indicate that by 1965, a senior worker in child welfare for a family services bureau could receive an annual salary of $4,400 while a social assistance senior worker could receive $4,000. Starting salary for a new child welfare caseworker would have been $3,600 per year.[19]

Whilst professional salaries may have held appeal, the working environment was not without its challenges. Marcel Arseneau, reflecting on his career, which began in 1960, and on the context for francophone regions, spoke of a lack of resources in communities, and a lack of resources in social services, in hospitals, and in child and family services. It was precisely this lack of resources that made the work so difficult. Further, he noted that the lack of financial resources for agencies rendered many people poor. There was no way for people to climb out of their situations. Living conditions were deplorable and even worse for those not eligible for unemployment insurance. He described such situations as characterized by deep misery.[20]

The theme of social workers as agents of social control continued from the earliest days of the profession. In the financial domain

> employees were often seen a bit like police who controlled the amounts given and who did investigations. Often they were called investigators or inspectors. They were not seen as social workers, but as investigators. The word investigator, stayed for a long time in the vocabulary, because they asked lots of questions, especially about incomes – if people worked, etc. It was a form of control because the counties had very little money, so they wanted to ensure the money was administered well.[21]

Arseneau concluded, “It may have been a poor perception of what the employees wanted to do.”[22] The value base of the profession even in its early days was steering qualified social workers away from punitive and restrictive roles and there was a growing acknowledgment of society’s failings in relation to economic hardship.

Tensions between untrained welfare workers and professionally trained social workers

Another theme that emerged during interviews with the earliest workers was the nature of the interface between the newly educated professional social workers who came onto the scene in the 1950s and 1960s, and people who had years, or even decades, of experience in social service positions. Some interviewees were more candid than others about the tensions they witnessed in this aspect of their working lives. Membership in the New Brunswick Association of Social Workers was potentially a contentious issue, depending on one's views about membership criteria (i.e., post-secondary education in social work or simply work experience):

> many people were sent away on bursaries to study psychology, social work, and psychiatry and those persons came back to the province. This was towards the end of the fifties. So you have this group of people who are functioning as social workers out in the community now being impacted by these professionals coming back from training in Halifax. It was not a happy meeting. There was conflict. The trained professionals were thought to have a huge body of knowledge and capabilities. "You have all the answers." The persons who had been doing the work out in the field personally felt that they couldn't measure up and frequently were put down by these professionals. They didn't value each other's strengths at all. I don't think it was ever resolved.[23]

Flora Jean Kennedy commented on the general societal response to freshly educated social work professionals making their debut:

> Most of the places I worked did not know what to do with social workers. You had to go in and tell them this is what I can do or you had to show them what you can do. Other places had the stance that you were a professional, a trained person, and therefore you are able to accomplish all these miracles, which was ridiculous. So there wasn't a very realistic attitude toward social work or social workers.[24]

The same interviewee responded to a question of what theoretical orientation she was taught by indicating, "We didn't use labels to describe our practice. How about 'situational social work?' Responding to what was. Who was the boss? Who were the comptrollers? How much money did they have? These were the restrictions that influenced what we did."[25]

Identity and recognition

Marcel Arseneau, who practised in the northern region of the province, also emphasized that part of their work as social workers was to be recognized as a profession by the general population; he stressed they needed to work hard to gain an identity, and one way was to form a professional association. He also mentioned this was a time period when social workers were in great demand as guest speakers at home and school associations, in service clubs, with volunteer organizations such as the Mental Health Association, at Women's Institutes, and 4H Clubs, as well as often serving as masters of ceremonies for different functions in the community. He estimates the number of professional social workers in 1960 as being approximately forty, with most being anglophones.[26]

Prevention

Social workers were often employed by Family Welfare Associations, which were the forerunners of today's Family Service Agencies. The following description portrays how one such association viewed its mandate and mode of operation in the mid-1960s:

> Lack of education, early marriages, drunkenness and unemployment ... these and other factors may create situations leading to disharmony, to conflict, to poor parent-child relationships or to strains between families of different generations ... The function of the Family Welfare Association is basically to provide case work service to help these people where they need to be helped, keeping in mind the importance of retaining a family as a social unit and not as a social problem. It also provides auxiliary services such as placing children in camps during the summer, care of grants and trust funds, locating housing, providing clothing and giving relief for fire victims. On a broader field, by the nature of its work, it has become an important factor in the field of community planning.[27]

A statistical summary provided for the year 1954 by the Family Welfare Association of Saint John reveals a categorization that reflects "client problems" of the times: Income: one hundred forty-eight; Marital Difficulties: fifty-nine; Unemployment: sixty-three; Indebtedness: forty-two; Known Sexual Immorality: four; Sexual Immorality Suspected: five; Begging Tendency: twenty.[28]

By 1963, the issues of housing and income were being granted far greater attention as evidenced by data generated in that year: Housing – substandard: fifty-three; Housing – needed: forty-two; Insufficient Income: one hundred sixty-one; Marital Difficulty: sixty-four; Indebtedness: fifty-four.[29]

Regarding domains of practice, a case work report from one family-counselling agency for the year 1964 highlighted that "more emphasis was also placed on family counselling. This was due in part to the addition to our staff of Mrs. Riives who had training and experience in Europe, as well as some Canadian experience. This trend to family counselling and preventive service we plan to develop further in the future."[30]

Civil defence

Civil defence was a national concern for social workers in New Brunswick as well. In 1956 Civil Defence Welfare Services provided a training course for board members of the CASW and branch presidents because they wished to involve professional social workers so that they could contribute to disaster planning in their own communities. Although organization for wartime disaster was not too well planned in New Brunswick by 1960, a special disaster committee was sanctioned by the attorney general's department that consisted of representatives from the Red Cross, the Salvation Army, Saint John Ambulance, the Canadian Legion, the RCMP, Forestry Services, fire marshal's resources, and the army. The coordinator for the Saint John area asked that a list of social workers and their locations be prepared for him, and one was drawn up for the provincial coordinator of welfare services as well.[31]

Community organization and advocacy

Another report emphasized the role of community planner and developer in addition to highlighting the importance of counselling couples and individuals:

> too often the efforts of Family Agencies are hindered by inadequacies in such essential services as public housing or inadequate social assistance rates. Unemployment or bare subsistence on a meagre income can render counselling services ineffective or even sometimes almost inappropriate in the face of need. Community planning and action are needed to combat some of the

> conditions detrimental to sound family life. A Family Agency can speak from first hand knowledge and experience and has a responsibility to give leadership in making known conditions and needs, and in finding solutions.[32]

A commitment to advocacy is also found in this commentary from an annual report of a family service agency:

> Another gap where families need aid is for the man who falls ill on the job and his wages stop immediately. Unemployment benefits, as we all know, have been a wonderful step in the right direction to alleviate suffering within the family when a man is laid off because the job is finished or work is slack, but there is no provision for illness ... It is a Family Agency that knows only too well the worry, discomfort, and mental anguish that can go on within a home where a man has been so stricken.[33]

The Moncton Boys Club began in 1957, preceded by Saint John, which had established one a few years earlier. The organization reflected a philosophy of community organizing among marginalized and often excluded populations. John Lutz, sponsored by the organization to pursue his master's in social work in Montreal, returned in 1959 to become director of the Moncton agency. He points out that even in the 1950s,

> that was still in the era where there was a charitable approach to providing services. And that was certainly so in New Brunswick. The thrust or the aims of the Boys Clubs of Canada were to provide services to poor kids, to kids in disadvantaged areas. And one of the elements was to select areas where there was a known high rate of delinquence.[34]

Stress and commitment

Father Frank MacDonald spoke candidly about a phenomenon that would today be referred to as "burnout" among human-service professionals. He recognized that in his context of being not only a parish priest but a social worker as well, his health and well-being were jeopardized. Within ten years of completing his master of social work degree, he had ulcers. In retrospect, he says, he should have asked which of the two roles he was to prioritize. By 1950, he states that he was no longer able to continue and, in his words, had not done anything for a year and a half, yet did not recognize that workload was to blame. He points out that church officials were oblivious to what social work encompassed in terms of human nature and that a medical doctor finally referred him to a psychiatrist, who questioned why as a parish priest he was also playing a full-time role as a social worker with its heavy demands.[35]

Much heart and optimism were undoubtedly needed in the face of daunting and overwhelming economic and social environments as the first professionally trained social workers appeared in New Brunswick, as the following reflection indicates:

> At the time I had a strong idealism, desire, and felt inadequate to the task. The task was much greater than the resources. There was satisfaction, but the task was overwhelming. There wasn't enjoyment. I remember at the time having a radical idea that everybody should have access to food and that there was a need for free food – that should be there but has never really come to pass.[36]

Professionally qualified social workers practising in New Brunswick up until the mid-1960s faced a number of challenges as individuals and as a group, challenges that had echoes across Canada. One might logically expect that in a profession in which advocacy for social justice has always been important, and which is also heavily weighted with female workers and service users, engagement with the women's movement would be a priority. Yet the Royal Commission on the Status of Women in early 1967 received submissions only from the New Brunswick Association of Social Workers and the chapters from Nova Scotia and Western Ontario; the national Canadian Association of Social Workers' leadership did not spend time voicing concern or support.[37]

Perusal of the more than 120 names of social workers in Appendix 2 reveals that many came to New Brunswick from elsewhere or left the province to pursue the educational qualifications that would enable them to become social work pioneers. They demonstrated commitment to organizing themselves as a professional body, first through formation of a chapter with Prince Edward Island social workers and in 1965 through forming the NBASW. Interviewees spoke of extensive travelling to meetings – Marcel Arseneau recalled driving three hours after a day's work in Campbellton to Moncton on poor highways to meet chapter members, before returning the same evening.

Determination, courage and persistence were undoubtedly required, given the constraints and limitations of the systems and domains within which they worked. In the next chapter we will consider experiences of the first Acadian social workers in New Brunswick's social work history.

8

The First Acadian Social Workers

LOUIS J. RICHARD

Introduction

The previous chapter focused on social workers who were practising in New Brunswick before the days of Equal Opportunity (1967). The majority were anglophones, although some of the Acadian social workers identified in the present chapter were also included. The author of this chapter, Louis J. Richard, had previously written a research paper on the first professionally trained Acadian social workers in New Brunswick related to the question of social work education for a minority group, which was the theme of his doctoral studies, undertaken in 1989, at the University of Bristol. In mapping out this book, the five original researchers quickly recognized that the earlier study would become central to the Acadian content.

This chapter examines the experiences of twelve Acadian social workers who began practising social work in New Brunswick between 1957 and 1964. The chapter is descriptive and has two objectives: first, to provide demographic and historical data on the earliest trained Acadian social workers; and second, to bring to light the experiences of the members of this group.[1] See Table 1 for a list of names and details.

As an Acadian and a social worker, Louis J. Richard was close in age to the first Acadian social workers; he graduated from the same professional school as nine of the twelve studied, just three years after the last member of the group, under conditions similar to those described by them.

When colleagues in the Moncton area in 1992 were asked the question, "Who were the first Acadian social workers working in New Brunswick?" the same thirteen names kept appearing. One of these was outside the

Table 1. List of first Acadian social workers by place of birth, school of social work, and year of graduation

1. Normand Clavet (Saint-Basile)	Maritime School of Social Work, 1957
2. Joseph Laviolette (Charlo)	Université de Montréal, 1957
3. Ronaldo Lavoie (Rogersville)	Maritime School of Social Work, 1958
4. Marcel Arseneau (Balmoral)	Maritime School of Social Work, 1960
5. Patricia Savoie-Savard (Kedgwick)	Université Laval, 1960
6. Leonard Delaney (Grang-Étang, NS)	Maritime School of Social Work, 1961
7. Jean-Paul Chiasson (Pointe-Verte)	Maritime School of Social Work, 1963
8. Normand Doucet (Petit-Rocher)	Maritime School of Social Work, 1963
9. Marc Gallant (Bathurst)	McGill University, 1963
10. Donald Richard (Cocagne)	Maritime School of Social Work, 1963
11. Willie Gibbs (Baie Sainte-Anne)	Maritime School of Social Work, 1964
12. Aldéo Losier (Tracadie)	Maritime School of Social Work, 1964

Note: All were born in New Brunswick, with the exception of Leonard Delaney, who was born in Nova Scotia

province on an extended leave, and another chose not to participate in the study. This left a total of eleven; however, at the end of the study, another participant joined. Eleven of the twelve were men, evidence that access to the extensive required number of years of preparatory education in the classics before graduate school was very limited and that roles as homemaker and educators were more highly promoted for Acadian women during the time. All participants fell into the category of raconteur, or storyteller, as they related willingly and enthusiastically their experiences as Acadian social workers.

Origins and Early Education

Nine of the twelve first Acadian social workers came from small rural communities in New Brunswick that were either wholly or almost entirely French-speaking. Two hailed from bilingual towns with a population of less than 10,000, while the twelfth was raised in a village in Nova Scotia.

French was the language spoken at home and in the primary school attended by all twelve members of this group. In five homes some English was spoken in addition to French because of a larger English speaking centre nearby, the presence in the community of a few English-speaking families (in one instance, a solely English-speaking family), or a family move in search of employment in a larger, and, inevitably, predominantly English-speaking centre in another part of the province.

Eight of the twelve first Acadian social workers completed high school in the French language. Given the unavailability of a public French-speaking school beyond grade seven in some of their home communities the remaining four had to attend English-language schools. One reported a change to an English-language school because his family had moved to a predominantly English-speaking community where education in French was unavailable at the time.

French-language education at the time varied greatly from one Acadian community to another depending on the particular community's resources. Fortunately for Acadian families with limited means, nationalistic groups offered college bursaries to Acadian students who studied in the French language. The system in place pleased parents very much as it included the high school portion in the French language, not often available in small communities, as stated earlier.

Le collège classique

The first Acadian social workers began and completed a baccalaureate of arts degree at a collège classique located in either Saint-Joseph (5), Bathurst (5), or Moncton (1) in New Brunswick, and Pointe-à-l'Église (1) in Nova Scotia. Each of these was operated by an arm of the Roman Catholic Church. The expression collège classique refers to an eight-year program of studies leading to a BA degree. Those studies began after grade eight and consisted of four years of high school, followed by four years of college. It must be remembered that the Acadian population of the day was predominantly rural, and since rural schools rarely offered education beyond the eighth grade in the French language, the collège seemed made-to-measure for those few Acadians who were fortunate enough to afford these studies.

In some collèges the eight-year period of studies was reduced to seven. That was the case, for example, at Collège Saint-Joseph, where four years of high school studies were reduced to three. The program of studies in a collège classique was similar from one school to another and based on the following subjects: French, English, Latin (Greek in some institutions), philosophy, literature, history, pure sciences, and mathematics.

That ensemble of studies led to a liberal arts degree and served as a prerequisite for studies leading to the professions.

Several factors prompted the first Acadian social workers in the choice of a collège. Proximity to their home communities and the possibility of studying in the French language appealed to five of them. Also, two of them made their decisions based on the positive reputation of the collège, as reported by other members of the community, an older sibling, or a distant relative. Another two chose simply to attend the same collège as that attended by a friend. One made a decision because it was recommended by the parish priest. Five other reasons, mentioned once each, were private source of funding, affordable, work available on site, popular for Acadians, and family tradition. (Some gave more than one answer.)

Work/Studies between BA and MSW Studies

The length of time between these two programs varied from zero to seven years. The majority who worked during this period found employment in the construction industry, in the social services, teaching and the armed forces; one worked as a clerk, and another as a psychiatric aide.

Several members reported hearing about social work through presentations made at their collège. In one instance, the informant allowed the notion of social work studies to mature during the last three years of his undergraduate studies. Another reported he credited his father's role as a parish counsellor as an important influence in his choice of studies. Lastly, one reported being increasingly attracted to social work during his work as an attendant in a hospital, not having heard about social work while in collège.

Social Work Studies

The first Acadian social workers studied social work during the late 1950s and early 1960s in one of four schools in eastern Canada. The two English-language institutions consisted of McGill University in Montreal and the Maritime School of Social Work in Halifax, while the two French-language schools were Université de Montréal and Université Laval in Québec City.

Both Montréal and Laval required from Acadians a full year of studies in the social sciences before admission to their master's programs in social work, because Acadians taught under the collège classique scheme received little or no content in the social and behavioural sciences. Acadians who studied at the Maritime School of Social Work were not expected to complete a full year of studies before admission; however, they were assigned readings in psychology and sociology. One informant who studied at the Maritime School agreed with the practice, as he was conscious of the absence of these two subjects in his liberal arts education. He added he felt his English-speaking classmates were better prepared than he was in those two areas crucial to a program of social work studies.

The reasons given for the choice of a particular school were reputation (3), proximity (3), only choice in the Maritimes (3), is a French-language university (1), suggested by a friend (1), admission was easy (1), and the opportunity to improve one's spoken English (1). (Some gave more than one answer.) At that time the program of studies was defined around the three fields of practice: casework, groupwork, and community organization.

Persons from New Brunswick studying social work during the 1950s and 1960s could receive financial assistance from the province. The provincial government of the day offered bursaries, with the condition that the recipient give back to the province one year of employment for each year of study. Under this scheme the Mental Health Branch of the Department of Health awarded bursaries to nine members of this group and the Department of Social Services awarded the other three. The reason for the variation in these numbers is that the policy of the Mental Health Branch of the day was to hire only persons with a master's degree. The Department of Social Services, however, continued for many years employing not only non-social workers but also, in some cases, persons without a university degree, which explains why they provided fewer bursaries than the Mental Health Branch.

While all twelve Acadian social workers completed undergraduate studies in the liberal arts in French, only two undertook social work studies in that language. Of the ten who studied in English, seven reported experiences related to language varying from quite difficult to a suspected incidence of discrimination. One informant reported certain problems arising in his fieldwork as he had to deal with "English-speaking clients in a totally English-speaking community." The suspected incidence of discrimination concerned three informants from the same class. They reported being the only ones asked to retake an exam. Since they were the only Acadians in the class and since none of them had failed an exam before (or after) that incident, they concluded there "might" be an instance of discrimination. Although they had no tangible proof, they all still remained suspicious some thirty years later. In discussing this incident they all stressed that the professor involved was a part-time lecturer and not a regular professor of the school.

Several informants reported the Maritime School of Social Work made them feel welcome, while another reported that a student whose attitudes towards minorities were "incorrect" was expelled (he did not elaborate). Another reported that "the School stated it was enriched by the presence of Acadians." According to another informant, some English-speaking students found the presence of Acadians somewhat "folkloric." In general, however, Acadian graduates gave high marks to the direction and full-time staff of the Maritime School of Social Work, although they pointed out there was "no content" on minorities.

A member who studied in French in Québec reported "they (the Québecois) tended to look down on the Acadians, and make fun of my spoken French, although I did not have a Moncton accent."[2] He added that if he had not helped his Québecois classmates in the translation of the social work literature, available almost exclusively in English at that time, the derogatory comments would have been more severe, and the result would have been a greater feeling of discomfort. Of this he was certain.

Thus the Acadian studying in English in Nova Scotia and the Acadian studying in French in Québec experienced similar reactions from the mainstream society: that of being singled out and somehow made to feel different.

Tales from Early Work Experiences

The first Acadian social worker started his career in the mental-health field in northern New Brunswick in 1957, and a few weeks later, he was joined by another.

The employment prospects that greeted the first Acadian social workers of New Brunswick during the 1950s and 1960s were in the agencies of social services and mental health. Offices of the social services were located in the larger centers. Mental-health services of the day were limited to the two psychiatric hospitals located in Saint John and Campbellton, as well as the three mental-health clinics located in the cities comprising the southern triangle of Fredericton, Saint John, and Moncton.

When the first Acadian social workers finished professional studies (1957–64), the English-speaking community itself had but a handful of trained social workers. Thus, the Acadians faced a society which, for the most part, had not yet formed an opinion of what a social worker was. At times members of the public referred to them as "child snatchers" or "government inspectors." The informants reported on the community's perception of them, in three distinct categories. One group consisted of the welfare workers with whom the new recruits interacted often; many were untrained, and some had only a high school education. These welfare workers looked upon the newcomers as "stars," a designation considered both "intimidating and validating," according to an informant. The terms "rare bird" and "learned person" were also reported. The members of the second group were professionals such as doctors, psychologists, and nurses, who generally had a positive reaction to the arrival of the social workers. A third group, made up chiefly of clergy and persons associated with the church, considered social work to be among the vocations, almost in the same category as the priesthood. Finally, the social workers reported being well regarded and that they were often invited to speak to community and service groups; they believed they were well remunerated and had a certain margin of work opportunities.

Below are accounts from the tales of the first Acadian social workers with respect to issues around languages. These reports revolve around direct service to the clientele, the judicial system, and the "Mini United Nations."

With respect to direct service, several reported feeling "more accepted" and experiencing "less apprehension" and "fewer prejudices" in Acadian homes.[3] Another stated he felt "more comfortable with Acadian families ... better able to establish a working relationship, and more at ease, even in difficult cases." It is interesting that this last informant volunteered that he experienced those feelings at a time in his life when he had been "fluent in the English language for some fourteen years."

The following is a recollection of a situation that took place in a juvenile court in 1965: as a young and inexperienced Acadian social worker, recalled the informant, he appeared before a judge in the course of his work in child protection. During the proceedings the judge openly expressed his intolerance towards this particular Acadian for being French-speaking. This incident "left a permanent scar ... I felt lucky with the knowledge of a second language, but also (felt) a handicap that everything was in English."

The expression "Mini United Nations" was introduced by two participants during separate face-to-face interviews. It refers to the many foreign languages of the practising psychiatrists in the two psychiatric hospitals mentioned above. Doctors treating patients at those two hospitals came from foreign countries at a time when those nationals were not in evidence in other parts of the patient's experience. According to an informant, in the Campbellton institution, which served most of the French-speaking mental-health patients of the province, the doctors came from Turkey, Romania, Italy, Korea, Hungary, and Czechoslovakia. The doctors from those countries all had a rudimentary knowledge of English, but not enough to navigate the nuances associated with the sensitive nature of the communication required in such a setting. French-speaking patients were at a further disadvantage. The informants who described this situation gave accounts of "poor communication" between doctor and patient. It was often left to the social worker to translate for the benefit of both patient and doctor.

Another incident related to language involved the supervisor of one of the members of the group. This supervisor suggested the social worker showed "a lack of respect" when he spoke in French to a colleague in his (the supervisor's) presence! This comment was heard in Moncton during the late 1970s.

Finally, one informant reflected on a personal stance on the matter of language: "I accept that I may not be a true militant, and may not have been aware of the situation, but nobody makes me do anything I don't want to, in 1964 or in 1992 ... There may be the attitude that we as a people had been so stepped on or crushed that we simply had to accept the situation."

Culturally Conscious Content (CCC) in Social Work Education?

It was stated earlier that this study of the first Acadian social workers was undertaken as part of a broader study, that of social work education for a minority group. The answers to only one question of the broader study are examined here. This question is the only one asked of the participants with respect to social work education for a minority. The question was, should a school of social work operating within a university whose mission is to serve an identifiable ethnic-language minority include – or be marked by – a specific emphasis of that minority?

This turned out to be a question that most members of this group had not considered before. One stated he had "never thought" about it, and another that he had "difficulty with that." One of the two educators[4] replied he had been asked the question but that it still left him "baffled." The twelve opinions fell into three categories, namely, the "no" or "no opinion," the "evolving" (explanation below), and the "yes" group.

The following arguments were advanced by the "no" side: "A social worker is a social worker, whether or not he (sic) belongs to a minority"; "There is not much difference between Anglophones and Francophones (as a client of Social Services)," and "That is not the question. I am more interested in the problem of a lack of a knowledge base in the area of mental health." This informant directed his thoughts to a particular concern of his; I recorded it and did not redirect the question.

The second category is called the "evolving" group. In this category the three informants moved from one position to another as they pondered and formulated their answer. The three positions are as follows:

> My gut feeling is that there are too many universal characteristics which are imperative to social work knowledge-building without the additional preoccupation of cultural-ethnic content. For example, pain is the same whether you are an Acadian or a member of the majority group. But, if I really want to understand the person, and analyse the problem at hand, I must, as an intervenor, be open and sensitive to cultural, social and ethnic differences, which could influence the perception of the problem, the adaptive mechanisms, and learned procedures which lead to the resolution of certain problems. In this sense it is applicable to every client.
>
> I have difficulty with that problem. I do not like to associate Acadians with the idea of a minority because of the pejorative aspect generally associated with the term "minority." I believe not only the B.S.W. curriculum but all curricula of the Université de Moncton should touch on minority issues. [But one must be] careful of the way it is presented. U de M graduates should be prepared to work everywhere in Canada. I would like to see U de M offer excellence in education versus service to Acadians. The Université should look out to other Francophones who would come here to study.
>
> I believe social work students of Université de Moncton possess special peculiarities of the Acadian minority; since most of those students are Acadians they cannot avoid it [Acadian reality] forever. The faculty is varied, that is, Acadian and non-Acadian, and that is good: it brings newness in programmes and approaches. [Acadian] culture is there, otherwise students would boycott [classes]. As an example, students from the Acadian Peninsula seem to feel comfortable as field work students and as graduates ... In the area of transmission of knowledge the American literature and research on Blacks, Jews and Hispanics indicated the importance [of cultural differences]. I do not think there has been this structured attempt at the Université de Moncton. There is an advantage to examining the differences among various Acadian regions.

In the third category, the five social workers who gave a "yes" answer spoke as follows:

> Yes, I think so. An Acadian is not a Français nor a Québecois ... yes ... on a cultural level ... yes, consciousness in this area is necessary, but there is the danger of pushing it too far because many graduates work with Anglophones.
>
> I have not given any thought to this question, but [I believe there is] the necessity of teaching regional differences, mentality, character, habits and customs.
>
> The Acadian [reality] goes further than the Francophone reality. It [includes] an economic underdevelopment, a political underrepresentation, social isolation and religious practices [which were] at the mercy of a dominant clergy.
>
> There exist elements of culture specific to the Acadian culture.
>
> Students [of social work] should be conscious of minority attitudes, with specific emphasis on the Acadian minority, as well as other minorities. They should know the history of Acadie and Canada as well as sociology and [should] recognize aspects of laws on bilingualism. [This is] misunderstood, not only in Canada, but in the United States and in Belgium.

One reply did not fit snugly into one of the three categories of no, evolving, and yes, although one could argue that it is closer to the evolving category than either of the other two. This participant thought that this matter was "something educators should consider."

Conclusion

The first Acadian social workers were overwhelmingly male and first-generation university graduates; they came from small communities mainly in New Brunswick. The pursuit of professional studies outside their province of birth probably represented the greatest geographical/cultural distance they had ever known. Supported by study bursaries they ventured east to Nova Scotia to study in English or west to the province of Québec to study in French. (One studied in English in the province of Québec.)

Members of this group studied what can be called mainstream social work in universities that did not touch on minority content or content arising from the Acadians' experience. Here the term mainstream is taken to mean the predominant content of the time and refers to sameness in subjects taught during the same period in various locations like Toronto, Québec, Halifax, and Moncton.

The inclusion of culturally conscious content in social work education carried out by and for a minority group has the important objective of refinement or honing of both the theoretical bases and the practice skills. As time went on, an appreciation for cultural strengths and uniqueness would lead Canadian social work schools to move into population-specific teaching and learning, to provide students with a better understanding of experiences of marginalized groups. However, during the decades when the first Acadian social workers were educated, there was no such appreciation within the halls of universities where social work programs were being offered.

9

Social Workers Experience Child Welfare: View from the Trenches

LAUREL LEWEY

In this chapter personal observations that help illuminate the past are provided through oral interviews with the earliest social workers and archival records pertaining to agents for the Children's Aid Societies (CAS) in the province.[1] The archival records and the secondary literature affirm the workers' recollections.

Historically, the CAS was not well funded. In addition, CAS agents were poorly paid; they often travelled thousands of miles each year to investigate reports of abuse or neglect or to provide services; had high caseloads; and had few resources to provide prevention services. For example, in 1931, when a member of the New Brunswick Provincial Police requested a cheque to cover expenses incurred in investigating a matter under the Children's Protection Act, he was told by the secretary treasurer for the municipality of Carleton that the county was overdrawn, who noted that "it is almost impossible to collect taxes in this county."[2]

Social workers in New Brunswick faced issues similar to those faced in other provinces. Margaret Anstey was a social worker and director of the CAS in Saint John. In 1932 she faced the issue of a ten-year-old child on the street selling potholders after school and into the evenings. Street trading had been identified as a danger by the Department of Labour in 1930.[3] Anstey published a public notice titled "Canada's Children and Street Trading," in which she referred to legislation in Ontario, where street trading was not permitted for boys under twelve and girls under sixteen years of age, while in Manitoba, street trading was not allowed for boys and girls under twelve. She explained that the new Children's Protection Act,[4] not yet declared, would require a licence from the juvenile court or county court judge for a girl under twelve or a boy under ten years of age. A child had to be found on the street after 9:00 p.m. to be picked up as a vagrant, while the CAS Protection Act (the title used by Anstey for the legislation) could apply if a child was "growing up in circumstances exposing such child to lead an idle or dissolute life." She acknowledged that this was difficult to prove and asked the public to notify the CAS on encountering a child engaged in street trading.[5]

In 1948 Edna Smith worked for the CAS in Albert County one-third of the time and in Westmorland County two-thirds of the time. She resigned from Albert County in 1954 and was replaced by a trained nurse.[6] In 1946 a CAS worker typically earned $146 per month and had no pension.[7] CAS workers put many miles on their vehicles. In his 1959 annual report, Howard Young, CAS worker for Northumberland County, reported that he had driven 21,090 miles.[8] Many CAS agents travelled with a CAS board member or "hitched a ride with nurses."[9] A typical workweek for CAS agents was six days a week.[10] In 1953 it cost $3.75 for a hotel in Truro.[11]

In 1951 Bobbie MacKenzie lived in Campbellton and was a CAS agent for Restigouche County. She and one other welfare worker were responsible for the whole county, from Jacquet River to Saint-Quentin and all settlements in between. She found the in-service training for CAS workers provided by the Department of Health and Welfare very useful. The training consisted of three summer schools paid for by the province and was taught by professors from the Maritime School of Social Work in Halifax.[12] Welfare workers from Mothers' Allowance joined in on the training.

MacKenzie reported that CAS workers "did it all"; that is, adoptions, apprehension, and child placement, but they did virtually no preventive intervention because they didn't have the time. Often, by the time they met with families, it was too late, meaning children were taken into care.[13] She learned of cases from a parish priest or clergy in the area or persons who were on the board of directors of the CAS. Her caseload would allow her to visit children in foster care about once every six months unless there was a problem, in which case she might visit the child again the next day.[14] Once child welfare was centralized with Equal Opportunity there were more specific standards, which was a good thing because, "I think probably over the years they found that not all foster homes were safe for children. There should have been more intervention in that way."[15] Approximately 5 percent of MacKenzie's work was in an Aboriginal community, and usually the chief would tell her about a precarious situation, and again she would most often just go in and take the children. MacKenzie felt there was a lack of preparation for the changes Equal Opportunity brought in. She recalled that the CAS where she worked had no notice that the Department of Health and Welfare would be taking over her office. She thinks it was on a Monday that a male and a female social worker arrived at her office stating that they were with the province of New Brunswick on behalf of the minister. There were more resources to draw from once services were centralized with Equal Opportunity, and she believes that "it was certainly better, no question about it."[16]

Previously when a child died, the overseer of the poor would pay for the funeral. Bobbie recalls, "I had one little fella die with rheumatic fever and I was just broken-hearted. There were two children in all those years that died. Anyways, he went out in style. They wouldn't do it for him when he was living and they needed something."[17] But, she also recalls that she didn't agree with the changes in adoption. She provided an example of a child who had been with a family for twelve years, and when the practice changed, all of a sudden he had to be adopted or be removed.[18]

When asked how adoptions were done in the 1950s, Flora Jean Kennedy replied, "Girls produced babies and couples came and wanted them, and they were brought together."[19] When asked where the babies went to in Saint John, she described the options as consisting of the Salvation Army home or the diocese. Edna Smith recalled, "One of the priests standing up at the altar and saying there is a nice little baby boy needing adoption. Any couple interested in adopting him please see me after Mass. That's how babies were distributed at the time."[20]

The Catholic Church was definitely involved in child welfare. Armand LeCouffe recalled, "the priest taking it upon himself to place a handicapped child or an illegitimate child on a large farm where the availability of food would not be an issue."[21]

Social workers witnessed a lot of poverty but thought that housing was much poorer in rural areas, where there was a greater risk of fire hazards and there existed drastic situations for which the provincial fire marshal had to be called. Vilma Kurol described a situation in which a child of fourteen and four infants lived in an army tent in the middle of January. She also recalled being called on a Sunday morning to the hospital because a baby had arrived frozen. It took two hours to revive the infant. When Kurol visited the home, she observed that she could see the sun through the boards of the house. She determined that it had been a very cold night, the fire had gone out, and the baby had almost frozen to death.[22] Kurol also recalled a time when representatives from various agencies got together and tried to relocate ten families to better housing through the United Fund.

In a parish outside of Moncton, Carol Proctor recalls visiting a home where six children lived with their very ill mother, no father in the picture, and no firewood in the house. She arranged for the Catholic Women's League to respond to this emergency, and two homemakers brought firewood in from the shed, got the fire going, and stayed with the children after the mother had been brought by ambulance to a hospital. The mother needed medical care in the hospital, and so the children had to be placed.[23]

Sometimes CAS workers had to be very direct with their clients. Howard Young, CAS agent for Northumberland County, wrote a memo that clearly expressed his frustration:

> This child is a habitual truant. I called at the home of _____ and was informed by the mother that ______ was not going to school because they did not want her to go, told me it was none of my business. I told her that if she did not send the child to school she would be taken away from her and put in a home where she would be able to go to school. I also told her to clean the house, this home is filthy.[24]

Or CAS workers had to challenge a request for assistance:

> In reply to your letter of December 6, I have received your letters, the reason for not calling is because, shortly after giving you clothing on my last visit, I was told that ______ had bought a car. I have seen him driving his car several times, therefore took it for granted that it was his car. Now we only have a certain amount of clothing to divide up among the needy families and do not consider a family with a car a needy family. If ______ will make an effort to support his family and I have any clothing to give you I will again call and give you some.[25]

The conclusion that having a car denotes a luxurious lifestyle to which poor or unemployed people should not be entitled is difficult to comprehend, particularly given the rural geography and distances between home and potential work. A means of transportation was and is essential, yet clearly according to the belief system of the 1940s, people in need of clothing or food were expected to be without a vehicle. The following comment from a helping agency also reveals judgmental attitudes and frustrations about families:

> Now I have made arrangements to have this family taken to the County Home before he gets back out of jail. She, while not so much to blame, is quite a hand at begging for public support and is ready to give her children to anyone. It seems that now she is stalling about going to the Alms House, she told me she was willing to go but she says now she has to store her furniture somewhere, etc. I have asked the Town Office to grant no more relief orders to her as the orders to take the family up have been signed.[26]

In response to an inquiry from a municipal authority:

> I have not checked in on this family recently, however, we have done a lot for them and still give Mrs. _______ a considerable amount of second-hand clothing when we have it. If her husband was a good a worker as she is a beggar, they could have a home for their family, and be independent.[27]

This CAS agent was quite cross with a single mother who inquired whether she could receive the money the recognized father had provided for her confinement after the alms (money, food, or goods provided in a charitable context) had paid for her expenses:

> We told you we would see that you had medical care if you would lay the charge against the putative father of your unborn child. This you did and through the alms, and they collected the money. You must remember this is not a profitable business, if you added my expenses to what you have received from the alms you will find the alms has very little left. However, Mr. ___ should have told you this. You must remember you got some alms orders, who do you suppose is to pay this and Dr. _______. You had better forget about the money and be thankful you did not end up in the Home of the Good Shepherd for a few years.[28]

CAS workers also demonstrated compassion about people's misfortunes, as this comment, also from Howard Young, indicates:

> I know this case quite well, there is no question they are in dire need, shortly after receiving your letter I called at this home to what clothing was most needed for the children. I secured some things from the Red Cross, however, they are in need of many things.[29]

Archie Smith tells a "cloak and dagger" story about transporting an "illegitimate" child away from its biological family to its adoptive family so no one would know where that baby went. Of course, "it was done with good intentions and all that but today it never would be allowed."[30]

And there were also success stories:

> I had a nice card and handkerchief at Xmas from ______ and a lovely long letter recently. I note by her letter she wishes to finish her education in the home and train for a nurse. I have advised Magistrate ______ about her progress and the security she feels since going to Truro. He assured me again that he would do everything in his power to keep ______ in the school until she is finished her education, as long as she is satisfied and happy about the matter. He feels as I do that ______ committed no wrong, and only sent there for protection. I trust you will excuse my tardiness in answering your letter, and again assuring you that everything possible will be done to help _______.[31]

CAS workers got to know their clients, as Archie Smith recounted:

> In the old days we held onto cases, and people didn't move around as much. If you had all the bad bastards in the world and no good ones, you would soon burn out. So you deliberately kept some of the good ones and you worked with them because that was your feedback. You might have ten heartbreakers in a day and then you would go at the end of the day and drop in and see so-and-so and have a cup of coffee or a cup of tea and then go home.[32]

Carol Proctor described the informal, caring nature of social work practice:

> I'd say to the kids, what do you kids want to do, do you want to have lunch at my house or do you want to go to a restaurant. Well, they wanted to go to my apartment, and I would do that. But, today you would probably stop at a restaurant and get them a fast-food hamburger. And it was different in my home. My husband would be home for lunch and he would know the children by their first names. They loved him, and he laughed and teased and gave them new toothbrushes and they thought they owned the world. So we did things differently.[33]

On one occasion Robert Thériault brought a newborn awaiting adoption to his home for one month. His own children cried so much when the baby left that he decided not to do that again.[34]

Flora Jean Kennedy was impressed with the work of the CAS agents:

> Now these agents were dedicated. They loved their kids and they knew them, providing the kids weren't too much of a problem. If a child was a "difficult" child, they could hardly wait until he reached the age of sixteen so he could move out of care. But for the child who was doing well in school or was cute, or a child that was disabled in any way, they would devote all their time and attention to them. They knew those children and loved them.[35]

Differences in ideological perspectives among social workers are evident. Differences in size of caseloads, and contrasts between the amount of resources available, particularly between the rural and urban communities, and even natural tendencies towards idealism may have influenced the perspectives social workers provide of the contexts of their experiences. Some social workers had more than three hundred cases each when services were integrated in the 1960s;[36] neglect of some clients would have been inevitable, and for children in the system, not having easy and immediate access to their social workers set up conditions that heightened their vulnerability, and more so in rural areas with long distances and poor road conditions.

It was previously mentioned that before 1955 child welfare workers responded to situations that were so badly deteriorated that children were usually apprehended and placed in protective care. Social workers were not in great supply, and devoting time to rehabilitate families was not supported. Carolyn Howlett recounted Edith Nutter's experience as an early child welfare worker:

> She had few protection cases. On one occasion she was required to take custody of a child who had been beaten and left for dead in a woodshed. His parents were long gone. She said no legal steps were ever taken to find the parents; the child was simply placed in foster care.[37]

During the 1950s there were few trained social workers in the province and across Canada, and most child welfare workers were trained in the social sciences or as teachers or nurses. There were no practice standards, and staff and agencies were on their own. Child welfare workers had to rely upon their own common sense and their own experience:

In Flora Jean's experience, almost 100 per cent of child welfare cases were poor families. Society of the day considered their poverty to be their own fault; they were seen as lazy and parasites of the community. Unmarried mothers were considered immoral. Foster parents were perceived as unquestionably good people who would never abuse a child. Foster children were expected to be grateful that some family would take them into their home, and they were expected to learn new ways of behaving. Abuse, particularly sexual abuse, was rarely taken into account.[38]

At times, social workers had to address unsafe conditions in receiving homes. For example, in 1961 Mary R. Bishop, executive secretary of the CAS in Saint John, described in detail to the county secretary the presence of rats in the receiving home, which necessitated transporting any infant children to foster homes. She outlined the steps that had been taken to rid the receiving home of the problem.[39]

When asked what significant changes for the better she witnessed during the period that she was in social work, Vilma Kurol replied,

I see changes for the better. The Social Assistance Programs have improved so tremendously, it's like day and night, you can't compare it anymore in spite of our restraint programs. I've seen the changes in more uniformity in providing service. I have seen the changes in decision making which is more group decisions or what I called it also democratic decision, it's not made any more by one person but there is two or three people involved in that group because we are dealing with other people's lives, especially children for whom we have to make decisions, and I still feel that group decisions is better than one individual person's decision. I still in proportion think the professional staff has increased which also adds to the quality of service, and the people who are dealing with people have to have all the abilities and capabilities and knowledge in order to give a proper service to the people. Also the laws, the change of laws, more comprehensive approach to the total family matter, this has been helpful to us social workers.[40]

Geraldine Lee, a case worker in the 1960s, declared that "we don't get enough written about the joys of social work, the pleasures that come from social work, the satisfaction."[41] Father Fred Whalen said that "the image I get in this era is a lot of good people, forging their way and trying to provide social services, without a lot of models or directions. They would take one step at a time and hope they were taking the right step."[42]

Conclusion

In this chapter the stories shared reveal some of the rewards and challenges of child welfare. Rewards were experienced through the informality of the work, which allowed for the development of close personal relationships with the children in one's caseload. The independence also allowed for a sense of pride when the worker managed a positive outcome in spite of the challenges. The lack of practice standards until Equal Opportunity arrived may also have made it possible for abuse to occur and contributed to a varied experience in quality of services. CASs were not well funded; agents were poorly paid; they covered wide geographical territories and managed large caseloads, which meant that social workers could respond only to crises. In the absence of problems, children in care might be checked on a maximum of two times per year. One seasoned social worker concluded that 100 percent of the cases were poor families, and that in rural areas, the housing conditions she encountered were the worst. Poor Law mentality meant that the poor were blamed for their own circumstances, which added to people's shame.

These stories also reveal that many of these challenges were alleviated by the changes brought in by Equal Opportunity. Practice standards were established; services were centralized; more resources were created; legislation was standardized; social assistance was improved; the disparity between anglophones and francophones was lessened; and rural New Brunswickers' access to education was improved, particularly for anglophones and francophones.

10

Ushering in Equal Opportunity

LINDA TURNER, LOUIS J. RICHARD, AND LAUREL LEWEY

Introduction

Inequalities heightened by New Brunswick's social welfare legislation fell short of providing care and support that enabled people to meet basic needs adequately and to maintain their dignity. The system's meagre provisions contributed to ongoing, sometimes centuries-long, injustices in the province. The time was thus long overdue for political leadership to emerge that would find solutions, sweeping in nature, to the problems and that would improve the situation – at least for anglophone and Acadian New Brunswickers, although Indigenous people in New Brunswick and across Canada would continue to be neglected, would soon be facing the Sixties Scoop, and would continue to be left to live in deplorable circumstances for many decades to come.

Between the years 1900 and 1960 the Acadian population of New Brunswick had grown from 25 percent to nearly 40 percent of the population.[1] Louis J. Robichaud's election as premier of New Brunswick on 12 July 1960, along with the subsequent introduction of the Equal Opportunity Program, was a step of gargantuan proportions in the trajectory of the Acadian people. This legendary leap into power was strongly and directly influenced by the historical and political processes of the day.

This chapter begins with an overview of the development of post-secondary institutions and the Deutsch Commission. A description of the successful developments in Acadian society leading into the mid-fifties and early sixties, when Louis Robichaud came on the political scene, follows. Biographical information about Robichaud that suggests why he attracted the attention of significant Acadians who supported him as a candidate completes the chapter. It would indeed be tempting to explore the "back room" party politics and the social networking associated with Acadians' piercing the loyalist-dominated epicenter of Fredericton society in 1960; but these issues are not central to the present discussion. This is not to suggest that the traditional matters of party politics were set aside for the 1960 election, but rather to give place to the unprecedented L'Ordre de Jacques Cartier (OJC), called La Patente, discussed below. The chapter concludes with observations about the significance of the Equal Opportunities Program for the province and New Brunswick's social work pioneers' perceptions of its value.

The Development of Post-secondary Institutions and the Deutsch Commission

Sheila Brown[2] refers to how "a unique system of higher education" evolved in New Brunswick, beginning with the establishment of the Academy in Fredericton in 1785 by the Anglican Church. The Academy later became known as King's College, then UNB in 1859 so that the university would not be associated with a particular religion. Mount Allison University was founded in 1839 in Sackville. The Mount Allison Wesleyan Academy for boys opened in 1843, while the Ladies College was established in 1854. Although Mount Allison University was established by Methodists and later the United Church was involved, the intent was that the university would be accessible to students from all denominations. The Roman Catholic school system established St. Michael's College, which opened in 1861 in Chatham, New Brunswick. It was renamed St. Thomas College in 1910 and was a high school and junior college until 1934, when it became an accredited university with degree-granting authority. The name was officially changed to St. Thomas University in 1960, and four years later was relocated to Fredericton. Several francophone institutions of higher learning were also established early in the history of New Brunswick. St. Joseph's in the Memramcook valley, which originally provided education for Acadian and Irish Catholics, was established in 1864. Collège Notre-Dame d'Acadie for girls, affiliated with St. Joseph's, was established three years later by the Sisters of Charity of Memramcook, but not until 1943 was Collège de l'Assomption established for boys. Eudist Fathers established Collège du Sacre-Coeur in 1889 in Caraquet, but it was moved to Bathurst in 1915. Affiliated with Sacre Coeur in 1960, the Collège Jésus-Marie was founded in Shippagan by the Sisters of Jésus-Marie. By 1946 another university for boys was established – St. Louis in Edmundston. Education for girls had been offered in St. Basile by Les Religieuses Hospitalières de Saint-Joseph in the late nineteenth century, however, before Collège Maillet was established in the community in 1949.

Jointly established by New Brunswick and Nova Scotia, along with the University of New Brunswick (UNB) and members of the forestry industry, and funded by the Department of Natural Resources in 1946, the Maritime Ranger School provided technical education in forestry. The New Brunswick School of Fisheries was established in 1959; the New Brunswick College of Craft and Design in the 1940s; and the United Baptist Bible Training School in 1949 by private investors. Five diploma schools of nursing were created in the 1940s: two in Moncton, and one each in Saint John, Bathurst, and Edmundston. By 1951 the provincial government was persuaded by the additional five institutions to grant them operating monies similarly to that which UNB received. The diploma schools were discontinued by 2000, however, when professional standards made a BA a requirement.

Consistent with its emphasis on social and economic reform, the Louis J. Robichaud government established the Deutsch Commission in 1961, chaired by John J. Deutsch. The government wanted to encourage a more highly educated population and particularly wished to provide opportunities for higher education to the francophone population. Recommendations by the Deutsch Commission (*Report of the Royal Commission on Higher Education*) adopted by the Robichaud government in 1962 resulted in greater public funds directed towards higher education, as well as the extension of UNB to Saint John and more educational options for francophones with the founding of the Université de Moncton and its formal affiliation with Bathurst, Shippagan, and Edmundston. These changes were considered radical at the time.[3]

L'Acadie in the Mid-twentieth Century

Naomi Griffiths, one of the most renowned authorities on Acadian history, said that "Acadian history … is a story of human passion and obstinacy, an affirmation of individual courage and beliefs, a statement of the rights of small settlements against the claims of large Empires, and, above all, a gloriously awkward compendium of exceptions to everybody's rules."[4] The 1955 definition of l'Acadie as being "aggressive, awake and progressive" in reference to the unfolding proliferation of Acadian institutions, movements, and organizations in the period is ample evidence of a social group becoming "un peuple à part entière," and it is a likely climate for the important changes that would be enacted during the 1960s. Emerging strengths included the appearance of a collection of organizations, initiatives, institutions, and movements, including the appearance of five francophone post-secondary institutions (mentioned previously) and ten clinics and hospitals. These developments further solidified the foundation created by earlier movements such as implementation of the Caisse Populaires financial cooperative institutions through the Antigonish Movement's adult-education model:

> Study circles were spreading like wildfire. In New Brunswick's Acadian regions, there were 200 study circles in 1936, 400 in 1937, 565 in 1940 and 744 in 1941. According to statistics published by New Brunswick Department of Agriculture, 60 Caisses populaires and 78 credit unions were founded between 1936 and 1941. The first Francophone Caisse populaire in New Brunswick was established in Richibouctou in August 1916, without much success, however. The oldest Caisse populaire to be a member of the Fédération des caisses populaires acadiennes, the Caisse populaire de Petit-Rocher, was established in December 1936.[5]

Another important Acadian achievement was the Assumption Life Insurance Company, begun in 1903 in Massachusetts but transferred to Moncton in 1913, that provided many young Acadians with scholarships to pursue university studies from the company's early days. Also numerous Catholic organizations, several of which had strong youth branches, the Home and School Association, Acadian student associations, many new regional schools, two French radio stations, a daily newspaper (Evangeline), and an Acadian bookstore La Librairie Acadienne, that played an important role in a cultural and literary explosion that reached beyond Canada's borders, all played their part in the gradual transformation that saw greater Acadian involvement and leadership in society.[6] When Université de Moncton would open its doors in 1963 to pursue its mission that included solidifying Acadian identity and Acadian society, it was standing on the hefty shoulders of movements and institutions that had emerged over many decades.[7]

Louis J. Robichaud

Louis J. Robichaud was the last of ten children born to Amédée Robichaud and Eugénie Richard on 21 October 1925 in the predominantly Acadian village of Sainte-Antoine located in Kent County, southeastern New Brunswick. Amédée owned and operated a general store and a saw mill; as well he acted as the post master and was active in matters of public education and the church where Louis sometimes accompanied him to meetings.[8] In the traditional Roman Catholic home discussions on education, religion, and politics were an everyday occurrence;[9] it was also a home where values of love, determination, and frugality were handed down from one generation to another.[10]

The early home life of the Robichaud boy called "Ti-Louis" set the tone for the formation of the man who would become the first elected Acadian premier of the province.[11] His father inspired him in the Liberal doctrine with hints of hero worshipping of then Premier Allison Dysart and Prime Minister Mackenzie King, both Liberals.[12] At age nine he was already keeping a scrapbook of things political, and at age twelve, without telling anyone, drove about six miles on a borrowed bicycle to hear Premier Dysart speak at a community picnic.[13]

Louis was noticed and received encouragement from people in positions of authority at every step of his formal education. They included the parish priest during his elementary studies at the local parish school and the Eudist priests of Sacré-Coeur Collège in Bathurst, who taught him to listen to adults talk about larger issues.[14] There he was reported to be "consistently average"[15] and later would be described as "not an intellectual."[16] However, belief in his own potential was apparently not dampened by such assessments, if he was even aware of them. Della Stanley describes how Louis J. Robichaud signed the 1947 time capsule of his BA graduation with the words, "Louis J. Robichaud, Premier of New Brunswick"[17] thirteen years before his election to power. The program of studies at Sacré-Coeur was le cours classique as described in Chapter 8. In general, he showed qualities of leadership and was very active in extra-curricular activities, including debating and sports,[18] both in Bathurst and later in Québec.

As a young man, Louis J. Robichaud had powerful and highly intellectual Acadian influences and mentors. Among them one of the most important was Father Clément Cormier, founding president of Université de Moncton (1963–7) and chancellor (1973–8) who started the School of Social Sciences in Moncton and who understood that economic development was essential. Père Cormier found ideologies that resonated with his ambitions for Acadians at Université Laval in Québec and at Columbia University. Cormier was a man of vision who had an appreciation for sociology and psychology. He had seen the potential of Father

Moses Coady's cooperative movement in Antigonish, Nova Scotia, and also used the momentum of Catholic organizations to economic advantage.[19] Parallels in the ideological and higher education pursuits between Père Clément Cormier and Louis J. Robichaud are evident, but there was also a close relationship between the two. As an example, when Robichaud's financial situation threatened the continuation of his studies at Laval, Cormier obtained approval for a student loan from the Caisse Populaire in Sainte-Antoine, Robichaud's home town.

As for Louis J. Robichaud's path through higher education beyond Bathurst, when he found he was unable to finance studies in a law-degree program[20] he instead pursued studies in the social sciences at Laval University between 1947 and 1949. During that time he became editor of a student newspaper directed to Acadians studying at Laval and Montréal universities.[21]

The teachings of a Dominican priest and the practical realities of governing constituted the two main interests for Robichaud during this period. Father Georges-Henri Lévesque, hereafter called Père Lévesque, had been a professor at the Dominican College in Ottawa during the 1930s and acted as dean of social sciences during Robichaud's stay at Laval.[22] During that period the entire Faculty of Social Sciences was "at war" with the government of the day led by Maurice Duplessis.[23] The situation became so embittered at one point that Duplessis cut off the stipend the government provided to Laval University because the latter refused to fire Père Lévesque.[24]

Père Lévesque was consistent throughout his teachings and writings in that he attacked and denounced the Duplessis regime for its "corporate" nature, which favoured the elites and the interests of multinational corporations.[25] Social justice, he believed, was not only a concept for discussion but one on which action had to be taken; the logical consequence of this credo was that matters of health, education, and social services would cease to be the domain of religious congregations and should become an integral part of state-sponsored and state-paid services. Therein lies the fodder, the moral fibre, for Robichaud's Program of Equal Opportunity twenty years later.

Robichaud registered in Père Lévesque's first-year course called La Morale et la technique de l'Action, designed to prepare students to become the modern leaders of the "future" in French Canada.[26] Père Lévesque preached the notion of a "political role" whereby the politician did not aspire personal gain but rather to enrich the society as a whole.[27] Robichaud often visited Père Lévesque in his office, and the two held many long conversations.[28] He also received encouragement from other young Acadians who would become notables.[29] At Laval he was introduced to notions of social justice including the need for social reforms, for state provision of the welfare of the poor, the unemployed, and the orphaned; he was also introduced to the notion that financial aid from the state would eventually become the norm, not the exception.[30] Complementing Père Lévesque's teachings – the practical bent of Robichaud's stay at Laval – were the hours and hours spent observing the debates of the Québec Legislative Assembly.

Père Lévesque's influence on Louis J. Robichaud is clearly evident from the creed he passed on to his students and which the young Robichaud absorbed: "... the belief in the human freedom to discover, report upon and remedy social, economical, industrial, and political injustices and inequalities."[31] Following graduation from Université Laval, Louis J. Robichaud returned to New Brunswick and began a legal apprenticeship in Richibuctou in 1949 (an alternative option for becoming a lawyer for individuals who did not attend law school). He was admitted to the New Brunswick bar three years later.[32]

Some of the epithets that describe Robichaud and which he used to his advantage in the political process include being a quick learner, being a hard worker, and being blessed with considerable energy.[33] He has been described as brash and pushy,[34] helpful, and a "bulldozer."[35] It is said that his youthfulness, compulsive drive and contagious energy inspired the Liberals.[36] In her appraisal of the person of "Ti-Louis," Stanley concludes that neither "heredity nor environment" was likely to produce a shy or introverted child in the Robichaud household.[37]

Louis J. Robichaud and New Brunswick Politics

In 1953 during Louis J. Robichaud's maiden speech, presented in French after he was first elected as member of the Legislative Assembly for Kent County, he spoke of ethnic harmony.[38] From that moment until his election in 1960 as premier, he addressed several major issues in the Legislative Assembly: workman's compensation, religious instruction in the schools, inshore fishermen,[39] and the saturation point of municipal taxation and forest resources.[40]

While confronting the governing Flemming Conservatives between 1952 and 1960 on issues like education reforms, Robichaud had the chance to develop his abilities in rebuilding the Liberal party and learning the ropes of the Legislative Assembly. His years as financial critic between 1957 and 1960 were especially useful in his grooming for the 1960 election, after his election as party leader in 1958.[41] Robichaud was at the forefront of many ventures. These included leading New Brunswick Liberals to the national party convention in Ottawa, accompanying Prime Minister Pearson on a tour of the northern part of the province, and acting as principal financial critic for the Liberal Party. He also attracted considerable press coverage because of his attacks on the government. Other opportunities included the campaigning itself as well as a variety of inter-provincial meetings,[42] and not forgetting that his earliest formative years were couched in a Liberal world.[43] As he felt very secure in his own seat in northern Kent County he was able to devote most of his attention to other parts of the province during the campaign.[44] Included in the grand scheme for the preparation for the 1960 election campaign was the hiring of John Edward Belliveau of Tandy Advertising in Toronto as advertising campaign manager.[45] As an image maker, Belliveau was a good choice as he was originally from Moncton and understood the religious and ethnic realities of the province.[46] Also, this was the first general provincial election to make extensive use of television.[47]

The real issue of the election was the hospital premium tax; implementation of medicare was a campaign promise of Robichaud's in the 1964 and 1967 election campaigns. Despite the Liberal government's strong and early declared support, New Brunswick would be the last province in Canada to introduce the program, and it would be Richard Hatfield's Conservative government that would do so.[48] Although it did not take the same priority in the Flemming program, it was destined to become "the most widely discussed issue" of the campaign.[49]

La Patente and Louis J. Robichaud's Rise to Power

The Catholic l'Ordre de Jacques Cartier, known as La Patente, exerted tremendous influence on Robichaud's election victory and on his government's subsequent decisions related to the civil service and education.[50] La Patente came into being in Ottawa on 22 October 1926.[51] It was a secret society for Roman Catholic men with the mission of countering the equally secretive societies of the Orangemen and the Masons; the element of secrecy was interpreted by Gérard-Raymond Laliberté as a response in kind in strategy and tactics.[52] Some seventeen francophones from the Ottawa area, many from the federal public service, were the original signatories of the order which received its letters patents on 4 October 1927.[53] Its immediate aim was to encourage the employment of French-Canadians among the English-dominated civil service,[54] and, by extension, to the political and social spheres. The secret order would attack the notion of individualism among French Canadians and replace it with the notions of unity and cooperation.[55] To accomplish its goal, it established cells in each of the Canadian provinces and continued its fight until its demise in 1965.

The OJC was divided into two groups, the superior council called la Chancellerie, and the recruiting body or local cell directed by a Commandeur.[56] The methodology employed by the order was described by Laliberté as an instrument at the service of the nation, an efficient means of joining existing forces and creative energies.[57] Due to the secretive nature of the order, it is difficult to report with accuracy on membership. Estimates vary from 1,000 in 1938 to as many as 40,000 in 1963.[58]

Activities of La Patente include the dossier for the development of separate schools of Ontario[59] and the collection of French-language books in Québec for distribution to less fortunate Francophone minorities in other parts of the country.[60] In 1954 the OJC was credited with the election of Montreal Mayor Jean Drapeau.[61]

The order established different goals in the different parts of the country where it operated. For example, priorities in New Brunswick during the 1930s were unique, reflecting regional needs. Thus the Commandeurs pushed for the development of an experimental farm in Fredericton, a penitentiary in Dorchester, and for the federal unemployment insurance offices.[62] In New Brunswick, all four cells, located in Campbellton, Caraquet, Edmundston, and Moncton, identified education as a priority.[63] During the same decade in Moncton the order lobbied for francophones to be appointed to positions of authority at the Canadian National Railway, a very important employer of the time.[64] Other areas targeted included French-language radio and television and the written media.[65] In 1936 members of La Patente created the Association acadienne d'éducation; its ultimate stated objective was to assure the survival of the Acadian people, Catholic and francophone.[66]

Two Acadians with involvement in La Patente in New Brunswick during the 1960s shared their insights on the connection between the order and the election on 12 July 1960 of the first Acadian premier of New Brunswick, Louis J. Robichaud. Former social worker Joseph Laviolette,[67] a member of the group of the first Acadian social workers examined in Chapter 8 and the director of the School of Social Work at the Université de Moncton from 1974 to 1982 recalled the workings of the order in New Brunswick. He served as Commandeur of the

Campbellton (Restigouche area) cell between 1959 and 1965. The total of some sixty men who made up the cell participated by invitation only. Members of the clergy did not attend meetings as a rule but were influential behind the scenes; for example, Laviolette recalls that a church prelate made arrangements for a meeting room in a local convent that housed a female religious order. To a question concerning spousal knowledge of La Patente, he replied his wife knew the male-only secretive order was francophone and sanctioned by the Catholic Church. He added he thought the other wives did not know any more. With respect to Robichaud's election, Laviolette recalled hearing the Grand Commandeur at a meeting in Moncton pass on the buzz word of the day: "Louis J. Robichaud." That endorsement made within the secrecy of the order was passed along by its members using the usual networks such as membership in community-minded organizations, including, of course, the political arena.

The second person who commented on La Patente is a senior civil servant who wished to remain anonymous.[68] He was hired during the 1960s and had the distinct impression that the government of Louis Robichaud was influenced by La Patente when it came to the appointment of qualified civil servants to assist him in the implementation of the program of Equal Opportunity. Robichaud wanted to assure that the civil service was well equipped and understood its role when dealing with different regions of the province. For example, Mr Robichaud was well aware that Acadian nationalist organizations had a keen interest in the vitality and survival of their language and culture. There were persistent rumours to the effect that some of those Acadians were also members of La Patente and therefore able to influence the government, not only for the recruitment of senior civil servants but also to negotiate within the government hierarchy on their behalf.

The young premier is portrayed by Stanley as having the vision and the ambition to change the structure of government administration throughout the entire province of New Brunswick: "Through a combination of courage, audacity and conviction, Louis Robichaud confronted the traditional, often antiquated, discriminatory and inefficient philosophies and structures of a then backward province and wrestled New Brunswick to the forefront of social change and government reorganization during a decade of power."[69]

The same anonymous civil servant added that soon after the election of the Robichaud government in 1960, one could see a backlash growing against the government, and this was more evident in the English-speaking areas of New Brunswick and especially in Fredericton because of its proximity and ties to the government administration. Some New Brunswickers wondered, "Why are there so many Francophones appointed to the cabinet of Louis Robichaud?"

In his master's thesis, François LeBlanc found the order to be active during the period 1950–65.[70] More importantly, he established a parallel between the years of stability or growth of the membership, on one hand, and the fervour of the nationalist (Acadian) sentiment on the occasion of the bicentenary of the deportation of 1755, on the other hand.[71]

The commemoration of the bicentennial of the Acadian Deportation was held between 15 August 1954 and 15 August 1955. During the 1953 to 1954 recruitment period, the *OJC* registered sixty-four new members, an increase of 174 percent. (The pattern was repeated in 1955 to 1956 with another increase of sixty members.) Those two periods represent the two greatest increases in the history of the Moncton cell of the Patente.[72] This élan was maintained until 1960, and some argue that it was responsible, in large measure, for the election of Louis J. Robichaud.

The Equal Opportunity Program

In the years prior to Robichaud's victory, a united approach by the Atlantic provinces had been nudging New Brunswick in a more positive economic and political direction. Lisa Pasolli claims that

> this Atlantic Revolution resulted in a number of highly publicized political and financial victories for the region, including the creation of the Atlantic Premiers in 1956, the introduction of equalization in the 1956 federal budget, Diefenbaker's $29.5 million loan to New Brunswick's Beechwood power project, and the earmarking of $25 million annually for four years for the region in the form of the Atlantic provinces Adjustment Grants.[73]

There were also important changes in legislation approved by New Brunswick's government immediately before the July 1960 Liberal victory, during the Conservative Party's final months in office:

> The spring session of 1960 was not entirely devoid of useful legislation. The Social Assistance Act introduced by the Flemming government was legislation of considerable importance in the history of social welfare in New Brunswick. Through this legislation four previous social welfare related acts were repealed: Mothers' Allowance Act; Support of the Poor Act; Legal

> Settlement Act; and the Municipal Homes Act ... The anachronistic Poor Law which had controlled aid for the poor and destitute in New Brunswick since 1786, was no longer the guiding instrument.[74]

The new government would soon demonstrate its commitment to economic and industrial development, including "expansion of the province's capacity to generate hydroelectricity and infrastructure support for the mining industry in northeastern New Brunswick."[75] However, the Liberal government elected under Premier Louis J. Robichaud would inspire nothing less than massive changes. The scope of the changes implemented would result in New Brunswick gaining national recognition for the first time from other provinces such as Ontario, Saskatchewan, and Québec, according to Stanley. She notes that "while they watched, New Brunswick had the audacity and courage to rush in where others feared to tread."[76]

When Robichaud first took the reins in 1960, the government landscape reflected five types of municipally based systems and a disarray of structures and justifications. Georges Cyr explains that New Brunswick consisted of

> fifteen counties, six cities, twenty-one towns, one village, and some seventy local improvement districts and local administrative commissions ... The municipal system was inconsistent in many respects ... representation within the various councils could vary from one municipality to the next. Within the county councils, the basic unit of representation was the parish. In nearly all cases, two councillors were elected in each parish ... instead of being based on a county's population, representation was determined by the number of parishes within a county. This resulted in councils that varied in constitution from one county to the next, for instance, from thirteen councillors in Albert to thirty-five in Charlotte.[77]

The Social Assistance Act saw the major financial responsibility for assistance to people facing economic disadvantage taken on by the provincial government, even though counties continued to be involved in its administration and distribution. By 1965 county-level governments existed no more, and all welfare responsibility was on the province's shoulders:

> The Social Assistance Act of 1960 made significant changes in the cost-sharing arrangements between the provincial and municipal governments.

> The municipality replaced the parish as the unit of local government and took responsibility for social assistance payments, no longer to be called "relief"; the provincial government for the first time contributed to social assistance payments; the province took on 50% of municipal administration costs; provision was made for the appointment of full-time municipal welfare officers; the Mothers' Allowance Act was repealed; the new Department of Youth and Welfare was set up.[78]

As an initial step the premier hired a consulting firm from Chicago, Public Administration Service (PAS). They submitted an evaluative report in 1962 about the civil service:

> PAS undertook studies of position classification, pay scales, and, eventually, an intensive study of the organization of the entire administration ... [their report] made it bluntly obvious that the current systems and practices of the civil service were inadequate, and their condemnation of the civil service extended into virtually every department and agency ... a new plan was needed to ensure that staffing was adequate to meet program requirements.[79]

The comprehensive plan and transformations took only a few years to come into being, thanks to the work of the Royal Commission on Finance and Municipal Taxation, chaired by Edward Byrne, with fellow commissioners Alexandre Boudreau, Arthur E. Andrews, Ulderic Nadeau, and Charles N. Wilson. It started its work in 1962 and presented its report to the legislature in 1963. Their task was to examine the complex problems related to finance and taxation in the province.

As mentioned in an earlier chapter, K.C. Irving's empire was pampered by tax laws that allowed the company to be taxed at rates not enjoyed by companies in other provinces. Irving was not about to placidly accept the notion of a restructuring and changes that could alter the luxurious tax requirements. DeMont describes the Law Amendments Committee hearings, where the public could address the parliamentary panel with concerns:

> There wasn't an empty seat in the house on December 14, 1965, when Irving began to speak in cold, unwavering tones to Norbert Theriault, the ill-fated minister responsible for piloting the Equal Opportunity program through its initial stages. Although claiming the program was fine in principle, K.C. called the Assessment Act "completely unacceptable" and

said that "no sane person is going to agree with the method." He added, "They should understand that some industries are liable to choke to death." "Others," he hinted, "may have to pull back on expansion plans."

DeMont continues:

Irving's diatribe continued for 12 brutal hours. Finally, Theriault could stand it no longer. Reading from a prepared statement late in the evening, he said that there had been a misunderstanding: "There is no provision in this act whereby existing tax concession agreements can or will be broken. Nor is there any intention by the government to break any such agreements." Irving, at least in the eyes of most New Brunswickers, had faced down the Robichaud government. The battle lines were plainly drawn.[80]

The Byrne Report, entitled *Report of the Royal Commission on Finance and Municipal Taxation in New Brunswick*, offered numerous recommendations:

transfer of financial responsibility for education from local to provincial government, and the reduction of the number of school districts from 422 to 60 (further reduced to 33 upon implementation); the transfer of financial and administrative responsibility for justice, public health and welfare from local to provincial government; the abolition of county government and the establishment of some ninety new villages; the assessment of all real estate, to be carried out by the provincial government and to be based on market value; a uniform real estate tax, levied and collected by the provincial government; a system of unconditional grants to municipalities for local services costs, plus equalizing grants to municipalities with an insufficient tax base to provide an acceptable level of quality of services; and a substantial increase in provincial sales tax.[81]

As Pasolli notes, "Robichaud and his advisors knew in 1960 that the civil service needed to be revamped, but they also knew that the people and resources to make that happen were lacking within the existing bureaucracy."[82] Faced with the recommendations, Robichaud hired a team of people with expertise in redesigning bureaucratic systems and implementing administrative change. Referred to as the "Saskatchewan Mafia," they had been essential to Tommy Douglas's Co-operative Commonwealth Federation government in that province. They included Donald Tansley who had designed and implemented the new Medicare system in Saskatchewan and who had the expertise to transform financial components of the government, the civil service and to some degree economic policy. The others were Robert McLarty, Paul Leger, Dr Graham Clarkson, Donald Junk, and Desmond Fogg. All contributed to the massive "overhaul" of the government's operations.

The Byrne Report designed ways that key services such as education, health, social welfare, hospitalization, justice, and taxation could be centralized and administered uniformly throughout the province. The report recognized that services varied substantially because the tax bases differed significantly among urban areas as well as between urban and rural communities. A result was that not only were essential social services lacking for those living in rural areas but, in addition, as a group, the largely rural francophone population experienced systemic discrimination.

The program was not without its critiques, however. Opposition to Equal Opportunity was expressed by citizens in provincial newspapers and principally by the editor of the Fredericton *Daily Gleaner* Michael Wardell; they expressed fear about possible negative effects the Equal Opportunity Program would bring to the delivery of government programs within New Brunswick.

Criticism came even from the pulpit, as reported by Stanley:

> in April 1966, the Reverand (sic) Alan Reynolds, minister at St. Paul's United Church in Fredericton, attacked the government during a broadcast service. In the guise of a sermon based on the uses and misuses of the word "Holy," Reynolds managed to work in his own personal criticisms of the premier and his new program. Reynolds implied that the "issues of legislative reform have been clouded by accusation ... from rumors and reports of corruption and evil doing in high places" ... He then asked whether such rumors were not founded on facts, facts which Reynolds proceeded to list. Among those alleged facts was the following, "is it not true that our Premier was almost penniless when first elected and is now rated reliably as worth somewhere between $600,000 to $2,000,000."[83]

Even in the face of such criticisms, the Liberals carried on with their agenda of sweeping changes for the province. In a seminal speech entitled "A Program for Equal Opportunity," delivered to the Legislative Assembly on Tuesday, 16 November 1965,[84] the Honourable Louis J. Robichaud, QC, stated,

> The disparities which are evident among the nations of our World and among regions of our nation exist in equal measure within our own

province. We expect people in a municipality where many lack dependable incomes to provide the same level of services as municipalities where incomes are steady and high. We can no longer close our eyes and hope for a God-given miracle to end these disparities which are contributing to an irreplaceable waste of our most treasured possession – our people.

Claude Bourque, in his 1972 thesis examining the Program for Equal Opportunity, noted,

> The Program for Equal Opportunity is often referred to as "the Robin Hood Program"; i.e., take from the rich and give to the poor. The resources of a province, it was felt by the Byrne Commission, should be distributed with some degree of equality and not totally returned in proportion to the contribution. If this does not occur, there is going to be regional disparity.[85]

In the monograph *The Programme of Equal Opportunity: An Overview*, Robert A. Young summarizes the program's achievements succinctly:

> The most general characterization one can make of the EO program is that it involved a reallocation of responsibilities and fiscal arrangements between the government of New Brunswick and the province's municipalities and other local bodies. The guiding principle was that all residents of the province should have access to a basic standard of service regardless of the fiscal capacity of the locality in which they lived.[86]

He continues:

> the integration of the province through the EO program was not only about growth; it was also about *social justice*. Simply put, there existed in New Brunswick areas of wracking poverty where subsistence agriculture and low-wage jobs were unable to create an adequate tax base to provide the services that might eventually improve their lot. The equalization system introduced in 1967, along with the uniform property tax, provincial assessment, and central funding for schools and social welfare, was designed to remedy some of the appalling conditions that prevailed in parts of the province. Wealthier municipalities would help subsidize the poorer ones, but perhaps the main redistributive dimension was along rural-urban lines. Most agricultural counties had poor services and yet taxes high enough to discourage effort and investment. (Kent, for instance, had a five percent tax rate, yet its per capita revenue was third lowest of the fifteen counties).[87]

Social workers and others affected had to plough through all the Social Assistance Act's criteria for eligibility in numerous areas. For example, medical, hospital, nursing, dental, optical, drugs, and dressings were excluded from the reimbursement (except in cases of long-term assistance, in which case Old Age Assistance would be reimbursed); school supplies could be included in the reimbursement claim; however, the federal government had held up claims for items such as mattresses and stoves; municipal homes were eligible under the Social Assistance Act, and municipalities were reimbursed for those.

Social Worker Reactions to the Byrne Report

Social workers interviewed for this research shared positive assessments of the importance and impact of Louis J. Robichaud's team's accomplishments through Equal Opportunity legislation. The massive reforms that came with the policy changes would serve to offer hope and greater economic, educational, and social stability throughout the province.[88] Social workers were involved in providing feedback as a body, as the following quotation demonstrates:

> When Louis J. Robichaud was elected on his Equal Opportunity thing, we were very busy studying even before it came out; we were privy to reports that we could study and look at and have some opinion on. I don't know how many of our opinions were incorporated, but at least it was workable. We felt that we could work with the government, and it was a great shock to us to see that the southern part of the province, Saint John with its industrialization and lots of money and Moncton that was pretty well off and Fredericton, [while] the North Shore was not. All that part of the country needed money, and Louis got it through his taxation. He took over taxation, justice, health, welfare and education.[89]

The impact of the new program on social service delivery in the province was unprecedented:

> It was hard for the mentality of people in New Brunswick to accept this massive change, but it was marvellous. In the end people were taxed, and he [Premier Robichaud] had the money from all the taxation and was able to build proper schools up north and try to get industries up north, improve the fishing services and the fish packing plants were no longer all down on the south shore; they were being developed and built up there. So, there was a great difference in how social services were offered and what social

> workers did, what the justice system was doing and what the health system was doing and we all worked more closely together. I think that made a massive difference in how social work was practised. Some of the "hominess" went out of it, truly, but by the same token it probably got more professional because we got more professional workers. They sent more people away on bursaries to get educated in social work. [90]

Another social worker's comment reflects the personal impact of the changes as well as admiration for what was being attempted: "it was 1960 when Louis became premier and he started this program that everyone paid a fair share of the taxes. My taxes went down by over two hundred dollars. The thing was that everyone had to pay their share, and that meant that there weren't any exclusions from it at all." He concluded: "That was a marvellous program, it really was."[91]

The social workers interviewed for this study agreed that the legislative changes and leadership brought about by Louis J. Robichaud were warmly welcomed. Finally, they would be working in a provincial context in which disparities and constraints that characterized day-to-day reality under the former legislation could be replaced by greater equality in educational and financial support and opportunities.

It is difficult to learn of the Robichaud legacy without developing great admiration for the leadership and passion the man and his government breathed into the province. Recognizing that within Robichaud's policies were woven belief in the necessity and value of government intervention, Michel Cormier also points out that strongly supporting a government interventionist agenda simultaneously served

> to circumscribe the power of K.C. Irving's corporate empire. The idea that the provincial government could become a player in the economy, that it could, as it were, influence the course of economic events was itself novel at the time. It is perhaps true that Robichaud was only taking part in a much wider trend, but that did not make it any less perilous to challenge the financial establishment and its ways. Ample proof of this was provided by the campaign that Irving waged against the social equality program and in favour of maintaining the generous tax concessions that he had negotiated with municipalities. Robichaud's riposte – namely, that if K.C. Irving wanted to run the province he would first have to get himself elected premier – has long since entered the history books.[92]

Income levels and education rank highly as relevant markers of government success and social and economic gains in a province. After

Equal Opportunity was implemented, Robert Young notes that "the New Brunswick economy enjoyed something of a spurt ... with income rising by 115 percent between 1967 and 1974."[93] The same author reports that educational aspirations were far from neglected:

> ... in the 1960s, the major focus of social programs was on education (rather than health, pensions, and social assistance, as came to be the case later). Improved education could translate directly into both greater social and individual welfare and increased economic productivity and growth. This was recognized in New Brunswick, and it was done through the EO program. But accomplishing it required some special expertise and a bold government committed to Equal Opportunity for all New Brunswickers.[94]

Conclusion

Louis J. Robichaud's accomplishments for New Brunswick in general and for Acadian New Brunswickers specifically are perhaps best highlighted by Margaret Conrad and James Hiller:

> Robichaud ensured that a majority of his cabinet members were francophones (sic) and set out to improve conditions in the poor, rural municipalities where most Acadians lived. While his "Program of Equal Opportunity" brought howls of a "French takeover" from many anglophones, it transformed New Brunswick's political landscape. The centralization of health and educational services, the establishment of a francophone university in Moncton in 1963, and the decision in 1969 to declare New Brunswick a bilingual province – the only one in Canada – underscored the growing power of the province's Acadian minority.[95]

The La Patente movement in the province had been successful in reaching its goals, and probably even surpassing the dreams of its membership.

The final word for this chapter is given to Louis J. Robichaud himself, an Acadian of humble beginnings, whose leadership reflected values of inclusion, social justice, and the importance of a collective approach. He indicated what the program signified to the province of New Brunswick by summarizing it as "a programme of evolution, not revolution, a programme for efficiency with democracy, a programme of equality."[96]

11
Conclusion

LAUREL LEWEY, LOUIS J. RICHARD, AND LINDA TURNER

New Brunswick's rich social work and social services histories have been directly informed by listening to stories related by dozens of former social workers, gathering archival material and considering numerous secondary sources. The colonial, economic, and historical contexts of service provision, as well as the realities of poverty in New Brunswick, constitute an important backdrop to the development of social care agencies and the evolution of child welfare. First-hand experiences as reported by the earliest social workers in the province open unique doors to the practices of the times, and understanding the experiences of the first Acadian social workers enables insights into the ways a professional minority group took their place in the social order of the province. Given that child welfare is primary to the social work profession, accounts of the realities encountered by clients and social workers in the child welfare field in New Brunswick are important.

Understanding the foregoing allows the massive significance of Equal Opportunity legislation for the profession of social work and for New Brunswickers to be better appreciated, as it heralded a new era for New Brunswick. However, we have also seen how the subsuming of Children's Aid Societies within the provincial structure imperiled Indigenous families. Despite New Brunswick being one of the four founding provinces of Canada in 1867, and despite the claim it staked when it became the country's first officially bilingual province a century later, its record of social welfare is less than praiseworthy.

There are three main threads that the authors consider the most prominent emerging from this book. The first is that the United Empire Loyalists represented the group with the most power: they were able to impose familiar colonial policies and practices that reflected their values. The second is the workings of a capitalist class that exploited the natural resources of the province for profit and that, through arbitrary hiring practices and pay rates, created a dependence of labour on capital. The third raises questions about the relative value of the assortment of religious, non-governmental, and charitable organizations, couched in Poor Law mentality, for those who experienced the greatest need. Nérée St-Amand aptly observes that "this book clearly demonstrates that we have evolved from emergency relief to basic rights for all, thanks to Louis J. Robichaud's vision in particular. Readers might wonder to what extent these basic rights are presently endangered by the dismantling of the welfare state and the privatization of social institutions."[1] One might wonder indeed.

The practices and culture that had sustained the Indigenous people of New Brunswick for centuries were significantly disrupted, first by the advent of French traders and members of religious orders; and then, most significantly and irretrievably, by the flood of United Empire Loyalists in the late 1700s. One of the stories that emerges from this book clearly reveals a pattern of colonial dominance that shaped and continues to shape substantive aspects of life in New Brunswick. The loyalists arrived as settlers in the territory with the promise of land by King George III, demonstrating the colonial assertion of their entitlement. With the British capture of Fort Louisburg in 1758, the British considered the French a conquered group, as well as the Indigenous inhabitants who were seen as their allies. The displacement and the destruction of the traditional lifestyle of Indigenous inhabitants continued in earnest at this point. In addition, most of the Acadians who would not declare allegiance to the British Crown were deported, and the lands they were forced to vacate were awarded to settlers. Acadians would eventually return to build settlements in other regions through the Maritime provinces. Gaining suffrage in 1810 and the ability to hold political office in 1830 made possible significant opportunities for Acadian men to become political actors in the province.

The imposition and dominance of the British colonial world view and accompanying policies and practices are evident. The rulers reflected the colonial assumption of superiority over systems that differed from the British system, and this assumption fuelled the lack of recognition of and respect for the peace and friendship treaties made with the Indigenous inhabitants. Instead, their lands were confiscated, therefore depriving them of the ability to sustain and govern themselves. The Indian Act ensured that Indigenous people were ruled and constrained by laws not of their own making. In addition, Indigenous inhabitants of the province were deprived of opportunities available to the settler populations, such as economic advantages, freedom of movement, freedom to engage in spiritual practices, equality in accessing education in their own language, and ultimately, when children were sent to the Shubenacadie Residential School, were deprived of the right to parent their own children. The fact that the Indigenous people were not able to vote federally until the 1960s demonstrates the extent to which Indigenous people were kept at the margins of citizenship within their own territory, although prior to this, adult males had been granted the right to vote in band elections. This assumption of superiority by the United Empire Loyalists extended to all subsequent groups of settlers in the province.

A second story that emerges through the writing of this book is that of the exploitation of natural resources by profit-driven capitalists. It is not surprising that the United Empire Loyalists asserted themselves as the victors of the struggle in the territory and therefore considered themselves free to dominate the exploitation of its natural resources for profit. Andrea Bear-Nicholas spoke of the gangs that were brought in specifically to harvest the timber and the subsequent pollution of the Nashwaak River that destroyed salmon stocks by the mid-1800s. Members of those groups unable to compete as owners or managers of capitalist enterprises would provide the ready and cheap labour force that was needed for such enterprises. In this book, examples were provided that revealed the arbitrary hiring practices and pay rates offered to workers, demonstrating the precarious dependence of labour on capital. It was mostly the wealthy who could exert their influence in the political arena, particularly until the francophone population began to exercise suffrage and hold political office.

The third significant thread identified by the authors concerns the creation and expansion of the assortment of religious, non-governmental, and charitable organizations that often provided the only buffer against starvation. New Brunswickers were able to survive but often at a cost to their self-respect. It has been shown how the social care provided in the province consisted of a patchwork of religious, non-government, and charitable organizations that were available to the settler populations. Many New Brunswickers needed to turn to those organizations as a result of illness or limitations, lack of employment opportunities, and marginalization owing to racism and discrimination. Women and children were particularly vulnerable and subject to societal assumptions that patriarchal (and often violent) rule was justified. They could be deprived of support if not deemed worthy and grateful recipients. This legacy of residual social welfare needed to be replaced with a comprehensive institutional response, if dignity and social justice were to enter into the fabric of service delivery.

Application of the British Poor Law system, with its embedded ideology, dominated the social care experience of both anglophone and francophone settlers of New Brunswick. Although the social care agencies available to francophone settlers were religion based, the British system was the one enacted through law in New Brunswick. The parish system provided for the distribution of goods to those most in need, yet the offerings varied depending on the location and, therefore, the relative wealth of a parish. Relief was parcelled out to those determined to be worthy of the assistance and was often accompanied by demeaning treatment, depending on the moralistic bent of those charged with the task of determining eligibility for and distributing relief. Social workers learned to navigate the rules and residency requirements as well as the individual biases of the gatekeepers of the resources.

Similar to what was occurring in North America and Europe, attitudes shaped by the eugenics movement provided the impetus for the categorization of mentally challenged individuals and instilled fear that somehow the larger society would be "infected" unless individuals deemed defective were contained. Moralistic judgments surrounded unmarried mothers; however most often these judgments were not applied to the men who impregnated them. The term "illegitimate child" wasn't abandoned until 1956 when the Illegitimate Children's Act was changed to the Children of Unmarried Parents' Act. Social workers were involved in securing this change through promoting language reflective of changing attitudes. The practice of housing the poor in almshouses, in what would later be called municipal homes, continued until 1966, when the last one closed during the Robichaud era.

When the changes associated with the Equal Opportunity Program began in the 1960s, social workers in the province had already been influenced by movements occurring in other parts of Canada to expand child welfare services and to move from institutional-care settings to those that most resembled family homes. While the first Children's Aid Societies were formed in 1914 in Saint John, 1916 in Fredericton and Moncton, and in Sackville in 1924, they served largely anglophone and Protestant families living in the respective counties of Saint John, York, and Westmorland. It was only in 1941 that other counties would begin to have access to these agencies. It would not be until 1953 that the CAS agencies no longer had to submit operational grants on an annual basis, a sign they were finally being seen as a permanent municipal expenditure. Another decade would pass before the province assumed responsibility for all child welfare and social assistance in 1965; most of the functions previously performed by the CAS agencies were taken over by 1967.

Orphanages did not begin to disappear until the 1950s, with the last one closing in 1966. However, Indigenous children were sent to Shubenacadie Residential School in Nova Scotia, beginning in 1929 until the school closed in 1967. Children received little actual education there, and because the operation of the school depended on their labour, the children were engaged in much physical work. During its lifetime, the Shubenacadie Residential School was also used to house children identified as being in need of care, including children whose parents could not afford to keep them. When the province began to provide child protection for Indigenous children in the 1960s, as a result of 1951 amendments to the Indian Act, the most common practice was to remove children from their homes and reserves and place them with non-Indigenous caretakers. This represented the New Brunswick version of the "Sixties Scoop" that occurred in other parts of Canada, until the chiefs from four reserves interrupted the practice by beginning to establish Indigenous child welfare agencies in the late 1970s.

Tracing the evolution of social care reveals an ad hoc, moralistic, and residual system that was difficult to navigate and was reflective of the unequal social relations. Only with the advent of Equal Opportunity did the gross inequalities begin to be addressed.

In light of the meager resources made available to the poor and needy in New Brunswick it is interesting to speculate on how the various groups looked after themselves and each other. Carolyn Ennis[2] provides insight into practices that occurred during her early years. Having no alternative, her working mother paid for family members to look after her children. Ennis described the role of the Grand Council, on which individuals and extended families could rely when there was a concern. This system no doubt provided the best and only safety net to Indigenous inhabitants, since provincial resources were unavailable and federal resources were so meagre. Other settler groups in rural areas probably were able to grow and hunt for most of their food. The Acadians cooperated in working bees, called the corvées, and developed a device called l'aboiteau used to irrigate their fields while preventing salt water from encroaching onto them. Acadians have always attached great value to a collective approach, necessary to their survival and an ongoing source of resilience. Thus the cooperative movement resonated with collectivism and played a valuable role in how they, as a group, looked after one another.

At this point it is apropos to return to underlying questions raised by Nérée St-Amand in the foreword to this book. He asked what might have been different if the social workers of the period had focused more on social change. He questions how things might have been different if a structural social work approach had been used. He goes on to encourage social work practices that eliminate poverty and violence rather than offer individualized assistance. Further, he asks, what if decent housing was a right, not a privilege, and what if decent working conditions were protected by law. Finally, he left us with the following thought-provoking question and claim: "What if we had taken another approach rather than relying on Mary Richmond's charitable philosophy ... it could be argued that the poor have been, and still are, more courageous than the people helping them."

The arrival of social workers was a significant step in the provision of social services in New Brunswick. The first anglophone social worker to work in New Brunswick was Elizabeth King in 1925, whereas the first Acadian was Norman Clavet of Saint-Basile in 1957. The first Indigenous social worker in the province was Malcolm Saulis, who worked in child welfare beginning in the 1970s.

Central to St-Amand's questions is speculation about how differently people's needs would have been addressed had social work practice incorporated a structural approach. Our social work predecessors worked with limited resources, and it was shown how children were taken from their homes when there was no alternative because of dangerous conditions. Social workers carried on with few resources and worked within a system that they did not have a role in designing – one that was also imbued with an antiquated ideology. Certainly compassion was expressed at the appalling conditions that children and families experienced.

It appears that historically, very few social workers in New Brunswick were employed in positions where they could affect social policy. It is apparent from the interviews conducted with former social workers that many worked around rules in order to obtain more provisions for those in need, which reflected a common strategy of good social workers.[3] There is, however, no evidence of structural social workers working in the province in these early years, nor were there councils, such as the Child Welfare Council in Toronto, where radical social workers could form coalitions with other radical social workers to effect social change. Although the CCF gained strength throughout the 1940s, there is no evidence of any lasting legacy until the early 1970s.

In conclusion, the administrative landscape that preceded Equal Opportunity consisted of five types of municipal-based systems ranging from parish to small village, to a municipality, a county, or a large centre like Saint John; there were great inconsistencies among the welfare institutions and services that responded to people in need. Nevertheless, it would appear that francophones prodded New Brunswick society forward once they had gathered the necessary ingredients with Louis J. Robichaud as the messenger. The guiding principal of the Equal Opportunity Program was that all citizens of the province should have access to a basic standard of services in the areas of health, education, welfare, and justice, regardless of the fiscal capacity of the locality in which they lived. The massive changes included the transfers of financial responsibility from the local to the provincial level in the areas mentioned above and a uniform province-wide tax base. The Robichaud government concluded, wisely, that the people and resources needed to make the proposed changes were lacking within the existing bureaucracy, and so experts were brought in. In practice, services would be centralized and administered uniformly throughout the province. The Byrne Report, which inspired the legislation of the Equal Opportunity Program, was considered in a positive light by the social work community. The social workers welcomed the changes that made a massive difference in how social work was administered and practised. The professionalization of social work became a focus. Although the number of social work positions was not as high as had been recommended, bursaries were provided for many of those wishing to pursue studies in social work.

What can be learned from the New Brunswick experience? One lesson is that a carefully designed and comprehensive program, such as Equal Opportunity, capable of remedying unequal access, is both possible and beneficial. Praise for the many positive outcomes of Equal Opportunity for the province of New Brunswick continues. The New Brunswick story should serve to inspire governments in any country that wish to remedy unequal access to health care services; educational or employment opportunities; affordable housing; affordable child care; shelter for those living in abusive relationships, or that wish to provide a remedy to the

Indigenous languages that are in peril. We as social work educators, practitioners, and citizens can insist on it.

The authors realize their role as one limited to that of initiator and explorer. Much research remains to be conducted to give a better understanding of the past in order to guide in shaping present and future policies. We wish future researchers good fortune in that venture.

Appendix 1

Origins of the New Brunswick Association of Social Workers (NBASW)

The professionalization of social work began in Canada when the Canadian Association of Social Workers (CASW) was formed in 1926. Following that, branches were formed in the larger Canadian cities. For example, the Toronto and Montreal branches were formed in 1927; the Hamilton, Ontario, and British Columbia mainland branches in 1928; and the Manitoba branch in 1930.

In order to form a branch of the CASW, five members had to meet the criteria to be considered a qualified social worker. These criteria varied over the years. Kathleen (Tally) Morrissy represented New Brunswick at national meetings of the CASW as a non–branch member at the time when there were insufficient members to form a branch in her province. An intermediate step for social workers in New Brunswick and in Prince Edward Island was to combine their numbers to form the New Brunswick–Prince Edward Island association in 1948. It was difficult to have meetings of this association for various reasons. One barrier was finding a meeting place that could house all the members. A second significant barrier was the weather. A third barrier was travel, as the New Brunswick members had to motor to Prince Edward Island to ensure a quorum for a meeting: this was before the days of the bridge, when travelling to the island was a very time-consuming business.

The New Brunswick–Prince Edward Island association wished to make key persons in the social welfare field aware that the branch had formed and to advise the ministers in both provinces of the assistance they could offer. From the end of 1956 to 1958, the types of educational programs offered at meetings included a variety of topics such as discussion of civil defence, public assistance in New Brunswick, the constitution of the association, recruitment and national personnel practices, provincial organization, the use of responsibility in casework practice, and social work in social action.

The New Brunswick–Prince Edward Island Branch was dissolved in 1958 when Carol Proctor became the first president of the New Brunswick branch of the CASW. At that time there were fifty social workers eligible to become members of this branch. "They met on a regular basis to discuss such issues as professional identity, salary standards, social work education, adoption practices, social action, the Byrne Report, relationships between social workers and welfare workers, employing qualified social workers in government, and provincial incorporation."[1] The first biennial report was dated 3 May 1960.

Incorporated in 1965, the NBASW was founded by Constance Harrison, E. Stanley Matheson, Murray Manzer, Carol Proctor, Marcel Arseneau, Joseph Laviolette, and Normand Clavet.

Appendix 2

Biographical Sketches of Social Workers and Social Welfare Workers in New Brunswick, 1925–1966

In this section, we provide, in alphabetical order, brief biographies of individuals identified as being social workers or in social work positions in the years up to 1967, when the Equal Opportunity legislation was passed. Information for the biographies was found in historical documents or published obituaries and was sometimes confirmed in interview data. We have included this to honour the many individuals who were in social work roles up to 1967. We apologize for any errors, omissions, or oversights in this initial collection of New Brunswick's social work pioneers. Very often women were identified on membership lists with the title of "Miss" or "Mrs." We have not included those titles unless the individual's gender would not otherwise be known. In addition, there are some people about whom the only information we currently hold is an entry of their names on a membership list. These individuals are listed separately at the end of this appendix.

The Maritime School of Social Work was created in Halifax in 1941 to serve Atlantic Canada. Graduates from its professional program would apply to one of five affiliated universities for a master's degree. Those universities were Saint Mary's and King's College (Halifax), Saint-Francis Xavier (Antigonish), Acadia (Wolfville) in Nova Scotia, and Mount Allison (Sackville) in New Brunswick. This scheme continued until the early 1970s, at which time the school became part of Dalhousie University.

Margaret Jean Algie. She held a BA and was from Moncton. She graduated with master of social work from the Maritime School of Social Work in 1954.

Dorothy Marion (Runnells) Allen. She had a BA in social sciences from Victoria College (University of Toronto) 1933. In 1935, she was working at the Montreal Day Nursery, and spoke on a panel to the casework section of the Montreal Welfare Council at McGill University about attending the national conference of social work in Atlantic City. Dorothy was a member of the New Brunswick–Prince Edward Island branch of the Canadian Association of Social Workers (CASW). She worked in Moncton. In 1955 she chaired the Program Committee. She died 1967.

Margaret Anstey. Margaret graduated with a diploma in social service from the University of Toronto in 1927. She was originally from London, England. In March 1929 her article titled "Italy Renascent," in which she was critical of Mussolini, was published in the journal *Social Welfare*. She had lived in Italy for several years and at that time was on the staff of the infants home. Margaret worked in the role of agent and/or director for the CAS in Saint John from 1930 until 25 July 1934, when she resigned her position as director due to ill health. She had been a caseworker on loan to the CAS from the Central Welfare Council in order to reorganize the CAS and implement modern casework practice.

Marcel Arseneau. Marcel obtained his BA at the Université Saint-Joseph in 1958. He later went on to receive his MSW at the Maritime School of Social Work in 1960. Marcel is one of the founding members of the NBASW. He was employed at the provincial hospital in Campbellton and was a district welfare supervisor. He worked in the areas of Tracadie, Caraquet, and Shippagan.

Barbara E. Bell. Barbara was a member of the New Brunswick–Prince Edward Island Branch, CASW, and probably worked in Fredericton, New Brunswick.

Marion H. (Machum) Bennett. Marion lived in Sackville, New Brunswick, and was a member of the New Brunswick–Prince Edward Island Branch, CASW, in December 1956. She died in 1981.

Harold Betts. Harold received his BA from Sir George Williams College in 1937 and a partial master's (Alberta). He received a diploma from the Toronto School of Social Work, and it is not clear if he completed an MSW degree. For many years he worked for the YMCA in Moncton as director of physical education. By 1948, he'd taken the position of assistant executive secretary with the Montreal Boys Association.

Mildred Bingay-White. She was from Saint John. She let her membership in CASW lapse the end of 1944 because she moved to Washington.

Dorothy Bishop. She attended Simmons College School of Social Work in Boston. Dorothy lived in Sackville, New Brunswick. She wrote the article "Some Implications of the Functional-Diagnostic Controversy," published in the *Social Worker* in February 1951. From 1949 she served as the executive secretary of the Children's Aid Society of Westmorland

County in Sackville. In 1956 she was secretary treasurer of the Children's Aid Society of Westmorland County. From 1956 to 1964 she worked with Moncton Family and Children's Services. She was an active member of the Committee for the Unmarried Mother and Her Child, New Brunswick–Prince Edward Island Branch, CASW.

Mary Bishop. Mary was a graduate of the McGill School of Social Work. At a meeting of the New Brunswick–Prince Edward Island Branch, CASW, Mary stated, "Perhaps CASW meant more to the social workers in this branch than in other parts of Canada, as the association, to them, brought enthusiasm and vitality." The March 1929 issue of *Social Welfare* published her article "The Older Girl and the Group." Formerly a child welfare agent (1946), she served as the executive secretary from 1949 to 1959 with the Saint John Children's Aid Society. She was also the director of the Protestant Orphans' Home. Mary served as a member of the National Membership Committee, CASW.

Elizabeth Bissett. Elizabeth went to New Brunswick from Ontario with one year of training and worked with the Saint John CAS. In 1974 she is cited in the Montreal *Gazette* speaking about adoption of older children, in her role as coordinator of the adoption-clearance service of the Nova Scotia Department of Social Services.

(Mrs) Bowman. In 1955, the minutes of the New Brunswick–Prince Edward Island Branch, CASW, indicate that she moved and so transferred her membership to another branch.

Ruth (Galbraith) Brittain. Ruth was employed with Department of Social Services, New Brunswick, throughout her career, in Mothers' Allowances.

Gertrude Butler. Gertrude was a graduate of the School of Social Work of the Catholic University in Washington and a graduate of the Maritime School of Social Work. She was hired in 1945 by the Catholic Welfare Bureau in Saint John and worked with Father MacDonald.

(Mrs) J.A.D. Campbell. Mrs Campbell lived in Clifton Royal, Kings County, New Brunswick.

(Mrs) David Chambers. Mrs Chambers lived in Saint John, New Brunswick and was listed as employed in CASW membership files.

Jean-Paul Chiasson. He obtained his BA at the Université Sacré-Coeur, in Bathurst, New Brunswick, in 1961. He then went on to receive his MSW at the Maritime School of Social Work in 1963. He was employed with Moncton Family and Children's Services as well as Child Welfare Services in Moncton.

Florence Christie. She was the executive secretary with the Family Welfare Association in Saint John in 1964. She was a long-time member of the New Brunswick Association of Social Workers and served as president from 1967 to 1968. Florence was also a member of the National Membership Committee, CASW.

Normand Clavet. Normand obtained his BA at the Université Sacré-Coeur, in Bathurst, New Brunswick, in 1951. He then went on to receive his MSW at the Maritime School of Social Work in 1957. He worked at the provincial hospital in Campbellton and at the Clinique d'Hygiène Mentale d'Edmundston. From 1960 to 1962, Normand served on the Terminology Committee, CASW.

Peter J. Collis. He lived in Lancaster, New Brunswick. For a period, Peter served as vice president of the New Brunswick–Prince Edward Island Branch, CASW.

Margaret Nason Collis. She was introduced to the New Brunswick–Prince Edward Island Branch, CASW on 15 November 1955, where it was noted that she moved to Fredericton, New Brunswick, and so her membership was transferred from the Nova Scotia Mainland Branch.

Bernardine Conlogue. Bernadine was born in 1912. She attended the Business College and received her Maritime School of Social Work certificate in 1964. Bernardine helped Father MacDonald set up the Catholic Welfare Bureau in Saint John in 1944. She stayed with the bureau until it was incorporated into the Family Welfare Association under Florence Christie. She became a child welfare consultant when Gerry Hickey became administrator.

Byrd Corbett. In 1939 she was employed with the Family Service Bureau in Saint John, and a member of the Advisory Committee for the "Household Service Practice House," which trained young women to become maids in households across Canada. She was also eligible to become a member of the CASW during the years from 1944 to 1946.

Reginald Craig. He obtained his MSW at the Maritime School of Social Work in Halifax in 1952. He was the first social worker at the Saint John General psychiatric wing. He also worked at the Mental Health Clinic in Saint John. From 1952 until 1956 he served as secretary of the New Brunswick–Prince Edward Island Branch, CASW. He left the Mental Health Clinic to work at the Ottawa Civic Hospital. From 1960 to 1962 he served on the Social Action and Social Policy Committee, CASW. In later years he became a well-known Maritime School of Social Work professor.

Evelyn Crowley. Evelyn worked at the Catholic Welfare Bureau in Saint John and was very involved in adoptions assessment and placement.

Leonard Delaney. Leonard received his BA at the Université Sainte-Anne, at Pointe-de-l'Église in Nova Scotia in 1955. He went on to obtain his MSW at the Maritime School of Social Work in Halifax in 1961.

June Dexter (Murphy). She attended the University of Toronto but apparently did not stay in the field long.

Anne Harrington Disher. In 1951 she joined the CASW and served as a New Brunswick representative on the Membership Committee. She was a member of the New Brunswick–Prince Edward Island Branch but resigned in 1955. She received her BA from Dalhousie University and her BSW from the University of Toronto. Anne was a social worker at the provincial hospital in Saint John.

John Wilson Donnachie. He received his BA at the University of New Brunswick and then obtained his MSW at the Maritime School of Social Work in Halifax. He was employed with the Department of Health and Social Services, Mental Health Division, in 1953 in Fredericton, New Brunswick. From 1952 to 1956, he served as treasurer of the New Brunswick–Prince Edward Island Branch, CASW.

Normand Doucet. He obtained his BA at the Université Saint-Joseph in 1961. He then earned his MSW at the Maritime School of Social Work in 1963. In southeastern New Brunswick, he is considered a pioneer because of the important role he played in establishing the social work departments at the Moncton and Georges Dumont hospitals, and as founding director of l'École de travail social, Université de Moncton.

Richard Duffy. From 1958 until 1969 he was a pensions inspector in Saint John, administering the Old Age Assistance, Disabled and Blindness Assistance Programs.

Eleanor Joyce Flood. Eleanor received an MSW at the Maritime School of Social Work in 1959. She was then employed with the Moncton Mental Health Clinic satellite and the provincial hospital at River Glade.

Marc Gallant. Marc received his BA at the Université Sacré-Cœur in 1958 and his MSW in 1963 from McGill. He was briefly employed with Child Welfare Services in Moncton. He was also a member of the CASW National Membership Committee.

Georgio Gaudet. He received his Maitrise en service social at Laval. Georgio was a member of the New Brunswick Association of Social Workers.

J. Willie Gibbs. He obtained his BA at the Université Saint-Joseph in 1962 and his MSW at the Maritime School of Social Work in Halifax in 1964. In 1966 he joined the Correctional Service of Canada and pursued a successful and lengthy career in that field.

Margaret H. Gibson. Margaret obtained her teachers' certificate and taught school from 1936 to 1941. She served in the Royal Canadian Air Force from 1942 to 1946. She received her MSW at the Maritime School of Social Work in Halifax in 1948 and was given an award donated by the chair of the school's board, Mr Justice Hall, for highest standing of a graduate in her final year. She worked with the Saint John Children's Aid Society and was the director in 1948. She also worked with the Moncton Welfare Bureau from 1956 to 1961. From 1959 to 1960, she was the president of the New Brunswick Branch, CASW.

Margaret Mary T. Gillis. She earned her MSW at the Maritime School of Social Work in 1957. In 1963 Mary was the supervisor of the Social Assistance Division, Department of Youth and Welfare, Fredericton. She also worked as a community development education officer for the Miramichi Indian Agency.

Catherine C. Giovannetti. She was born in Pictou, Nova Scotia, and worked in Saint John. She is listed as a member of the New Brunswick Branch, CASW, 1958 to 1960. She obtained her master's degree from the Maritime School of Social Work in 1946. She worked two years for a Catholic adoption agency in Saint John and an additional sixteen years for the Province of New Brunswick. At one point in her career, she was head of the Foster Parents Association, helping to place children in foster care and providing ongoing support and training for foster parents.

Sister Lorraine Godin. In 1969 she was a social worker II, acting supervisor of Child Welfare.

C.F.A. (Helen) Graham. Helen worked at the Dr. William F. Roberts Hospital School and later became director. She was also employed in the mental health field in Saint John and Fredericton. She served as treasurer for the New Brunswick Branch, CASW, circa 1960–1; the Study for Competence, 1960–2; and the constitution committee in 1962.

Dorothy Grantmyre. She worked in Saint John, New Brunswick, and was a member of the New Brunswick–Prince Edward Island Branch, CASW, circa 1956.

Mr Green. He was a member of the New Brunswick–Prince Edward Island Branch, CASW, in 1954 and served on the Publicity Committee that year.

Arthur Gregg. Arthur was listed in the CASW membership files as eligible to become a member circa 1944–6.

Elizabeth Gunter. Circa 1960–1, Elizabeth was the director of Fredericton's Welfare Department. She also worked with the Kingsclear agency.

Kay Hamilton. Kay was a CAS agent for Carleton County, working in Woodstock, circa 1960–1. Before 1967, she was a welfare worker III, and a former CAS employee. She supervised one welfare worker II and one clerk-steno.

Dorothy (Stanton) Hanusiack. Dorothy lived in Fredericton, New Brunswick. She was listed as employed circa 1960–1. She received her BA from St. Francis Xavier University in 1949.

Dora Hargrove. Circa 1960–1, she was executive director of Oromocto Welfare, town of Oromocto.

Constance (Connie) Harrison. Constance graduated with a BA in sociology in 1942. In the fall of 1946, she went to the Toronto School of Social Work. She worked for the CAS and the Special Projects Branch of the YWCA while in Toronto. In 1955 she returned to work in Saint John and got a job with the Lancaster DVA Hospital, where she worked for six years until 1961. Constance was the president of the New Brunswick Association of Social Workers from 1964 to 1965 and the New Brunswick representative on the Membership Committee, CASW, from 1960 to 1961.

Catherine Henley. She came to New Brunswick from Ohio in 1955 and was noted as a prospective member of the New Brunswick–Prince Edward Island Branch, CASW. She was supervisor of psychiatric social work for the Mental Health Division of the Department of Health and Social Services. Previously, she had worked in Toronto, Ontario, in psychiatric social work.

Gerald Francis Hickey. He earned his MSW from the Maritime School of Social Work in 1961. He was then employed with the Saint John Children's Aid Society and Moncton Family and Children's Services, where he was the director. In 1969 he was a district welfare supervisor.

Frances Irwin. She was listed as attending a New Brunswick Branch meeting in Saint John in 1960.

Ruth Jenkins. Ruth worked as a CAS agent in St. Stephen in 1948.

Phyllis Keating. She lived in Salisbury and Bathurst and was a registered social worker. In 1968 she was employed by the Mental Health Clinic in Fredericton.

Flora Jean (Sears) Kennedy. She obtained her BA from the University of New Brunswick and her MSW from the Maritime School of Social Work in 1954. Her placements during her MSW included the Welfare Department with former students from the school in Truro and also the Child Guidance Clinic. She also attended MSW training on a mental-health bursary. Flora Jean then worked for several years at the provincial hospital in Saint John and transferred to the Catholic Welfare Bureau, where she served as the director until the Equal Opportunity Program came into effect. She also worked as child welfare supervisor, Department of Youth, in Fredericton and later became regional director of Fredericton Region. She was co opted by the provincial office to design new child welfare legislation, and once that was finished became director of planning and evaluation. She served as the New Brunswick representative, Membership Committee, CASW, and from 1960 to 1961 on the Publicity and Interpretation Committee for the New Brunswick Branch, CASW. She was later a member of the New Brunswick Association of Social Workers.

Dorothy King. Dorothy was a social service worker who worked on the survey of welfare services conducted by Charlotte Whitton in Moncton in 1939.

Elizabeth King. She was born in New Brunswick. In 1905 she received a BA, and in 1907 an MA from Acadia University. In the summer of 1918 she attended the American Red Cross Summer Course in Social Work. She worked at the Ottawa Welfare Bureau in a secretarial position and then as an investigator on the Ontario Mothers' Allowance Commission. Elizabeth then became a senior investigator for the commission. Then in 1928 she took the New School for Social Work Course in behavioural problems of children. She moved from Ottawa to New York City and worked as a visitor for the Family Welfare Society of Queens and the Brooklyn Bureau of Charities. It appears that she moved to New Brunswick from New York. King was hired as survey staff for Charlotte Whitton's survey on New Brunswick child welfare in Saint John (1927–30). Whitton was a well-known social worker and director of the Canadian Council on Child Welfare and sought to promote modern social work practices. Whitton had hoped that King would oversee the establishment of the Family Welfare Bureau, the Council of Social Agencies, and to be closely involved in the revamping of social work in Saint John.

Marg Kinghorn. Marg lived in Fredericton in 1956 and she also lived in Saint John. She worked with Lorna Warneford in Saint John.

Vilma Kurol. Vilma took a three-year course in social work, which she completed in 1941 in Estonia, in Europe. She worked three years in Estonia and one in Austria. In 1953 she came to Canada and got her first job with the Children's Aid Society in child protection in Saint John under the supervision of Mary Bishop. She also worked at the Saint John Mental Health Clinic.

Raymonde Marie Landry. She obtained a BA at St. Thomas College and then took a two-year course at Laval University. She worked for the Moncton Municipal Welfare Bureau. She was also survey staff for Charlotte Whitton and the New Brunswick Child Welfare Survey, 1927–30. She became a member of the CASW in 1948.

Joseph Laviolette. In 1957 he received a mental-health bursary to complete his MSW at the University of Montreal. From 1957 to 1964 he worked at the provincial hospital in Campbellton. He was involved in the organization of the volunteer services for the hospital from 1964 to 1970. He then moved to Joliette to work in the addictions clinic in 1965. Later, he taught at the Université de Moncton where he was Director of its École de travail social.

Ronaldo Lavoie. He received his BA at the Université Saint-Joseph and then obtained his MSW at the Maritime School of Social Work in Halifax in 1958. He went on to work with the Moncton Mental Health Clinic. During 1960 to 1961 he served on the Program Committee of the New Brunswick Branch of the CASW.

Armand LeCouffe. Armand worked most of his life for social services as an administrator, was on the board of the Dalhousie Nursing Home, and served as president of the local Golden Age Club. He served as president of the Provincial Federation of Senior Citizens, was a school board superintendent in the mid-sixties and a recipient of the Paul Harris Award (Rotary).

J. Gérard LeBlanc. He was sent for one year of training and was hired in 1945 under Robert Scott in the Child Welfare Division of the Provincial Department of Health and Social Services in Fredericton. Scott had previously been alone in that division, which had been created in 1941 and was housed in the Department of Health until the amalgamation with Social Services. LeBlanc was assigned to the provincial program to promote awareness of the work of the Children's Aid Society. He was also a member of the New Brunswick Association of Social Workers.

Ronald LeBlanc. He earned a master's degree in Ottawa, worked for the New Brunswick Department of Social Services and taught at the École de travail social at the Université de Moncton.

Paul-Émile LeClair. He obtained his MSW at Laval University in 1963. He worked at the Boys' Industrial Home in Saint John. He was then employed with the New Brunswick Central Reformatory in Kingsclear, New Brunswick. He was listed as a new member of the CASW in 1963.

Geraldine Lee. Geraldine attended night school to earn a BSW. She began working at the CAS in Saint John in 1965 and initially worked with unmarried parents.

Emile Leger. First social worker in Kent County. He studied at Collège Saint-Joseph de Memramcook and the Halifax seminary. He was director of Child Protection for the Ministry of Social Services for twenty-five years.

Marie-Marthe Léger. She earned an MSW at Université Laval. Her thesis (1960) was entitled Équation des besoins et des ressources du point de vue d'un service aux mères du service social de Portneuf. She worked at the provincial psychiatric hospital in Campbellton.

Una Lennam. She worked for the Province of New Brunswick at the Department of Youth and Welfare in Fredericton with the Welfare Division and transferred to another branch in 1961.

Fay Ethel (Nagle) Levine. Fay was born in Winnipeg and raised in Alberta. She held graduate and post-graduate degrees from University of British Columbia, University of Toronto, and the London School of Economics. She was coordinator of adoptions for New Brunswick and was a community-based family therapist.

J. Aldéo Losier. He received his BA at the Université Sacré-Coeur in Bathurst. He then obtained his MSW at the Maritime School of Social Work in 1964 and worked at the provincial hospital in Campbellton.

John Lutz. John received his BA from Sir George Williams University (eventually Concordia). He was the director of the Moncton Boys and Girls Club from 1957 to 1959. He received scholarships from the New Brunswick government and the Boys and Girls Club to acquire his MSW, which he obtained from McGill University in Montreal in 1966. He then returned as the director of the Moncton Boys and Girls Club from September 1966 to August 1968.

Mr David MacAulay. He was the dean of men at Mount Allison University.

Father Frank MacDonald. He obtained his MSW at the University of Montreal, which was a two-year program (he did placement with Catholic Welfare Bureau in Montreal and Catholic Children's Aid Society in Toronto). He co-founded the Catholic Welfare Bureau in June 1941, which was one of the operating units of the Catholic Charities. These units included the Catholic Welfare Bureau, the St. Patrick's Orphanage in Silver Falls, the infants' home (next to St. Joseph Hospital) for unwed mothers and their babies, and the Mater Misericordiae Home for senior citizens. Father MacDonald resigned from CASW membership in May 1963.

Helen Macdonald. She lived in Saint John, New Brunswick, and worked for Children's Aid Society in Saint John. From 1952 to 1956, she was a New Brunswick–Prince Edward Island Branch member.

Margaret (Morgan) MacDonald. Margaret obtained her MSW at the Maritime School of Social Work in 1950. She was the founder of the Moncton Hospital Psychiatric Department.

Stan MacDonald. He became a member of the New Brunswick–Prince Edward Island Branch, CASW, in 1955. He was connected to the northern New Brunswick region.

William (Bill) A. Macdonald. Bill lived in Saint John, New Brunswick. He was the president of the New Brunswick–Prince Edward Island Branch, CASW circa 1952–6. In 1955 he was a social worker in the Department of Veterans' Affairs.

Harvey MacEachern. Harvey was employed with the "Provincial Hospital for Nervous Diseases" (renamed Centracare in 1978) in Lancaster, New Brunswick circa 1963.

Roberta (Bobbie) MacKenzie. Bobbie began to work as a CAS agent for Restigouche County in 1951. Approximately 5 percent of her work was with a First Nations community. She experienced the transition brought about in child welfare because of Equal Opportunity. After a five-year secondment from the province, Bobbie was later hired by Eel River Bar First Nation as director of child and family services.

Murray Manzer. Murray was born and raised in Woodstock, New Brunswick. He obtained his MSW at the Maritime School of Social Work in Halifax in 1957. He worked as a psychiatric social worker in the provincial hospital in Saint John, New Brunswick, and the Mental Health Clinic in Fredericton, He was director of the Welfare Department, City of Fredericton, circa 1960. He worked for the Federal Department of Indian and Northern Affairs (DINA) from the late 1960s until he retired in 1980. On his retirement from the DINA, he was hired by the Union of Nova Scotia Indians to help them develop services and programs and establish the Mi'kmaq Family and Children's Services of Nova Scotia.

Dorothy R. Marshall. Dorothy was a member of the New Brunswick–Prince Edward Island Branch, CASW; she resigned from the New Brunswick Branch on 20 April 1963. In 1956 she worked as a nurse in the TB clinic in Saint John. In Toronto she worked in the Good Samaritan Group. She was reported in 1956 as "presently nursing but plans to continue in social work."

Edmund Stanley (Stan) Matheson. Originally from Sydney Mines, Cape Breton, he received his BA at Mount Allison and went on to earn his MSW at the Maritime School of Social Work in Halifax, and was class valedictorian for his 1951 graduation. He was employed at the provincial psychiatric hospital in 1951 in Saint John and was the first social worker to work in the mental health clinic. Stan was the president of the New Brunswick Association of Social Workers from 1965 to 1967. He was the

New Brunswick representative of the National Membership Committee, CASW.

J. Alyre Mazerolle. He lived in Moncton, New Brunswick, and as a social worker, worked for the Moncton CAS. He became a member of the New Brunswick–Prince Edward Island Branch, CASW, in 1956.

Louis McGinn. He earned his MSW at the Maritime School of Social Work in Halifax in 1963. He was employed with the Saint John Children's Aid Society Child Welfare Services in Moncton, as well as with the Correctional Service of Canada. Louis was also a member of the New Brunswick Association of Social Workers.

Patricia (Dillon) McGinn. Patricia obtained her MSW at the Maritime School of Social Work in Halifax in 1963.

Clarence McKenzie (note: spelled Mc and Mac in files). Clarence was a native of Nova Scotia who gained extensive experience in the field of public welfare in British Columbia. He was appointed as the director of welfare for the Municipality of Saint John on 10 October 1961, according to the New Brunswick Branch, CASW.

Laura Rosalie McLaughlin. She was born in Saint John. She obtained her MSW at the Maritime School of Social Work in 1952. She was then employed at the New Brunswick Boys' Industrial Home in Saint John. She was first employed by the Province of New Brunswick as a social worker with the Mental Health Clinic in Saint John and later as director of the Department of Social Work at Centracare, a position she held until her retirement in 1981. Circa 1960–2, she served on the Standards of Practice in Health and Medical Care Committee for the New Brunswick Branch, CASW.

(Mrs) D. Lewis C. Miller. She lived in Fredericton, New Brunswick, after having done social work in Scotland. In 1956, she became a member of the New Brunswick–Prince Edward Island Branch, CASW.

Francis Montgomery. She was from Montreal and had been educated at the University of Pennsylvania. She was a faculty member at McGill University before moving to Halifax, where she became one of the original faculty members of the Maritime School of Social Work. In 1952 she was a member of the New Brunswick–Prince Edward Island Branch, CASW, while being assistant director of the Maritime School of Social Work, a position that brought her to the province often, for recruitment and promotion of the profession. In 1956 she represented social work on career day at Moncton High.

Nettie Moore. Nettie Moore was a CAS worker from 1948 to 1961. In 1951 she served as secretary treasurer of the New Brunswick Association of Children's Aid Societies.

George Morris. Circa 1960–1, George was the executive director, CAS, York County, Fredericton.

Kathleen (Tally) Morrissy. Tally attended Simmons College in Boston in 1933 and earned a BSW degree. She was a founding member of the New Brunswick–Prince Edward Island Branch of CASW. She was supervisor of the Department of National Health and Welfare (Family Allowance Division), working out of Fredericton. Tally was the only social worker hired by Family Allowances to determine eligibility.

Helen Morrison. As of 20 November 1964, Helen had worked thirty-seven years in social work. She was employed with the Lancaster DVA Hospital. Helen was also a branch convener for the association and was employed as a child welfare officer in Charlottetown in 1953. She served as secretary of the New Brunswick Branch, CASW, from 1960 to 1961.

Rosaire Nadeau. He lived in Edmundston, New Brunswick, and spent five years at College Saint Joseph in Memramcook, attended Saint Dunstan's University for his BA, and went to University of Montreal for his MSW. His career begin in federal public service in 1954 with the Unemployment Insurance Commission. In 1964 he became manager of the Canada Employment Centre in Edmundston.

Margaret Nelson. She studied at the Maritime School of Social Work from 1956 to 1958 but received her MSW degree from Mount Allison University in 1958. She worked at the "Provincial Hospital for Nervous Diseases" in Lancaster, New Brunswick, during the summer of 1957 and after graduation until she resigned in August 1959. She also attended a New Brunswick Branch, CASW, meeting in 1961.

Edith Nutter. In 2012 she was living in Perth, Ontario. She grew up in Prince Edward Island. She graduated in 1945, and lived from 1951 to 1957 in Woodstock, where her husband was rector and later became archbishop at Christ Church Cathedral. She worked for the Saint John River Indian Agency in 1966. Her first job was as a child welfare worker.

Mary Katherine O'Connell. She was from Campbellton, New Brunswick. She received her teacher's certificate diploma and taught school from 1933 to 1936. She completed an MSW at the Maritime School of Social Work in 1948. She was employed at the Saint John CAS, but in 1955 it was noted that she transferred to another branch.

Mary Evelyn O'Leary. She was from Rexton, New Brunswick. A member of the Sisters of Saint Martha, she earned an MSW from Boston University. She was executive director of the CAS for Sunbury County. In 1969 she was acting supervisor welfare worker II.

Fredda Peden. She worked with the Department of Veterans Affairs in Saint John, New Brunswick. She joined CASW in 1948 and was branch convener of membership and was appointed as a corresponding member of the Membership Committee, CASW.

Annie Peters. Annie worked as a CAS agent in Carleton County. She died in 1956 in a car accident.

Carol Proctor. She obtained her BA at Mount Allison University and then attended the Maritime School of Social Work in the fall of 1948, but didn't go back for her second year, as she married and started working. Carol did go back to finish her MSW in 1960. From 1949 to 1951 she was employed with the Westmorland County Children's Aid Society. She began working with unwed mothers in 1952 and continued there until she retired in 1986. She worked for the New Brunswick government in the Mental Health Division, Department of Health and Social Services, located on North King St. in Moncton. She was also employed at the Mental Health Clinic in Moncton. Carol then became the director of Social Services while in this position. During her employment, she also acted as the coordinator of community services. In addition, Carol worked with parents to start an Association for Cerebral Palsy and Mentally Retarded Children and assisted with the formation of a board to create an adult-services program and housing board. In 1955 she participated in Sunday forums broadcast on the radio station CKCW through Mount Allison University. Between 1962 and 1970 she served as a member of the executive and board of the CASW. In 1965 she was founding member of the New Brunswick Association of Social Workers.

Grace Reynolds. She received her training as a social worker at Columbia University. On 21 October 1961, she became the new director of the Moncton Family and Children's Services. Grace was also employed with the Moncton Welfare Bureau from 1963 to 1964. From 1960 to 1962 she served on the Education for Social Work Committee of the New Brunswick Branch, CASW.

(Joseph) Donald Richard. Donald obtained his BA at the Université Saint-Joseph in 1960 and earned his MSW at the Maritime School of Social Work in Halifax in 1963. He was then employed with Child Welfare Services in Moncton. By 1969 he was a social worker II.

Jean-Bernard Robichaud. In 1966 he worked as a CAS agent for Gloucester County in Caraquet. He was president of the Université de Moncton from 1990 until 2000.

Jennie Robinson. In 1926 Jennie was in the senior category of CASW's membership. She was the first superintendent at the Interprovincial Home for Young Women in Moncton, New Brunswick (a residence designed to provide a home-like atmosphere for women committed by the courts). Originally from Sweetsburg, Quebéc, she also worked in Alberta in a facility for young women before coming to New Brunswick. She attended the CASW's conference in Montreal in 1926. By 1927 she was no longer employed at the home.

Margaret Rowley. She was from Saint John, New Brunswick. She was the first known New Brunswicker to graduate from Maritime School of Social Work (1943, second graduating class).

Gérald Savoie. He transferred out of the Canadian Association of Social Workers in the New Brunswick Branch. He was employed at the provincial hospital in Campbellton.

Patricia Savoie-Savard. She attended the Collège Notre-Dame d'Acadie in Moncton and received an MSW from Laval University in 1960. She was employed in Saint John. Patricia was also employed with the Department of Health and Social Services, Mental Health Division, Saint John. She was noted as being present at a New Brunswick Branch CASW meeting in 1961.

Edmund Harper Sewell. He lived in Fredericton. In 1961 he was noted as present at a New Brunswick Branch meeting of the CASW and that he was chairman of the Membership Committee. He was born in Caraquet, and graduated from the University of New Brunswick in 1953 with BA and BEd degrees. He received an MSW from McGill University. He also attended the University of New York, and worked at Indian Affairs.

Archie Smith. In 1960, he worked at the Boys' Industrial Home. Although he didn't complete his social work education, he was hired in Saint John in 1966 as a CAS agent because they needed a male worker.

Edna Myrna Smith. She was from Elgin, New Brunswick. Edna obtained her teachers' certificate and then served in the Royal Canadian Air Force (WD) from 1942 to 1946. She completed her MSW at the Maritime School of Social Work in 1948. She was the supervisor of child welfare in the province from 1961 to 1964. Edna was also a Children's Aid Society agent in Albert and Westmorland Counties in New Brunswick. She was a Children's Aid Society agent for Albert County from 14 April 1948 until she resigned in October 1954. She started the Albert County Children's Aid Society and shared an office with Grace Reynolds.

Everett Richard Sullivan. He obtained his MSW at St. Patrick's College in Ottawa. He was employed at the provincial hospital in Lancaster, New Brunswick in 1963

Robert Thériault. He was an agent for Children' Aid Society for Madawaska County from 1946 to 1964, as well as an attendance officer for the Madawaska County school board, which paid his salary. Starting in 1964 he became a full-time agent when the Children's Aid Society became financed by the Province of New Brunswick (50 percent), the Municipality of Madawaska (25 percent) and the City of Edmundston (25 percent).

Freda E. Vickery. She was educated at Normal School and did not obtain a BA. After her husband's death in the war in 1945, however, she was encouraged to get training, so she completed two years of social work. She received her MSW at the Maritime School of Social Work in 1950. In 1956 Freda was in Munich, Germany, and wrote to J. Ernest Anderson (a provincial director in social service delivery) regarding employment in New Brunswick. She was originally hired by Fred McKinnon as the senior social worker in mental health for the province of New Brunswick. She then started the Department of Health and Social Services, Mental Health Division in Fredericton, and was director of social services at the IWK Children's Hospital.

Lorna Warneford. She was the executive secretary of the Family Welfare Bureau in 1948 and worked in that capacity until 1955. She was a founder of the New Brunswick–Prince Edward Island Branch, CASW, and held positions of secretary and president as well as chairing various committees. She died on 6 January 1956, and an appreciation of her life and work was presented at a New Brunswick Branch, CASW, meeting by Mrs J.B. Bishop.

Fred Whalen. He worked at the Catholic Welfare Bureau in Saint John from 1952–6 and sometimes travelled to annual meetings of county councils to share information.

Barbara White. She was trained as a social worker. She was employed with the Welfare Department for the City of Fredericton and the Westmorland County Children's Aid Society.

O. J. (Jean) White. She obtained her BA and BS at the University of Manitoba. She became a member in the New Brunswick–Prince Edward Island Branch, CASW, in 1954.

Joan Wilson. She was born in Providence, Rhode Island. She received her BA from the University of Toronto and her MSW from the Maritime School of Social Work. Joan moved to Saint John after working at the Welfare Department, Halifax, and worked with Louis McGinn. She was the executive secretary of the Children's Aid Society in Saint John circa 1963. Later in her career she became a manager and supervisor of

Children's Aid in Toronto, where a scholarship in her name was created after her death.

Doris Wylie. Circa 1960–1, Doris was the executive director, CAS, and had thirteen years' experience with the agency in Victoria County. By 1969 she was a welfare worker III.

Dan Young. In 1945 Dan wrote to the Membership Committee of the CASW on behalf of New Brunswick prospects for membership.

The follow list is of individuals whose names surfaced in relation to social work in New Brunswick before 1967 but about whom details are not available:

Mr Cushing. New Brunswick Branch member in 1961.

Pamela Gillespie

Carolyn Lock

Helen Steeves. She lived in Hillsboro, Albert County.

Mrs R.C. Stevenson. Fredericton, New Brunswick.

Mrs Watson. She left the province in 1960.

Mary Louise White. BA, University of New Brunswick.

Walter Wood. He lived in Petitcodiac.

Notes

Foreword

1 Richard Duffy, interview by Brian Ouellette, 9 May 2001.
2 Welfare Services in Moncton, 1939, Library and Archives Canada, Canadian Council of Social Development fonds, MG 28 I10, vol. 132, p. 34.
3 Twenty-Seventh Annual Meeting Case Work Report, 5 March 1957, Provincial Archives of New Brunswick, Saint John County Council collection, RS156, file E/CG, p. 3.

1 Introduction

1 Putnam, *The Enforcement of the Statutes of Labourers*, iii.
2 Fred Whalen, interview by Brian Ouellette, 9 May 2001.
3 Archie Smith, interview by Brian Ouellette, 10 May 2001.
4 Richard Duffy, interview by Brian Ouellette, 9 May 2001.
5 Archie Smith, interview by Brian Ouellette, 10 May 2001.
6 Donald Richard, interview by Brian Ouellette, 11 April 2001.
7 The research assistants who undertook archival work include Veronique Brideau, Deborah Cammack, Judy Teakles, and Andrea Watson; assistant Melanie Melanson conducted interview transcription.
8 Alway, *Critical Theory and Political Possibilities*, 27.
9 Weinberg, "Structural Social Work: A Moral Compass for Ethics in Practice."
10 Fred Whalen, interview by Brian Ouellette, 11 May 2001.

2 A History of the Peoples of New Brunswick

1 According to A. Bear Nicholas, Wəlastəkwewiyik is the traditional name for Maliseets, but because there are several versions of the name and at least

two competing orthographies, a decision has been made by the Maliseet chiefs of New Brunswick to continue using "Maliseet" until a collective decision can be reached on these issues (Bear Nicholas, personal communication with Laurel Lewey, 21 September 2016).

2 Bear Nicholas, "The Role of Colonial Artists," 27.
3 Dickason, *Canada's First Nations*, 73.
4 Ibid., 108.
5 Ibid., 107.
6 Paul, *We Were Not the Savages*, 52.
7 Chute, "Algonquians /Eastern Woodlands," 42.
8 Bear Nicholas, "The Role of Colonial Artists," 27.
9 Finkel, *Social Policy and Practice in Canada*, 18–19.
10 Ibid., 21
11 Carolyn and Dan Ennis, interview by Laurel Lewey, 23 February 2007.
12 Paul, *We Were Not the Savages*, 1.
13 Chute, "Algonquians /Eastern Woodlands," 46.
14 Havard, *The Great Peace of Montreal of 1701*, 34, 122.
15 Paul, *We Were Not the Savages*, 76.
16 Norbert Finzsch defines the process of settler imperialism as one that "could only be implemented in conjunction with gentlemanly elites." Cited in Bear Nicholas, "The Role of Colonial Artists," 27.
17 Dickason, *Canada's First Nations*, 231.
18 Paul, *We Were Not the Savages*, 176.
19 Dickason, *Canada's First Nations*, 231.
20 Ibid., 230.
21 Ibid., 231.
22 Ibid., 231.
23 Upton, "The Origins of Canadian Indian Policy," 51.
24 Ibid., 59.
25 From the Aboriginal Affairs, Government of New Brunswick website: "According to the Indian Register System from Aboriginal Affairs and Northern Development Canada (AANDC), as of December 31, 2014, there were approximately 15,249 First Nations people in New Brunswick, 9,366 on reserve and 5,883 off reserve." Retrieved 31 December 2016 from http://www2.gnb.ca/content/gnb/en/departments/aboriginal_affairs/fnc.html.
26 Stats Canada reports that in its 2011 survey, almost half of First Nations people (46 percent) were under the age of 25 (48 percent of those living on a reserve and 45 percent of the off-reserve population), and also notes, "In 2011, the median age of First Nations people was 27.6; the off-reserve

population was older (29.3) than those living on a reserve (26.4). Both groups were younger than the non-Aboriginal population, whose median age was 43.6." "Aboriginal Peoples: Fact Sheet for New Brunswick," Statistics Canada website. Retrieved 31 December 2016 from http://www.statcan.gc.ca/pub/89-656-x/89-656-x2016005-eng.htm.

27 The following description of the centre is found on the University of New Brunswick's website, "Mi'kmaq-Wolastoqey Centre": http://www.unb.ca/fredericton/education/mmi/:

> "Epjila'si! / Kulahsihkulpa! / Welcome! The Mi'kmaq-Wolastoqey Centre (MWC), located on traditional territory of Wolastoqiyik at the University of New Brunswick Fredericton, provides a learning environment for Indigenous students to develop a strong cultural foundation as well as academic and professional skills, and offers opportunities for all UNB students and faculty to become familiar with Mi'kmaq and Wolastoqey histories, cultures, contributions and treaty rights through principles of respect, sharing, harmony, acceptance and unity in diversity. MWC promotes the professional growth and self-determination of First Nations through its programs, services, and research."

28 From "About MMNN," *Mi'kmaq Maliseet Nations News* website: "The MMNN is a First Nation owned, community focused monthly newspaper with a particular expertise in Mi'kmaq culture. The objectives of the newspaper are to celebrate and lift people up/lift their spirits with an emphasis on positive stories and success stories in the Mi'kmaq community, to archive and record history, to educate, and to provide information on current stories and events that have relevance to the Mi'kmaq and Maliseet people in Atlantic Canada." Retrieved 18 July 2017 from http://www.mmnn.ca/about-mmnn/.

29 Howe, *Debriefing Elsipogtog.*

30 Rudin, *Remembering and Forgetting in Acadie,* 12.

31 The term *Acadia* was possibly inspired by the expression *Arcadia,* a region of classical Greece, which became a symbol of a traditional idealized rural setting in Greek and Roman bucolic poetry. The term "La Cadie" was already being used in 1603 before the "discovery" of Acadia by Henri IV, the then king of France, when referring to commissioning the services of officers to oversee sea and land exploration (see Griffiths, *Contexts of Acadian History*).

32 Later, as Acadian settlements became established in the Grand Pré Nova Scotia area and beyond, Acadians developed a co-operative activity they called a *corvee,* or working bee, employed widely in the construction of

buildings and *aboiteaux*, a device employed to irrigate low-lying lands and at the same time protect them from the salt water.

33 Griffiths pointed out that as early as 1650 "the (Acadian) community had a bilingual capacity, that is, there was always someone who knew English as well as French in the settlements." ("Perceptions of Acadians," 104)
34 Faragher, *A Great and Noble Scheme*, 468–9.
35 Daigle, "L'Acadie de 1604 à 1763," 19.
36 Ibid., 36.
37 Faragher, *A Great and Noble Scheme, 99.*
38 Daigle, "L'Acadie de 1604 à 1763,' 22–3.
39 Faragher, *A Great and Noble Scheme*, ix.
40 Ibid., 467–8.
41 Ibid., 467.
42 Ibid., 468.
43 Ibid., 467.
44 Ibid., 468.
45 Candow, *The Deportation of the Acadians*, 2.
46 Ibid., 6.
47 For a concise account of events associated with the expulsion, the reader is referred to Roy, "Settlement and Population Growth in Acadia," in *Acadia of the Maritimes*. In that chapter, she covers, among other topics, the expulsion, the escapees, the dispersal and the resettlement.
48 Paul, *We Were Not the Savages*, 152.
49 "Those Who Disappeared," Acadian.org website. Retrieved 20 November 2016 from https://www.acadian.org/genealogy/families/acadian-family-names/those-who-disappeared/. (Credit given on website to Stephen White, Parks Canada, for the information.)
50 Arsenault, *History of the Acadians*, 159.
51 They were not yet full citizens of the nation. The rights of Acadian men to vote and, later, to hold office, would not come until 1810 and 1830 respectively (Garner, *The Franchise and Politics in British North America*, 54–72). Acadian women, like other women in New Brunswick, would wait until 1919 for the same right ("Provincial Elections History," Elections New Brunswick website. Retrieved 14 January 2018 from http://www.electionsnb.ca/content/enb/en/about-us/history.html). Meanwhile Indigenous people in Canada did not receive the right to vote in federal elections until 1960.
52 Clement Cormier, "Université de Moncton: Historique," Centre d' études acadiennes, 1975. Retrieved 1 January 2017 from http://www.umoncton.ca/umcm-ceaac/files/umcm-ceaac/wf/wf/pdf/umhist.pdf.

53 Taillon, "Ce secrétariat permanent d'éducation."
54 McKee-Allain, "Une minorité et la construction de ses frontières identitaires," 530.
55 Sirois, "Évolution de l'enseignement public au Madawaska," 6.
56 Poirier, "La Loi Scolaire de 1871 au N.-B. et ses répercussions," 141.
57 Taillon, "Ce secrétariat permanent d'éducation," 16.
58 Savoie, *L'Éducation des petits Acadiens*, 14.
59 The École de travail social is housed in a Université de Moncton building that bears the noted educator's name.
60 McKee-Allain, "Une minorité et la construction de ses frontières identitaires," 531.
61 McKee-Allain, "La place des communautés religieuses de femmes," 3–8.
62 Landry and Lang, *Histoire de l'Acadie*, 310.
63 Gallant, *Les femmes et la renaissance acadienne*, 211.
64 Berthelot, "Les Acadiennes font entendre leur voix." Retrieved 30 december 2016 from https://www.gazettedesfemmes.ca/5372/les-acadiennes-font-entendre-leur-voix/.
65 Landry and Lang, *Histoire de l'Acadie*, 319.
66 McKee-Allain, "Rapports ethniques et rapports de sexes en Acadie."
67 Berthelot, "Les Acadiennes font entendre leur voix." Retrieved 30 December 2016 from https://www.gazettedesfemmes.ca/5372/les-acadiennes-font-entendre-leur-voix/.
68 Larracey, *Resurgo: The History of Moncton*, 172.
69 Bell, *Early Loyalist Saint John*, 17.
70 Wallace, *The United Empire Loyalists*, 26.
71 Rees, *Land of the Loyalists*, 55.
72 Ibid., 1–2.
73 René Lévesque exhibition, *Le New Carlisle des années 1920 et 1930/The New Carlisle of the 1920s and 1930s*, in the Kempffer Centre, New Carlisle, Québec, visited by Louis J. Richard on 22 October 2016.
74 "Our History," University of New Brunswick website. Retrieved 23 October 2016 from http://www.unb.ca/aboutunb/history/.
75 Bell, *Early Loyalist Saint John*, 57.
76 Freedman, *Sissiboo River Redemption*, 147.
77 Rogers, "A Historical Geography of the British Colonies," 244.
78 "The First Three Black Lawyers in Canada," Osgoode Society for Canadian Legal History website. Retrieved 5 October 2017 from https://www.osgoodesociety.ca/encyclopedia/three-first-black-lawyers-in-canada-robert-sutherland-abraham-walker-delos-davis/.

79 "Abraham Beverley Walker," New Brunswick Black History Society website. Retrieved 25 January 2017 from http://www.nbblackhistorysociety.org/professionals.html.
80 Conrad and Hiller, *Atlantic Canada: A Region in the Making*, 180.
81 Gillard, "The Black Church in Canada," McMaster University website. Retrieved 24 April 2016 from http://www.mcmaster.ca/mjtm/1-5.htm.
82 An interesting history of one of Moncton's founding families, the Steeves, who originated from the seven sons of Heinrich Stief was compiled by Philip Earle Steeves. Retrieved 24 October 2015 from https://www.steeves250.com/sites/default/files/Brief%20Steeves%20History-Revised%20Sep%2015.pdf.
83 Evans, "Irish Settlement Patterns in New Brunswick," Irish Canadian Cultural Association of New Brunswick website. Retrieved 5 September 2017 from http://newirelandnb.ca/irish-settlement-patterns/.
84 Soucoup, *Know New Brunswick*, 18.
85 Buckner and Reid, *The Atlantic Region to Confederation*, 316.
86 Campey, *With Axe and Bible*, 128.
87 Cadogan, "Our Lebanese Legacy," 36.
88 "The History of the Jewish Community in Saint John," Atlantic Jewish Council website. Retrieved 24 April 2016 from https://theajc.ns.ca/history/the-jewish-community-of-saint-john/.
89 Jewish Immigrant Aid Services Canada. Retrieved 24 April 2016 from JIASC http://www.jias.org/JIAS/jiasweb.htm.
90 Seager, "Minto, New Brunswick," 100.
91 "Les archives inédites de 'Monsieur Montréal', le maire Camillien Houde (1889–1958)," Archives Montréal website. Retrieved 9 September 2017 from http://archivesdemontreal.com/2017/08/16/les-archives-inedites-du-maire-camillien-houde/.
92 "Focus on Geography Series, 2011 Census, Province of New Brunswick," Statistics Canada website. Retrieved 19 July 2017 from http://www12.statcan.gc.ca/census-recensement/2011/as-sa/fogs-spg/Facts-pr-eng.cfm?Lang=Eng&GC=13.

3 Historical, Economic, and Political Contexts of Service Provision

1 Bent, *Determined to Prosper*, e-book.
2 "Agriculture, Aquaculture and Fisheries: The Formative Years (1860–1910)," Government of New Brunswick website. Retrieved 31 December 2016 from http://www2.gnb.ca/content/gnb/en/departments/10/agriculture/content/history/years.html.

3 "Agriculture, Aquaculture and Fisheries: Building on Foundations Laid (1910–1950)," Government of New Brunswick website. Retrieved 31 December 2016 from http://www2.gnb.ca/content/gnb/en/departments/10/agriculture/content/history/foundations.html.
4 Ibid.
5 "Agriculture, Aquaculture and Fisheries: The Years of Change (1950–1983)," Government of New Brunswick website. Retrieved 19 July 2017 from http://www2.gnb.ca/content/gnb/en/departments/10/agriculture/content/history/change.html.
6 Ibid.
7 "Building on the Foundations Laid (1910–1950)," Government of New Brunswick website. Retrieved 9 September 2017, www2.gnb.ca/content/gnb/en/departments/10/agriculture/content/history/foundations.html.
8 Conrad and Hiller, *Atlantic Canada: A Concise History*, 92.
9 Bear Nicholas, "The Role of Colonial Artists," 31.
10 Ibid., 32.
11 Ibid., 51.
12 Wynn, *Timber Colony*, 152.
13 Meek, *Lumbering in Eastern Canada*, 24.
14 Ibid., 24.
15 Soucoup, *Logging in New Brunswick*, 10.
16 Meek, *Lumbering in Eastern Canada*, 25.
17 Soucoup, *Logging in New Brunswick*, 170.
18 Ibid., 171.
19 "New Brunswick's Fisheries of the Past," Government of New Brunswick website. Retrieved 30 December 2016 from http://archives.gnb.ca/Exhibits/ArchivalPortfolio/TextViewer.aspx?culture=en-CA&myFile=Fisheries.
20 Ibid.
21 Slumkoski, *Inventing Atlantic Canada*, 90.
22 Fuller, "The Loyalist Quaker Settlement," 77.
23 Slumkoski, *Inventing Atlantic Canada*, 89.
24 Ibid., 89.
25 Martin, *Gesner's Dream*, 19.
26 Ibid., 20.
27 Seager, "Minto, New Brunswick," 100.
28 Martin, *Gesner's Dream*, 15.
29 Ibid., 46.
30 Ibid., 14.
31 Ibid., 282.

32 “Maritime provinces”: Nova Scotia, New Brunswick, and Prince Edward Island; “Atlantic provinces”: these three and Newfoundland. The latter did not become part of Canada until 1949.
33 Howell, “The 1900s: Industry, Urbanization, and Reform,” 164.
34 Ibid., 175.
35 Forbes, “The 1930s: Depression and Retrenchment,” 281–2.
36 Ibid., 282.
37 “Welfare Services in Moncton Report,” 1939, Library and Archives Canada (hereafter LAC), Canadian Council on Social Development fonds (hereafter MG 28, I 10), vol. 132, p. 5.
38 *Labour Gazette* XVIII (May 1943), cited in Cassidy, *Public Health and Welfare Reorganization*, 396, 727–8.
39 Whalen, “Social Welfare in New Brunswick,” 60.
40 Ibid., 60.
41 Forbes, “The 1930s: Depression and Retrenchment,” 291.
42 Ibid.,” 291.
43 Cassidy, *Public Health and Welfare Reorganization*, 404.
44 The Campbellton Provincial Hospital served the counties of Victoria, Madawaska, Restigouche, Gloucester, Northumberland, and francophone areas of Kent County at that time.
45 Marcel Arseneau, interview by Brian Ouellette, 11 April 2001.
46 Pepin, *Life and Poverty in the Maritimes*, ARDA Project #15002, Minister of Forestry and Rural Development Ottawa, 1968, 30.
47 Thorburn, *Politics in New Brunswick*, 83.
48 Slumkoski, *Inventing Atlantic Canada*, 17.
49 Hoyt, *A Brief History of the Liberal Party of New Brunswick*, 55.
50 Slumkoski, *Inventing Atlantic Canada*, 18.
51 Conrad and Hiller, *Atlantic Canada: A Concise History*, 189.
52 Ibid., 198.
53 DeMont, *Citizens Irving*, 82.
54 Conrad and Hiller, *Atlantic Canada: A Concise History*, 198.
55 Savoie, *Harrison McCain*, 327–8.
56 “Provincial Elections History,” Elections New Brunswick website. Retrieved 24 July 2017 from http://www.electionsnb.ca/content/enb/en/about-us/history.html.
57 Spray, *The Blacks in New Brunswick*.
58 “Provincial Elections History,” Elections New Brunswick website. Retrieved 24 July 2017 from http://www.electionsnb.ca/content/enb/en/about-us/history.html.

59 "Provincial Elections History," Elections New Brunswick website. Retrieved 24 July 2017 from http://www.electionsnb.ca/content/enb/en/about-us/history.html.
60 "Provincial Elections History," Elections New Brunswick website. Retrieved 24 July 2017 from http://www.electionsnb.ca/content/enb/en/about-us/history.html.
61 Lewey, "A Near Golden Age," 93–4.
62 Seager, "Minto, New Brunswick," 118.
63 Hoyt, *A Brief History of the Liberal Party of New Brunswick*, n.p.
64 G.H. Castleden, Report to National Executive on the New Brunswick CCF Branch, 12 October 1943, LAC, CCF and NDP file, MG 28, New Brunswick: Organization, 1934–1958, IV1, vol. 34, p. 1.
65 Lewey, "A Near Golden Age," 96.
66 Boyko, *Into the Hurricane*, 43.
67 Comment made in correspondence by Dana Mullen, provincial secretary of the CCF in New Brunswick during this period to Fred Young, Maritime director of organizing for the CCF, who operated out of Halifax. 8 July 1949, letter from D. Mullen to F. Young, Provincial Archives of New Brunswick, MC724, Catalogue of Documents Dealing with the History of the CCF Party in NB (1944–1949), box 2373, file Maritime Director of Organization.
68 Broadfoot, *Ten Lost Years*, 12.
69 Wynn, *Timber Colony*, 153.
70 Frank and Reilly, "The Emergence of the Socialist Movement," 85–6.

4 Poor Law Legislation and the Poverty Experience

1 de Schweinitz, *England's Road to Social Security*, 28.
2 Whalen, "The Nineteenth-Century Almshouse System," 54.
3 Jennissen and Lundy, *One Hundred Years of Social Work*, 4.
4 Cassidy, *Public Health and Welfare Reorganization*, 393.
5 Carol Proctor, interview by Brian Ouellette, 2 November 2000.
6 Cassidy, *Public Health and Welfare Reorganization*, 120.
7 Whalen, "Social Welfare in New Brunswick," 55.
8 Carol Proctor, interview by Brian Ouellette, 2 November 2000.
9 Richard Duffy, interview by Brian Ouellette, 9 May 2001.
10 Craven, *Petty Justice*, 372.
11 A.B. MacKinnon to Mr Edmund F. Richard, Alms House Commissioner, Rogersville, N.B., with c.c. to J.H. Conlen, 8 April 1937. Provincial Archives

of New Brunswick (hereafter PANB), Northumberland County Council collection (hereafter RS153), container 28568, folder E27a12.
12 Boychuk, *Patchworks of Purpose*, 31.
13 Finkel, *Social Policy and Practice in Canada*, 58.
14 Whalen, "Social Welfare in New Brunswick," 59.
15 Boychuk, *Patchworks of Purpose*, 30.
16 Whalen, "Social Welfare in New Brunswick," 59.
17 Finkel, *Social Policy and Practice in Canada*, 49.
18 Whalen, "Social Welfare in New Brunswick," 60.
19 Myers, "The Governance of Childhood," ii.
20 Whitton, "Agencies Established Under Present Legislation," 148–50.
21 Welfare Services in Moncton Report, 1939, Library and Archives Canada (hereafter LAC), Canadian Council on Social Development fonds (hereafter MG 28, I 10), vol. 132, p. 26.
22 Welfare Services in Moncton Report, 1939, LAC, MG 28, 1 10, vol. 132, p. 28.
23 Richard Duffy, interview by Brian Ouellette, 9 May 2001.
24 Touzel, "Public Welfare Services in New Brunswick Survey."
25 Whalen, "Social Welfare in New Brunswick," 55.
26 Alton, "The Selling of Paupers by Public Auction in Sussex Parish," 94.
27 Whalen, "Social Welfare in New Brunswick," 56.
28 Cassidy, *Public Health and Welfare Reorganization*, 401.
29 Ibid., 402.
30 Bourque, "Accomplishments and Shortcomings," 31.
31 Finkel, *Social Policy and Practice in Canada*, 101.
32 Ibid.
33 Robert J. Fanjoy, Queen's County (Gagetown) Municipal Taxation, 10 September 1951, PANB, Saint John County Council collection (hereafter RS156), file E10a, p. 1.
34 Forbes, "The 1930s: Depression and Retrenchment," 276.
35 Strong, *Public Welfare Administration in Canada*, 227.
36 Whalen, "Social Welfare in New Brunswick," 60.
37 Letter from R.J. Hill, Assistant Superintendent to Warden and Members of Council Municipality of Northumberland, Newcastle, N.B., 30 December 1955, PANB, RS153, file E5a. Note that the CNIB Maritime Division was formed in 1938. By 1950 there were eight offices in the Maritimes providing services to 3,000 clients in New Brunswick, Nova Scotia, and Prince Edward Island. The Fredericton office of CNIB was officially opened in 1956, becoming the ninth office in the Maritimes. The

Halifax School for the Blind became a public institution in 1975 under the new name Atlantic Provinces Special Education Authority (APSEA) (Personal communication between Laurel Lewey and Ruth Edmonston 14 November 2016).

38 Flora Jean Kennedy, interview by Brian Ouellette, 20 October 2000.
39 Carol Proctor, interview by Brian Ouellette, 2 November, 2000.
40 Howlett, *The Story of Child Welfare in New Brunswick*, 9.
41 New Brunswick Government, *Report of the New Brunswick Committee on Reconstruction*, Fredericton, 1944.
42 Forbes, "The 1930s: Depression and Retrenchment," 275–6.
43 Ibid., 276.
44 Ibid., 276.
45 Finkel, *Social Policy and Practice in Canada*, 49.
46 Carol Proctor, interview by Brian Ouellette, 2 November 2000.
47 Ruth Brittain, interview by Brian Ouellette, 22 June 2001.
48 Whitton, "Agencies Established Under Present Legislation," 148.
49 McKay, *Reasoning Otherwise*, 225.
50 Renfree, *Heritage and Horizon*, 234.
51 *Annual Report from the Acting Superintendent of the Interprovincial Home for Young Women* (Miss Walker), 29 January 1929, PANB, Interprovincial Home for Young Women fonds: [1920–1983], MC1268, F9086, & F9087.
52 *The Actual Provision of Relief*, 1932, PANB, Chief Medical Officer cum Deputy Minister of Health collection (hereafter RS136), file N1b4.
53 Forbes, "The 1930s: Depression and Retrenchment," 275.
54 The inference is that the overseer sometimes borrowed money to be able to offer financial assistance to those in need.
55 Forbes, "The 1930s: Depression and Retrenchment," 279.
56 Blaney, "Tracing Classed and Gendered Relations," 14.
57 "The History of Canada's Public Pensions," Canadian Museum of History website. Retrieved 29 July 1017 from http://www.historymuseum.ca/cmc/exhibitions/hist/pensions/cpp-a28-wcr_e.shtml.
58 A.B. MacKinnon, Municipal Inspector, to Mr Edmond F. Richard, Alms House Commissioner, Rogersville, N.B., 13 February 1935, PANB, RS153, container 28568, folder E27a12.
59 LAC, Welfare Services in Moncton, 1939, MG 28, I 10, vol. 132, 33.
60 Ibid.
61 Ibid., 34.
62 Finkel, *Social Policy and Practice in Canada*, 50 (Original source: Mariana Valverde, "The Mixed Social Economy as a Canadian Tradition," *Studies in*

Political Economy 47 [Summer 1995]: 42; Michael S. Cross, ed., *The Workingman in the Nineteenth Century* [Toronto: Oxford University Press, 1974], 201).

63 Welfare Services in Moncton, 1939, LAC, MG 28, I 10, vol. 132, 35.

64 Ibid., 34.

65 Family Welfare Association, Ltd. Saint John, N.B., Report on Families on Relief, 1938, PANB, RS156, file E7c6.

66 Canadian Welfare Council, "Saint John Agency Surveys Relief Families," 47–9.

67 Report of Field Work in Moncton, N.B., November 27 to December 22, 1939, Welfare Services in Moncton Report, LAC, MG 28, I 10, vol. 132, p. 17, pp. 9, 22.

68 Cassidy, *Public Health and Welfare Reorganization*, 41.

69 Richard Duffy, interview by Brian Ouellette, 9 May 2001.

70 Antonine Maillet, interview by Andre Vignault, *Growing up Acadian*, CBC, video, 8 June 1980, http://www.cbc.ca/archives/entry/growing-up-acadian.

71 Richard Duffy, interview by Brian Ouellette, 9 May 2001.

72 Archie Smith, interview by Brian Ouellette, 10 May 2001.

73 Archie Smith, interview by Brian Ouellette, 10 May 2001.

74 Ruth Brittain, interview by Brian Ouellette, 22 June 2001.

75 Richard Duffy, interview by Brian Ouellette, 9 May 2001.

76 A.B. Gilbert, County Secretary, to R.H. Scott, Provincial Child Welfare Officer, Fredericton, N.B., 2 July 1952, PANB, RS156, file E11a.

77 Howard Young, CAS worker, Northumberland County to Kathleen Morrissy, Supervisor of Welfare Services, Fredericton, 31 August 1950, PANB, RS153, file E15b13.

78 Richard Duffy, interview by Brian Ouellette, 9 May 2001.

79 Saint John Social Welfare Workers' Association, brief on relief, 24 April 1950, PANB, RS156, file E9f, pp. 7–9.

80 Twenty-Seventh Annual Meeting Case Work Report, 5 March 1957, PANB, RS156, file E7d, p. 3.

81 John McKendy, personal communication with Brian Ouellette, 29 January 2003.

82 Saint John Social Welfare Workers' association, brief on relief, 24 April 1950, PANB, RS156, file E9f, p. 9.

83 Saint John Social Welfare Workers' Association, brief on relief, 24 April 1950, PANB, RS156, file E9f, p. 7–9.

This is a shortened version of their recommendations: "1. We believe the Municipality should recognize the right of its citizens to financial assistance in their own home as long as their need continues. This, of course, has reference to the practice of presenting the Municipal Home as a solution to the problem. 2. We feel that the present practice of considering relief as an adjunct to the Municipal Home is impractical. 3. The Municipality should not take responsibility for employables. The Rowell-Sirois commission very clearly showed that the Municipalities are not at all able to care for large-scale relief, and that only the Dominion Government has the taxing power to deal with the problem. It recommended that the unemployables should be the responsibility of the Municipality. 4. Eligibility: (a) we feel that the practice of requiring applicants for relief to show that they paid taxes for three successive years is unjust and unlawful. (b) We feel a person should not be denied relief because of an asset which is unrealizable, such as the shack or old truck which we have described previously. (c) Wives and children should not be denied help because of the delinquency of the breadwinner. 5. (a) We feel that assistance should be in the form of cash rather than orders. (b) Relief should be adequate to meet the needs of the family. It should be based on existing costs of food, fuel, rent and other essentials. (c) Relief should be administered by an agency or a person only where there is definite experience that people are unable to handle it themselves."

84 Saint John Committee on Public Assistance Correspondence and Final Report of the Joint Committee 1959–1960, PANB RS156, file E7d.

85 Howard Young, CAS agent, Northumberland County, received the publication "comparative meal costs for one person" from the Dept. of Health and Social Services, Maternal and Child Health Division, on 7 December 1959. PANB, RS153, file E15a2.

86 Brown, "New Brunswick," 201.

87 1963 Annual Report presented on 25 February 1964 at the 34th Annual Meeting Family Services Association, pp. 1–2. PANB, RS156, fileE7c6.

88 Ibid., p. 2.

89 Bourque, "Accomplishments and Shortcomings," 25.

90 Ibid., 9.

91 Ibid., 10.

92 Tremblay, "Moving Beyond the Urban/Rural Divide," 344, citing Fitzpatrick, "New Brunswick: The Politics of Pragmatism," in Martin Robin, *Canadian Provincial Politics: The Party Systems of the Ten Provinces* (Scarborough, ON: Prentice-Hall, 1972), 116.

5 Origins and Development of Social Care Agencies and Networks

1 Social workers were those with university degrees in social work. Social welfare workers performed tasks similar to social workers but did not

possess social work degrees. Children's Aid Society (CAS) workers conducted child welfare work with or without social work degrees.

2 Finkel, *Social Policy and Practice in Canada*, 43.

3 Duguay, *Child Care in New Brunswick*, 16.

4 "About Us: Our History in Canada," YWCA Canada website. Retrieved 22 October 2017 from http://ywcacanada.ca/en/pages/national/history).

5 The first YMCA in Canada was established in Montreal, 9 December 1851.

6 Minutes of the Annual Meeting of the N.B. Association of Children's Aid Societies, October 9 and 10, 1962, held in the Old Town Hall in Oromocto, first page. Provincial Archives of New Brunswick (hereafter PANB), Northumberland County Council collection (hereafter RS153), file E16. The citation in the minutes was by Miss McCaron, who presented a paper on the philosophy of adoption and recent changes.

7 New Brunswick Protestant Orphans' Home letter of appeal dated 6 April 1925, signed by D.C. Clark, President, and H. Usher Miller, Secretary. PANB, Chief Medical Officer *cum* Deputy Minister of Health collection (hereafter RS136), file p1c1.

8 Ibid.

9 Max Baxter, Secretary of N.B. Protestant Orphan's Home, to A.B. Gilbert, County Secretary's Office, Saint John, 14 December 1950. PANB, Saint John County Council collection (hereafter RS156), file E7c.

10 Archie Smith, interview by Brian Ouellette, 10 May 2001.

11 Acts of the General Assembly of Her Majesty's Province of New Brunswick. Passed in months of February and March 1895. Fredericton: G.M. Fenety, Publisher, p. 406.

12 As of 31 March 1928 the agency was $12,000 in debt. The pamphlet read, "our greatest drawback has been the fact that during this period few men of wealth have come to our aid with large donations as given to other worthy work, and many in passing have splendidly remembered other similar institutions but we have always been overlooked, yet our endorsements are evidence of proof that we have maintained high institutional ideals, and our efforts have not been surpassed." Seventh Annual Report of the Nova Scotia Home for Colored Children. Canada's Only Orphanage for Neglected and Orphaned Colored Children, 1928. PANB, RS136, file P1c4, p. 4.

13 Vilma Kurol, interview by Karen Hill, 17 February 1984, Oral History of Social Work in Canada Project, Canadian Association of Social Workers, Ottawa.

14 Flora Jean Kennedy, interview by Brian Ouellette, 20 October 2000.

15 Children's Aid Society of the County of Saint John. PANB, RS156, file E10a, p. 5.

16 Built Heritage Files, Home of the Good Shepherd, second floor, Resurgo Centre (Moncton Museum), 20 Mountain Road, Moncton, NB, E1C 2J8.

17 Louis Richard, personal communication with former school director (1974–82) Jos Laviolette, 23 September 2016.

18 Salvation Army Correspondence re: Evangeline Hospital and Home for Unwed Mothers, PANB, Albert County Council collection (hereafter RS146), file E1e.

19 Salvation Army Correspondence re: Evangeline Hospital and Home for Unwed Mothers, PANB, RS146, file E1e. The girls/women ranged from thirteen to thirty-three years.

20 The Salvation Army Evangeline Hospital Extension, Saint John. Brief presented to the Council of the Municipality of the City and Council of Saint John, 8 May 1956. PANB, RS156, file E7c4.

21 Annual Report of the Family Welfare Association Limited, Saint John, New Brunswick. Brief to the Municipality of the County of Saint John, 1963, PANB RS156, file E7c6, p. 2.

22 Annual Report of the Saint John Family Welfare Association, 1963. PANB, RS156, file E7c6.

23 Nowlan, *A Century of Service*, 148.

24 Ibid., 149.

25 E.F. Leahey, Executive Director of the Catholic Youth Organization, to His Worship the Mayor and the Common Council, City of Saint John, 16 January 1958, p. 1. The centre was located at the corner of Cliff and Waterloo Streets. The executive director made the point that "people today confuse 'recreation' with 'wreck creation'" (p. 1) but assured the mayor and council that all programs at the centre were supervised. He also pointed out that many children have their first shower at the centre, "since a bath or shower is a luxury unheard of in many homes" (p. 2)., PANB, RS156, file E7c3.

26 E.F. Leahey, Executive Director of the Catholic Youth Organization, to His Worship the Mayor and the Common Council, City of Saint John, 16 January 1958, PANB, RS156, file E7c3, p. 1.

27 Annual Report of the Saint John Family Welfare Association, 1953, PANB, RS415, file E2g4.

28 Finkel, *Social Policy and Practice in Canada*, 29.

29 Godin, Carmen, *L'Histoire des Politiques Sociales au: N.B. de 1605 à nos Jours* (unpublished paper, 1987), in Howlett, *The Story of Child Welfare in New Brunswick*, 10.

30 D'Amour, *Les Filles de Marie-de-l'Assomption Sur les Chemins de l'Évangile.*

31 Rev. F.T. Whalen to A.B. Gilbert, Secretary-Treasurer, Municipality of Saint John. 9 January 1954. PANB, RS156, file E7c8.

32 Duguay, *Child Care in New Brunswick*, 12.
33 Ibid.
34 Ibid., 13.
35 Rev. F.T. Whalen to A.B. Gilbert, Secretary-Treasurer, Municipality of Saint John, 9 January 1954. PANB, RS156, file E7c8.
36 Hébert, Thaddeus, Secretary-Treasurer, to Mr R.S. Carpenter, Municipal Affairs Officer, Department of Municipal Affairs, Fredericton, 14 January 1960. PANB, Madawaska County Council collection (hereafter RS152), file E2/2b.
37 L'Assistance Sociale-Welfare. Factures – Familles Nécessiteuses – par paroisses (Invoices – Social Assistance), 1958, Saint-André. PANB, RS152, file E1/1k.
38 "Pioneers, Ploughs and Politics: New Brunswick's Planned Settlements," PANB website. Retrieved July 21, 2017 from http://archives.gnb.ca/exhibits/plannedsettlements/TextViewer.aspx?culture=en-CA&t=Allardville&p=1of19.
39 Wəlastəkwewiyik is the traditional name for Maliseets, but since there are several versions of the name and at least two competing orthographies, a decision has been made by the Maliseet chiefs to continue using "Maliseet" until a collective decision can be reached on these issues. Bear Nicholas, personal communication with Laurel Lewey, 21 September 2016.
40 Bear Nicholas, personal communication with Laurel Lewey, 21 September 2016.
41 Shewell, *"Enough to Keep Them Alive"*, 41.
42 Finkel, *Social Policy and Practice in Canada*, 57.
43 Fingard, in "The New England Company and the New Brunswick Indians," describes the London-based New England Company as being founded in New England in 1649 by Puritans, making it the oldest of the English missionary societies, which was administered by middle-class loyalist Anglicans, 29.
44 Peck, *The Bitter with the Sweet*, 27.
45 Fingard, "Women's Organizations," 30.
46 Ibid., 33.
47 Peck, *The Bitter with the Sweet*, 31.
48 Ibid., 32.
49 Bear Nicholas, "The Role of Colonial Artists," 40.
50 Bear Nicholas, "The Role of Colonial Artists," 48–9.
51 Fingard, "Women's Organizations," 42.
52 Walls, "'Part of that Whole System,'" 377.
53 Ibid., 365.

54 Ibid., 365.
55 Ibid., 368.
56 Ibid., 365.
57 Ibid, 364–7.
58 Paul, *We Were Not the Savages*, 220.
59 Olsen, *The Politics of the Welfare State*, 85–6.
60 Library and Archives Canada (hereafter LAC), Indian and Northern Affairs Canada (hereafter INAC), Indian Affairs record group (hereafter RG 10), vol. 8886, file 55/29–6, Pt. 1.
61 Knockwood, *Out of the Depths*, 16.
62 Walls, "'Part of that Whole System,'" 363.
63 Chrisjohn et al., "Genocide and Indian Residential Schooling," 237.
64 Ibid., 241.
65 Walls, "'Part of that Whole System,'" 369.
66 Knockwood, *Out of the Depths*, 22.
67 Ibid., 47.
68 Ibid., 28.
69 Ibid., 18.
70 Ibid., 29.
71 Ibid., 38.
72 Ibid., 33.
73 Ibid., 18.
74 Ibid., 41–2.
75 Ibid., 63.
76 Ibid., 114–17; 149–56.
77 Walls, "'Part of that Whole System,'" 373.
78 Ibid., 385.
79 Phillipson, *Linguistic Imperialism Continued*, 202.
80 Chrisjohn and Young, *The Circle Game*, 63.
81 Bear Nicholas, personal communication with Laurel Lewey, 21 September 2016.
82 Carolyn and Dan Ennis, interview by Laurel Lewey, 23 February 2007.
83 Finkel, *Social Policy and Practice in Canada*, 272.
84 Forbes, "The 1930s: Depression and Retrenchment," 283.
85 Shewell, *"Enough to Keep Them Alive"*, 233.
86 Ibid., 237.
87 Letter dated 4 February 1946 to Nora Lea from R.H. Scott, LAC, Canadian Council on Social Development fonds (hereafter MG 28, I 10, vol. 117), file Department of Citizenship and Immigration, Indian Affairs 1938 47.

88 Letter dated 4 February 1946 to Nora Lea from R.H. Scott, LAC, MG 28, I 10, vol. 117, file Department of Citizenship and Immigration, Indian Affairs 1938–1947.
89 Sinclair et al., "Aboriginal Child Welfare," 213.
90 Shewell, *"Enough to Keep Them Alive"*, 193.
91 Ibid., 333.
92 Bohaker and Iacovettta, "Making Aboriginal People 'Immigrants Too,'" 457.
93 Ibid., 429.
94 Ibid., 446.
95 Ibid., 456.
96 Dickason, *Canada's First Nations*, 320.
97 Ibid., 329.
98 Laurel Lewey, personal communication with Harry Sock, Director of Child and Family Services, Elsipogtog, 24 November 2015.
99 Laurel Lewey, personal communication with Harry Sock, Director of Child and Family Services, Elsipogtog, 24 November 2015.
100 LAC, INAC, RG 10, vol. 8886, file 55/27-5-1, Welfare of Indians – Welfare 1955–61. Letter dated 7 January 1955 from J. Ernest Anderson, Director of Old Age and Blind Assistance Board, Fredericton to E.J. Blakely, Superintendent of Miramichi Indian Agency, Rogersville, NB.
101 Letter dated 4 September 1963 from Mary McBroom, Department of Youth and Welfare, Fredericton to B.G. Clench, Superintendent, Indian Affairs Branch, Woodstock, LAC, INAC, RG 10, vol. 8366, file 54/29-4, pt. 2, Welfare of Indians – Care of Children.
102 LAC, INAC, RG 10, vol. 8366, file 54/29-4, pt. 2, Welfare of Indians – Care of Children.
103 LAC, INAC, RG 10, vol. 8886, file 55/29-6, pt. 1, Miramichi Agency – Foster Home – Eel Ground 1949–62. Press release dated 7 July 1964, No. 64-14, Department of Citizenship and Immigration from the Hon. Rene Tremblay, Minister and Superintendent General of Indian Affairs.
104 LAC, INAC, RG 10, vol. 8886, file 55/29-6, pt. 1, Miramichi Agency – Foster Home – Eel Ground 1949–62.
105 Letter dated 6 October 1964 from H.S. MacNeill to Dr Mirtle, National Health and Welfare, LAC, INAC, RG 10, vol. 8366, file 54/29-4 pt. 2, Welfare of Indians – Care of Children.
106 Ibid.
107 H.S. MacNeill, Superintendent to Ruby Taylor, social worker, town of Oromocto, 18 February 1964, LAC, INAC, RG10, vol. 8366, file 54/29-4, pt. 2, Welfare of Indians – Care of Children.

108 LAC, INAC, RG 10, vol. 8886, file 55/29–6, pt. 3.
109 LAC, INAC, RG 10, vol. 8886, file 55/29–6, pt. 1. Miramichi Agency – Foster Home – Eel Ground 1949–62. Brief Introduction to Child Welfare Services, 15 February 1968. Regional Welfare Workshop, 20–2 February 1968 by R.J. Tobin, Welfare Consultant, p. 2.
110 LAC, INAC, RG 10, vol. 8886, file 55/29–6, pt. 1, Miramichi Agency – Foster Home – Eel Ground 1949–62. Brief Introduction to Child Welfare Services, 15 February 1968, Regional Welfare Workshop, 20–2 February 1968 by R.J. Tobin, Welfare Consultant, pp. 4–5.
111 Shewell, *"Enough to Keep Them Alive"*, 41.

6 The Evolution of Child Welfare

1 Carol Proctor, interview by Brian Ouellette, 2 November 2000.
2 Fredericton Community Survey Report, 1930, Library and Archives Canada (hereafter LAC), Canadian Council on Social Development fonds (hereafter MG 28, I 10), vol. 42, file 187.
3 The Victorian Order of Nurses was created, not without controversy, in Saint John largely through the efforts of the Council of Women in 1897–9 for the purpose of attending to issues of public health (Campbell, *Challenging Years, 1894–1979*).
4 History of Child Welfare in Ontario Family & Children's Services of Guelph and Wellington County. Retrieved 21 October 2016 from http://www.fcsgw.org/about-us/history-of-child-welfare-in-ontario/
5 D'Amours, "Survol historique de la protection de l'enfance au Quebéc."
6 Child Protection Services, Fredericton Community Survey, 1930, LAC, MG 28, I 10, vol. 42, file 187.
7 Child Protection Services, Fredericton Community Survey, 1930, LAC, MG 28, I 10, vol. 42, file 187.
8 Child Protection Services, Fredericton Community Survey, 1930, LAC, MG 28, I 10, vol. 42, file 187.
9 Its declared objectives were:
 1st. To carry out the provisions of all ACTS for the protection of children, in receiving and providing homes for neglected and dependent children;
 2nd. To systematically agitate against all that tends to rob children, of the right to grow up in an atmosphere of purity and moral cleanliness.
 3rd. To prosecute parties who contribute towards the delinquency of children.

4th. To create a sentiment for the establishing of wholeness uplifting influences, such as small parks, gymnasiums, free baths, social centres, and the like.

5th. To maintain an educational campaign on subjects relating to child protection. From the constitution of the Children's Aid Society of the city and parish of Moncton authorized under the "Children's Protection Act 1916," Moncton Children's Aid Society General, 1917, 1924, 1939. Provincial Archives of New Brunswick (hereafter PANB) Moncton Municipal collection (hereafter RS418), file F3l.

10 Howlett, *The Story of Child Welfare in New Brunswick*, 19.
11 Ibid., 13.
12 Duguay, *Child Care in New Brunswick*, 30.
13 Tillotson, "Democracy, Dollars, and the Children's Aid Society," 84.
14 From 1918 to 1920 Whitton had worked at the Social Service Council of Canada as assistant secretary to Dr John Shearer. In 1920 Whitton was made the honorary secretary of the newly formed Canadian Council on Child Welfare to oversee child welfare activities for the Social Service Council, which she did until 1941 (Jennissen and Lundy, *One Hundred Years of Social Work*, 6).
15 Duguay, *Child Care in New Brunswick*, 18.
16 Myers, *The Governance of Childhood*, 357.
17 Ibid., ii.
18 Ibid., 366.
19 Ibid., 302.
20 Ibid., 369.
21 Ibid., 371.
22 Ibid., 380.
23 Ibid., 1.
24 Ibid., 19.
25 Ibid., 247.
26 Ibid., 247.
27 Ibid., 345.
28 Ibid., 1.
29 Guildford, "The End of the Poor Law," 69.
30 Duguay, *Child Care in New Brunswick*, 19.
31 Minutes of meeting of Toronto Branch CASW, 24 March 1943, LAC, CASW fonds (hereafter R3418-0-3-E), vol. 35, file 14.
32 Maines, "Through the Years in CASW," 30.
33 Guest, *The Emergence of Social Security in Canada*, 132.
34 Duguay, *Child Care in New Brunswick*, 22.

35 Flora Jean Kennedy, interview by Brian Ouellette, 20 October 2000.
36 This was ahead of Manitoba, where social workers were just beginning to improve the adoption process (Jennissen and Lundy, *One Hundred Years of Social Work*, 97).
37 Hick and Stokes, *Social Work in Canada*, 146.
38 Flora Jean Kennedy, interview by Brian Ouellette, 20 October 2000.
39 Ibid.
40 Carol Proctor, interview by Brian Ouellette, 2 November 2000.
41 Cahill, *Butterbox Babies*, 15.
42 Balcom, "Scandal and Social Policy," 11.
43 Ibid., 17.
44 Flora Jean Kennedy, interview by Brian Ouellette, 20 October 2000.
45 Minutes of the Annual Meeting of the N.B. Association of Children's Aid Societies, October 9 and 10, 1962, held in the Old Town Hall in Ormocto, first page, PANB, Northumberland County Council collection (hereafter RS153), file E16.
46 Myers, "The Governance of Childhood," 357.
47 Howlett, *The Story of Child Welfare in New Brunswick*, 16.
48 Minutes of the Annual Meeting of the N.B. Association of Children's Aid Societies, October 9 and 10, 1962, held in the Old Town Hall in Oromocto, first page. PANB, RS153, file E16.
49 Duguay, *Child Care in New Brunswick*, 21.
50 Ibid.
51 Minutes of the Ninth Annual Meeting of the N.B. Association of Children's Aid Societies, October 9, 10, 11, 1956, at the Lord Beaverbrook Hotel, Fredericton, p. 2, Panel on Clothing for Wards, PANB, RS153, file E16.
52 Minutes of the Annual Meeting of the N.B. Association of the Children's Aid Societies, October 9 and 10, 1962, held at the Old Town Hall, Oromocto, pp. 4–5, PANB, RS153, file E16. Specifically, resolutions stated, "BE IT RESOLVED that the Provincial Government be asked to cooperate with this Association in a study to establish a non-ward care service in New Brunswick for certain determined types of cases, and to study the possibility of having non-ward care services included in those already given by the Children's Aid Society, and that the definition of a 'foster home' be amended" (p. 4). "BE IT RESOLVED that the resolution regarding the Deserted Wives and Children's Act be passed at the annual meeting of the N.B. Association of Children's Aid Societies October 11th and 12th, 1960, be reviewed by the appropriate department of the government in the light of more recent studies on the Act made locally and nationally" (p. 4). "BE IT RESOLVED that the Department of Youth and Welfare be approached to make a study

of services to the delinquent children released from a place of safety" (p. 4). "BE IT RESOLVED that the Attorney General's Department be approached to amend the Adoption Act. (a) to set a definite period of one year after a final adoption, after which no appeal can be made. (b) that the Department of Youth and Welfare be requested to make provisions for a notice of the granting of an adoption order to the adoptive parents and that the original order be filed in the Department. (c) that birth re-registration be automatic with the granting of the final adoption order. (p. 4). (d) that an affidavit be required of the person making the adoption report (p. 5). (e) that a medical consent be obtained with the parent's consent to adoption" (p. 5).

53 Annual Reports Children's Aid Society 1962–1965 PANB, RS 147, E13 a2. The annual report 1963 is signed by Kay Hamilton, CAS Agent for Carleton County.

54 Report of committee on the unmarried mother and her child presented to the New Brunswick Association of the Children's Aid Societies, October 11, 1955. Committee members on the Unmarried Mother and Her Child were Rev F.T. Whalen, Mary R. Bishop and Mrs Hugh McGinn. PANB, RS153, file E16.

55 Social Assistance, Child Welfare, Children's Aid Society, PANB, RS136, file S 3c.

56 Memo dated 1 April 1956, re: maintenance of wards and children of Unmarried Parents Act by J.G. LeBlanc, Director of Welfare, PANB, Albert County Council collection (hereafter RS146), file 2A1.

57 Minutes of the Ninth Annual Meeting of the N.B. Association of Children's Aid Societies, October 9, 10, 11, 1956, held at the Lord Beaverbrook Hotel, Fredericton, p. 4, Legislation & Resolutions Committee, PANB, RS153, file E16.

58 Madawaska County, Mothers Allowance Commission, 1960, PANB, Madawaska County Council collection (hereafter RS152), file E2/1b.

59 Manzer, Murray, Director of Welfare. Letter to Alderman L.C. Poore, City Hall, Fredericton, 6 August 1965, Fredericton Municipal Welfare, PANB, Gloucester County Council collection, RS149, file F1.

60 Howlett, *The Story of Child Welfare in New Brunswick*, 23.

61 Ibid., 25–30.

62 Butler, "The Dark Side of Honouring Dr. Helen MacMurchy."

63 O'Brien, *Framing the Moron*, 3.

64 O'Brien and Bundy, "Reaching Beyond the 'Moron,'" 158.

65 McLaren, "Stemming the Flood of Defective Aliens," 190.

66 Ibid., 192.
67 Dyck, *Facing Eugenics*, 9.
68 Grekul, Krahn, and Odynak, "Sterilizing the 'Feeble-Minded,'" 361.
69 Baker, "Institutionalizing Eugenics," 64.
70 Feebleminded Children, Report from Canadian Council on Child Welfare, 1927, PANB, Records of the Chief Medical Officer Cum Deputy Minister of Health 1719–1971, (hereafter RS136), file N163, p. 2.
71 Duguay, *Child Care in New Brunswick*, 24.
72 Letter dated 24 January 1929, to Charlotte Whitton, Executive Director of the Canadian Council on Child Welfare, addressed to the Admiral Beatty Hotel in Saint John from the Chief Medical Officer, who was Dr George G. Melvin, Canadian Council of Child Welfare. PANB, RS136, file N1b3.
73 Panel on medical care for wards. Minutes of the Ninth Annual Meeting of the N.B. Association of Children's Aid Societies, October 9, 10 and 11, 1956, PANB, RS153, file E16.
74 Report dated 4 May 1957, by the New Brunswick Co-Coordinating Council for the Handicapped presented at the Annual Meeting N.B. Council for the Handicapped, PANB, RS136, file S4.
75 Annie Peters, CAS agent in Carleton County, to Howard Young, CAS agent, Northumberland County, 11 August 1950, PANB, RS153, file E15a1, General 1948–1954.
76 Fred Blair, Secretary, York County Liberal Association, to Honourable Louis J. Robichaud, Premier of New Brunswick, September 1963, PANB, RS416, file 155.
77 H. Usher Miller, President's Office Children's Aid Society, Saint John, to W.A. Ross, County Secretary, Saint John (n.d.) indicated that one hundred child refugees from Britain would be arriving. A letter dated 29 June 1940, from the County Secretary to the President of the Children's Aid Society indicated that additional staff was authorized. PANB, Saint John County Council collection (hereafter RS156), file E10a.
78 L.T. Tingley, Secretary, Albert-Westmorland Children's Aid Society to Arnold Bowes, Secretary-Treasurer, Municipality of Westmorland and George Blight, Secretary-Treasurer, Municipality of Albert, 30 September 1940, Albert County Council Health and Welfare Children's Aid Society Correspondence 1928, 1961, PANB, RS146, file E5a.
79 Ethel Murphy, on behalf on the Moncton University Women's Club to Major Rouse, 13 July 1940. PANB, RS418, file F1a.
80 Guest, *The Emergence of Social Security in Canada*, 54.
81 Ibid., 63.

82 Finkel, *Social Policy and Practice in Canada*, 101.
83 Guest, *The Emergence of Social Security in Canada*, 59.
84 Ibid., 59.
85 Ibid., 62.
86 LAC, MG 28, I 10, vol. 134, file 600, New Brunswick Survey 1948–1949.
87 Howard Young to "deadbeat dad," 2 December 1953, PANB, RS153, file E15 b13.
88 Blaney, "Tracing Classed and Gendered Relations," 15.
89 Ibid., 147.
90 Howard Young, CAS agent, Northumberland County. Letter in response to a query. December 28, 1961, PANB, RS153, file E15a2, General Correspondence 1955–1962.
91 R.H. Scott, Provincial Child Welfare Officer, to Howard Young, CAS worker for Northumberland County, 1948, PANB, RS153, file E15a1, General 1948–1954.
92 R.H. Scott, Provincial Child Welfare Officer to Howard Young, CAS worker for Northumberland County, 1949, PANB, RS153, file E15a1, General 1948–1954.
93 R.H. Scott, Provincial Child Welfare Officer to Howard Young, CAS worker for Northumberland County, 1949, PANB, RS153, file E15a1, General 1948–1954.
94 Kathleen Morrissy, for the Regional Director of Family Allowances, to Howard Young, CAS worker for Northumberland County, 1954, PANB, RS153, file E15b2, B1948–1961.
95 Kathleen Morrissy, for the Regional Director of Family Allowances, to Howard Young, CAS worker for Northumberland County, 1954, PANB, RS153 file E15b2, B 1948–1961.
96 Howard Young, CAS worker in Northumberland County, to J.G. LeBlanc, Director of Welfare, Department of Health and Social Services, Fredericton, 1958, PANB, RS153, file E15b9, J1951–1961.
97 Vilma Kurol, interview by Karen Hill, 17 February 1984, Oral History of Social Work in Canada Project, Canadian Association of Social Workers, Ottawa.
98 Howard Young, CAS worker for Northumberland County, 6 April 1959. Letter recommending that a mother be allowed to adopt her natural child. PANB, RS153, file E15b13, M1948–1962.
99 Vilma Kurol, interview by Karen Hill, 17 February 1984, Oral History of Social Work in Canada Project, Canadian Association of Social Workers, Ottawa.
100 Howard Young, CAS agent, Northumberland County, December 1955, PANB, RS153, file E15b12, Mc and MAC, 1948–1962.

101 Howard Young, CAS agent, Northumberland County, to municipal authorities, 1956, PANB, RS153, file E15b 12, Mc and MAC, 1948–1962.

102 Letter dated 15 December 1951, from the New Brunswick Association of Children's Aid Societies, Social Assistance, Mother's Allowance, PANB, RS136, file 1a, New Brunswick Association of Children's Aid Societies.

103 Minutes of the Ninth Annual Meeting of the N.B. Children's Aid Societies, October 9, 10, 11, 1956, held at the Lord Beaverbrook Hotel in Fredericton, p. 4, Legislation & Resolutions Committee, PANB, RS153, file E16.

104 Brigadier J. Ernest Anderson, of Mother's Allowance Commission, to Helen Morrison, Chief Welfare Officer, Charlottetown, PEI, 22 April 1953, PANB, RS136, file S1a.

105 J. Ernest Anderson, Director of Mother's Allowance in Fredericton, to H.B. Mersereau, Secretary Treasurer, N.B. Provincial Command, Saint John, N.B. 16 November 1950, PANB, RS136, file S1a.

106 J. Ernest Anderson, Director of Mother's Allowance to H.B. Mersereau, Secretary Treasurer, N.B. Provincial Command, Saint John, N.B., 16 November 1950, PANB, RS136, file S1a.

107 Mildred Bridgeford, Executive Secretary, Twenty-ninth Annual Meeting, Case Work Report, 13 February 1958, PANB, RS156, file E7c6, p. 2.

108 Memo dated 13 February 1953, from Howard Young, CAS worker in Northumberland county, PANB, RS153, file E15b4, D 1949–1962.

109 Letter dated 28 August 1954, from Howard Young to J.E. Anderson, Director of Mothers' Allowance, Fredericton. Anderson replied to Young on 31 August 1954 that the woman was awarded Mothers' Allowance in the amount of $65 per month effective 1 August, but that the first cheque wouldn't be forwarded from his office until 8 September. PANB, RS153, file E15b3, C 1949–1962.

110 Letters dating from September 1949 to March 1950 between Howard Young, CAS agent, Northumberland County, and Freda Peden, supervisor, Social Services Division, Dept. of Veteran's Affairs, Saint John, PANB, RS153, file E15a1, General 1948–1954.

111 Letter dated August 11, 1950, from Annie Peters, CAS agent in Carleton County to Howard Young, CAS agent in Northumberland County, PANB, RS153, file E15a1, General 1948–1954.

112 Mary Bishop to Howard Young, 18 April 1950, PANB, RS153, file E15a1, General 1948–1954.

113 Minutes of the Ninth Annual Meeting of the N.B. Association of Children's Aid Societies, October 9, 10, 11, 1956, held at the Lord Beaverbrook Hotel in Fredericton, p. 2, the round table discussion in French, PANB, RS153, file E16.

114 Minutes of the Ninth Annual Meeting of the N.B. Association of Children's Aid Societies, October 9, 10, 11, 1956, held at the Lord Beaverbrook Hotel in Fredericton, pp. 3–4, minimum standards in education of wards, PANB, RS153, file E16.
115 Minutes of the Annual Meeting of the N.B. Association of Children's Aid Societies, October 9 and 10, 1962, held in the Old Town Hall, Oromocto, PANB, RS153, file E16, p. 5.
116 Letter dated 16 July 1958, to Mrs Russell Crothers, Assistant Secretary, Women's Institute, Sussex from a CAS agent, PANB, RS156, file E10a.
117 Letter to non-branch members of CASW, submitted by Kathleen (Tally) Morrissy, 24 October 1957, LAC, R3418-0-3-E, vol. 17, file 12.
118 William R. Duffie, Minister of Youth and Welfare, New Brunswick, to David Smith, County Secretary, Saint John, N.B., 27 May 1965, PANB, RS156, file E7a.
119 David Smith, County Secretary, to Honourable H.R. Duffie, Minister of Youth and Welfare, Fredericton, 23 June 1965, PANB, RS156, file E7a.
120 Howlett, *The Story of Child Welfare in New Brunswick*, 23.
121 Nettie Moore, CAS agent, Fredericton, to Howard Young, CAS agent, Northumberland County, 27 June 1965, in which she states, "As you know, it is not allowed by law for them to be placed for adoption in other than a Protestant family. This fact, of course, would prevent permanent placement of any of these children with their Catholic relatives." PANB, RS153, file E15b3, C, 1949–1962.
122 Nettie Moore, CAS agent, Fredericton, to Howard Young, CAS agent Northumberland County, 26 October 1956, in which she stated, "Furthermore, I believe we would hesitate to place them, or any child, in a home where one parent is Catholic and the other is Protestant." PANB, RS153, file E15b12, Mc and MAC, 1948–1962.

7 A Portrait of New Brunswick's Earliest Social Workers

1 Cassidy, *Public Health and Welfare Reorganization*, 405.
2 Jennie Robinson, Superintendent, The Interprovincial Home for Young Women, to Mr Geo. C. Blight, Hopewell Cape, N.B., 15 November 1927, Provincial Archives of New Brunswick (hereafter PANB), Albert County Council collection (hereafter RS146), container 14549, file E2D.
3 Myers, *The Governance of Childhood*, 385.
4 Report of Field Work in Moncton, N.B., November 27 to December 22, 1939, Library and Archives Canada (hereafter LAC), Canadian Council

on Social Development fonds (hereafter MG 28, I 10), vol. 132, p. 17. (Suggestions for Welfare Council and social worker in Moncton) Charlotte Whitton involved, p. 35.

5 Hancock, *The Story of the Maritime School of Social Work*, 65.

6 LAC, CASW fonds (hereafter R3418–0-3-E), vol. 31, folder 15, New Brunswick-PEI Branch 1948–1950.

7 "Social Workers Hold Meeting," Charlottetown *Guardian*, 13 March 1952, p. 9.

8 Stanley Matheson, interview by Linda Turner and Louis Richard, 11 October, 2005.

9 Jennissen and Lundy, *One Hundred Years of Social Work*, 196.

10 LAC, R3418–0-3-E, Non-Branch members New Brunswick, vol. 17, file 12.

11 Hancock, *The Story of the Maritime School of Social Work*, 77

12 Archie Smith, interview by Brian Ouellette, 10 May 2001.

13 Report of Field Work in Moncton, N.B. November 27 to December 22' 1939, Welfare Services in Moncton Report, LAC, MG 28, I 10, vol. 132, p. 17 (Suggestions for Welfare Council and social worker in Moncton) Charlotte Whitton involved, p. 30.

14 Jennissen and Lundy, *One Hundred Years of Social Work*, 47.

15 Report of Field Work in Moncton, N.B. November 27 to December 22, 1939, Welfare Services in Moncton Report, LAC, MG 28, I 10, vol. 132, p. 17 (Suggestions for Welfare Council and social worker in Moncton), p. 107.

16 Report of Field Work in Moncton, N.B. November 27 to December 22, 1939, Welfare Services in Moncton Report, LAC, MG 28, I 10, vol. 132, p. 17 (Suggestions for Welfare Council and social worker in Moncton), p. 107.

17 Carol Proctor, interview by Brian Ouellette, 2 November 2000.

18 Ibid.

19 Municipality of Westmorland Inter Office Memo: Approved Salary Schedule presented to Mrs. P. (Mrs. Phillip) Bishop from C. Max Amos, PANB, Westmorland County Council collection (hereafter RS159), file B1/24, 1965.

20 Marcel Arseneau, interview by Brian Ouellette, 11 April 2001.

21 Ibid.

22 Ibid.

23 Flora Jean Kennedy, interview by Brian Ouellette, 20 October 2000.

24 Ibid.

25 Ibid.

26 Arseneau, "Le travailleur social des années '80."

27 Twenty-fifth annual meeting case work report, Family Welfare Association, Saint John N.B., 1954, presented February 21, 1955, PANB, Saint John County Council collection (hereafter RS156), file E7c6.
28 Twenty-fifth Annual meeting case work report Family Welfare Association, Saint John N.B., 1954, presented 21 February, 1955, PANB, RS156, file E7c6.
29 Family Welfare Association of Saint John, 34th Annual Casework Report for 1963, presented, 25 February, 1964, PANB, RS156, file E7c6.
30 Family Welfare Association of Saint John, 34th Annual Casework Report for 1963, presented 25 February, 1964, PANB, RS156, file E7c6.
31 Minutes and biennial report 1960–2, 4 October 1960, LAC, MG 28, I 441, container 31, file 14. File title: "New Brunswick Branch, Includes minutes and biennial report Date 1960–62."
32 Family Welfare Association of Saint John, 34th Annual Casework Report for 1963, presented 25 February, 1964, PANB, RS156, file E7c6, p. 4.
33 Family Welfare Association of Saint John, 34th Annual Casework Report for 1963 presented 25 February, 1964, RS156, file E7c6.
34 John Lutz, interview by Linda Turner, 11 January 2007.
35 Father Frank MacDonald, interview by Brian Ouellette, 1 May 2001.
36 Fred Whalen, interview by Brian Ouellette, 9 May 2001.
37 Jennissen and Lundy, *One Hundred Years of Social Work*, 251.

8 The First Acadian Social Workers

1 A mail-out questionnaire and an interview are the two principal research tools employed in this study.
2 The inference here is that the French spoken in the Moncton area is considered by many to contain many anglicisms and have a more limited French vocabulary than the French spoken by those Acadians who live in the northern and north eastern parts of the province.
3 Many interviews were held in the client's home at that time as opposed to an office.
4 Two of the twelve members of the group of the first Acadian social workers spent the greater part of their professional careers teaching at the École de travail social of the Université de Moncton.
5 The Maritime School of Social Work was created in Halifax in 1941 to serve the region. Graduates from its professional programme would apply to one of five affiliated universities for a master's degree. Those universities were Saint Mary's and King's Colleges (Halifax), St. Francis Xavier

(Antigonish) and Acadia (Wolfville) in Nova Scotia, and Mount Allison (Sackville) in New Brunswick. This scheme continued until the early 1970s, at which time the school became part of Dalhousie University.

9 Social Workers Experience Child Welfare

1 The oral interviews relied on in this chapter were conducted by Brian Ouellette, Louis J. Richard, Linda Turner, Laurel Lewey, and Katherine Marcoccio. Additional interviews were retrieved from the Karen Hill fonds at the Library and Archives of Canada (hereafter LAC) and the New Brunswick Association of Social Workers (NBASW) office in Fredericton, NB. Comments of CAS agents were found in records stored at the Provincial Archives of New Brunswick (hereafter PANB).
2 Asst. Commissioner of the N.B. Provincial Police, Fredericton, to the Secretary Treasurer for the municipality of Carleton, 27 July 1931, PANB, Carleton County Council collection (hereafter RS147), file E13a1.
3 Children's Aid Society Case Files 1929–1966 (Restricted Access), PANB, Saint John County Council collection (hereafter RS156), file e-1.
4 Revised Statutes in effect since 1927 according to Duguay, *Child Care in New Brunswick*, 23.
5 Children's Aid Society Case Files, 1929–1966 (Restricted Access), PANB, RS156, file e-1.
6 Unsigned letter, no date on letterhead, but text of letter states that Edna Smith resigned from Albert County CAS in 1954 and that a trained nurse succeeded her, PANB, Albert County Council (hereafter RS146), file E5a. Unsigned letter indicates that on 17 May 1948, Edna Smith began to work in both counties, PANB, RS146, file E5b.
7 Robert Thériault, interview by Brian Ouellette, 22 November 2000.
8 PANB, Northumberland County Council collection (hereafter RS153), file E15a2.
9 Robert Thériault, interview by Brian Ouellette, 22 November 2000.
10 Flora Jean Kennedy, interview by Brian Ouellette, 20 October 2000.
11 Ibid.
12 Bobbie MacKenzie, interview by Laurel Lewey, 14 August 2006.
13 Ibid.
14 Ibid.
15 Ibid.
16 Ibid.
17 Ibid.

18 Ibid.
19 Flora Jean Kennedy, interview by Brian Ouellette, 20 October 2000.
20 Ibid.
21 Armand LeCouffe, interview by Brian Ouellette, 3 May 2001.
22 Vilma Kurol, interview by Karen Hill, 17 February 1984, Oral History of Social Work in Canada Project, Canadian Association of Social Workers, Ottawa.
23 Carol Proctor, interview by Brian Ouellette, 20 November 2000.
24 Memo by Howard Young, dated 28 April 28, 1948, PANB, RS153, file E15b11, L 1947–1962.
25 Howard Young to Mrs ___________, 19 December 1954, PANB, RS153, file E15b8, H 1947–1962.
26 Letter dated 18 February 1948, from Canadian Legion, PANB, RS153, file E15b13.
27 Howard Young, letter dated 19 December 1962, PANB, RS153, file E15b4.
28 Howard Young, CAS agent, Northumberland County, to Miss _____, April 1950, PANB, RS153, file E15a1.
29 Howard Young, to J.G. LeBlanc, assistant child welfare officer, Fredericton, 11 February 1950, PANB, RS153, file E15a1.
30 Archie Smith, interview by Brian Ouellette, 10 May 2001.
31 Howard Young to Mrs _____, 16 March 1955, PANB, RS153, file E15b8, H 1947–1962 (Restricted).
32 Archie Smith, interview by Brian Ouellette, 10 May 2001.
33 Carol Proctor, interview by Brian Ouellette, 20 November 2000.
34 Robert Thériault, interview by Brian Ouellette, 22 November 2000.
35 Flora Jean Kennedy, interview by Brian Ouellette, 20 October 2000.
36 Geraldine Lee, interview by Brian Ouellette, 6 June 2001.
37 Howlett, *The Story of Child Welfare in New Brunswick*, 14.
38 Ibid., 16.
39 Mary R. Bishop to C. Smith, County Secretary, Saint John, 28 December 1950, She reported, "a cat was brought in; rat poison and traps employed, and any existing wall openings were closed off ... The firm of Campbell and McNulty, Exterminators, were consulted and they advised the most effective poison and suggested that if, at the end of ten days rats were still present, that exterminations would be the only remedy." PANB, RS156, file E10d1.
40 Vilma Kurol, interview by Karen Hill, 17 February 1984, Oral History of Social Work in Canada Project, Canadian Association of Social Workers, Ottawa, p. 39.
41 Geraldine Lee, interview by Brian Ouellette, 6 June 2001.
42 Fred Whalen, interview by Brian Ouellette, 9 May 2001.

10 Ushering in Equal Opportunity

1 Doucet, "Politics and the Acadians," 309.
2 Brown, "New Brunswick," 216
3 Ibid., 204.
4 Griffiths, *The Acadians*, xi.
5 "A Story of Determination: The roots of co-operation in New Brunswick," UNI Financial Corporation website. Retrieved 5 September 2017 from https://www.uni.ca/en/nous/contenu.cfm?id=2053.
6 Michaud, *Epilogue l'Acadie*, 208–9.
7 Cimino, "Ethnic Nationalism among the Acadians of New Brunswick," 139.
8 Stanley, *Louis Robichaud*, 3.
9 Ibid., 4.
10 Ibid., 2.
11 Two Acadians, unelected, served on an interim basis as premier before Robichaud; they were Aubin-Edmond Arsenault in Prince Edward Island, 1917–19, and Pierre Veniot in New Brunswick, 1923–25.
12 Stanley, *Louis Robichaud*, 3.
13 Ibid.
14 Ibid., 6.
15 Ibid., 7.
16 Ibid., 14.
17 Ibid., 9.
18 In 1946 he took the initiative of arranging an "unprecedented" hockey game between Collège Sacré-Cœur in Bathurst and Collège Saint-Joseph in Saint-Joseph, thus playing a part in opening lines of communication between the northern and southern French-speaking areas of New Brunswick (Stanley, *Louis Robichaud*, 9).
19 Massicotte, "Portrait d'un 'fondateur dans l'âme,'" 6.
20 Stanley, *Louis Robichaud*, 9.
21 Ibid., 8.
22 Ibid., 10.
23 Cormier, *Louis J. Robichaud*, 39–40.
24 Ibid., 37.
25 Ibid., 36.
26 Stanley, *Louis Robichaud*, 11.
27 Cormier, *Louis J. Robichaud*, 39.
28 Ibid., 38.
29 They included Adélard Savoie, the second president of the université (and his brother-in-law). Also included were Bernard Jean, who served as speaker

for the provincial assembly from 1963 to 1966, when he was named attorney general, and Martin Légère, recognized as the founder of the Acadian cooperative movement.

30 Stanley, *Louis Robichaud*, 10.
31 Ibid., 11.
32 Ibid., 13. In that period, it was possible to gain admittance to the bar without studying law at university, if an individual could successfully apprentice with a law firm.
33 Stanley, *Louis Robichaud*, 5.
34 Ibid., 5.
35 Ibid., 9.
36 Ibid., 31.
37 Ibid., 5.
38 Ibid., 19.
39 Ibid., 21.
40 Ibid., 30.
41 Ibid., 33.
42 Ibid., 34.
43 Ibid., 13.
44 Ibid., 25.
45 Belliveau, *Little Louis and the Giant KC*, 20.
46 Stanley, *Louis Robichaud*, 36.
47 Ibid., 40.
48 Marchildon and O'Byrne, "Last Province Aboard."
49 Stanley, *Louis Robichaud*, 44.
50 The work of G.-Raymond Laliberté, *Une société secrète*, published in 1983, remains the most authoritative source on the ordre, and material in this section was drawn extensively from its first chapter, "Fondation, structures et financement de l'Ordre de Jacques-Cartier," 37–80.
51 Laliberté, *Une société secrète*, 38.
52 Ibid., 42.
53 Ibid., 38.
54 Ibid., 40.
55 Ibid., 42.
56 Ibid., 43.
57 Ibid., 22.
58 Ibid., 37.
59 Bertrand, "L'Ordre de Jacques Cartier," 36.
60 Ibid., 38–9.

61 Laliberté, *Une société secrète*, 21.
62 Bertrand, "L'Ordre de Jacques Cartier,"30.
63 Savoie, "Un siècle de revendications scolaires au Nouveau-Brunswick," 57–99.
64 Bertrand, "L'Ordre de Jacques Cartier," 31.
65 Ibid., 34.
66 Ibid., 35.
67 Interviews carried out with Joseph Laviolette by Louis J. Richard on February 3 and 23 and March 10 and 14, 2016.
68 Interviews carried out with the informant by Louis J. Richard on February 15 and 24 and March 10 and 14, 2016.
69 Stanley, *Louis Robichaud*, 228.
70 Leblanc, "Membership, leadership et activisme," 102.
71 Ibid., 72.
72 Ibid., 26.
73 Pasolli, "Bureaucratizing the Atlantic Revolution," 131.
74 Stanley, *Louis Robichaud*, 37.
75 Desserud, "The Political Economy of New Brunswick," 113.
76 Stanley, *Louis Robichaud*, 227.
77 Cyr, "The 1967 Municipal Reform in New Brunswick," 137.
78 Bourque, "Accomplishments and Shortcomings," 24.
79 Pasolli, "Bureaucratizing the Atlantic Revolution," 132.
80 DeMont, *Citizens Irving*, 83.
81 *Report of the Royal Commission on Finance and Municipal Taxation in New Brunswick* (Byrne Report), University of New Brunswick website. Retrieved 7 August 2017 from http://www.lib.unb.ca/Texts/NBHistory/Commissions/ES81E/byrne_1E.html.
82 Pasolli, "Bureaucratizing the Atlantic Revolution," 126.
83 Stanley, *Louis Robichaud*, 146.
84 The original proposals can be found in the Byrne Report.
85 Bourque, "Accomplishments and Shortcomings," 30.
86 Young, "The Programme of Equal Opportunity," 23.
87 Young, "The Programme of Equal Opportunity," 27.
88 *Report of the Royal Commission on Finance and Municipal Taxation in New Brunswick* (Byrne Report), University of New Brunswick website. Retrieved 7 August 2017 from http://www.lib.unb.ca/Texts/NBHistory/Commissions/ES81E/byrne_1E.html.
89 Carol Proctor, interview by Brian Ouellette, 2 November 2000.
90 Ibid.

91 Richard Duffy, interview by Brian Ouellette, 9 May 2001.
92 Cormier, "The Robichaud Legacy," 190–1.
93 Young, "The Programme of Equal Opportunity," 32.
94 Young, "The Programme of Equal Opportunity," 34–5.
95 Conrad and Hiller, *Atlantic Canada: A Concise History*, 193.
96 *Montreal Gazette*, Friday Feb. 18, 1966, Article "New Brunswick – A difference in political philosophies"

Conclusion

1 Foreword, 4.
2 Carolyn and Dan Ennis, interview by Laurel Lewey, 23 February 2007.
3 Lewey, "Nothing to Fear but Fear," 267–9.

Appendix 1

1 Carol Proctor, interview by Brian Ouellette, 2 November 2000.

Bibliography

Akman, Dogan. *Policy Statements and Public Positions of the Canadian Association of Social Workers*. St. John's, Newfoundland: Memorial University of Newfoundland, 1972.

Alton, Grace. "The Selling of Paupers by Public Auction in Sussex Parish." *Collections of the New Brunswick Historical Society* 16 (1961): 93–110.

Alway, Joan. *Critical Theory and Political Possibilities*. Westport, CR: Greenwood Publisher, 1995.

Arsenault, Bona. *History of the Acadians*. Montreal: Leméac, 1978.

Arseneau, Marcel. "Le travailleur social des années '80." Conference paper presented to social workers of the Bathurst region, February 13, 1980.

Baker, Leslie. "Institutionalizing Eugenics: Custody, Class, Gender and Education in Nova Scotia's Response to the 'Feeble-minded', 1890–1931." PhD diss., University of Saskatchewan, 2015.

Balcom, Karen. "Scandal and Social Policy: The Ideal Maternity Home and the Evolution of Social Policy in Nova Scotia, 1940–51." *Acadiensis* 31, no. 2 (Spring 2002): 3–37.

Bear Nicholas, Andrea. "The Role of Colonial Artists in the Dispossession and Displacement of the Maliseet, 1790s–1850s." *Journal of Canadian Studies* 49, no. 2 (Spring 2015): 25–86.

Bell, David Graham. *Early Loyalist Saint John: The Origins of New Brunswick Politics 1783–1786*. Fredericton: New Ireland Press, 1983.

Belliveau, John Edward. *Little Louis and the Giant KC*. Hantsport, NS: Lancelot Press, 1980.

Bent, David. *Determined to Prosper: The Story of Sussex Co-op the Oldest Agricultural Society in the World*. Moncton, NB: Measuring the Co-operative Difference Research Network, 2011.

Bertrand, Gabriel. "L'Ordre de Jacques Cartier et les minorités francophones." In *Francophonies plurielles: Colloque du Regroupement pour la recherche sur la francophonie canadienne organisé dans le cadre du congrès annuel de l'Association canadienne-française pour l'avancement des sciences (ACFAS) (Chicoutimi, 1995, et Montréal, 1996)* edited by Gratien Allaire and Anne Gilbert, 13–58. Sudbury, ON: Institut franco-ontarien, 1998.

Blaney, Elizabeth. "Tracing Classed and Gendered Relations in Education and Social Welfare Policy Discourses in New Brunswick." PhD diss., University of New Brunswick, 2006.

Bohaker, Heidi, and Franca Iacovettta. "Making Aboriginal People 'Immigrants Too': A Comparison of Citizenship Programs for Newcomers and Indigenous Peoples in Postwar Canada, 1940s–1960s." *Canadian Historical Review* 90, no. 3 (Sept. 2009): 427–61.

Bourque, Claude. "Accomplishments and Shortcomings of the Program for Equal Opportunity in New Brunswick: People Services." BA thesis, St. Francis Xavier University, 1972.

Boychuk, Gerard William. *Patchworks of Purpose: The Development of Provincial Social Assistance Regimes in Canada.* Montreal & Kingston: McGill-Queen's University Press, 1998.

Boyko, John. *Into the Hurricane: Attacking Socialism and the CCF.* Winnipeg, MB: J. Gordon Shillingford Publishing, 2006.

Broadfoot, Barry. *Ten Lost Years, 1929–1939: Memories of Canadians Who Survived the Depression.* Markham, ON: Doubleday, 1973.

Brown, Sheila. "New Brunswick." In *Higher Education in Canada: Different Systems, Different Perspectives,* edited by Glen A. Jones, 189–219. New York & London: Routledge, 1997.

Buckner, Phillip A., and John G. Reid, eds. *The Atlantic Region to Confederation: A History.* Toronto: University of Toronto Press, 1994.

Butler, Don. "The Dark Side of Honouring Dr. Helen MacMurchy." *Ottawa Citizen,* 5 October 2012. www.ottawacitizen.com/health/darkside+honouring+Helen+MacMurchy/7346152/story.html.

Cadogan, David. "Our Lebanese Legacy." *Saltscapes* 13, no. 1 (Jan.–Feb. 2012): 36–9.

Cahill, Bette. *Butterbox Babies.* Toronto: Seal Books, 2006.

Campbell, R. Philip. *Challenging Years, 1894–1979: 85 Years of the Council of Women in Saint John.* Saint John: self-published, 1981.

Campey, Lucille. *With Axe and Bible: The Scottish Pioneers of New Brunswick, 1784–1874.* Toronto: Natural Heritage Books, 2007.

Canadian Welfare Council. "Saint John Agency Surveys Relief Families." *Canadian Welfare Summary* 15, no. 1: 47–9.

Candow, James E. *The Deportation of the Acadians.* Grand-Pré, NS: Société Promotion Grand-Pré, Parks Canada, 2003.

Cassidy, Harry. *Public Health and Welfare Reorganization: The Postwar Problem in the Canadian Provinces.* Toronto: Ryerson Press, 1945.

Chiasson, Father Anselme. *Petit manuel d'Histoire d'Acadie de 1867* à 1976. Moncton: Librairie Acadienne, 1976.

Chrisjohn, Roland, Tanya Wasacase, Lisa Nussey, Andrea Smith, Marc Legault, Pierre Loiselle, and Mathier Bourgeois. "Genocide and Indian Residential Schooling: The Past is Present." In *Canada and International Humanitarian Law: Peacekeeping and War Crimes in the Modern Era*, edited by Richard Wiggers and Ann Griffiths, 229–66. Halifax, NS: Dalhousie University Centre for Foreign Policy, 2001.

Chrisjohn, Roland, and Sherri Young, with Michael Maraun. *The Circle Game: Shadows and Substance in the Indian Residential School Experience in Canada.* Penticton, BC: Theytus Books, 1997.

Chute, Janet. "Algonquians/Eastern Woodlands." In *Aboriginal Peoples of Canada: A Short Introduction*, edited by Paul Robert Magocsi, 38–81. Toronto: University of Toronto Press, 2002.

Cimino, Louis Francisco. "Ethnic Nationalism among the Acadians of New Brunswick: An Analysis of Ethnic Political Development." PhD diss., Duke University, 1977.

Comacchio, Cynthia. *The Infinite Bonds of Family: Domesticity in Canada, 1850–1940.* Toronto: University of Toronto Press, 1999.

Conrad, Margaret R., and James K. Hiller. *Atlantic Canada: A Concise History.* Don Mills, ON: Oxford University Press, 2006.

Conrad, Margaret R. and James K. Hiller. *Atlantic Canada: A Region in the Making.* Toronto: Oxford University Press, 2001.

Cormier, Michel. *Louis J. Robichaud: une révolution si peu tranquille.* Moncton: Les Éditions de la Francophonie, 2003.

Cormier, Michel. "The Robichaud Legacy: What Remains?" In *The Robichaud Era, 1960–70: Colloquium Proceedings*, 187–98. Moncton: The Canadian Institute for Research on Regional Development, 2001.

Craven, Paul. *Petty Justice: Low Law and the Sessions System in Charlotte County, New Brunswick, 1785–1867.* Toronto: University of Toronto Press, 2014.

Cyr, Georges. "The 1967 Municipal Reform in New Brunswick." In *The Robichaud Era, 1960–70. Colloquium Proceedings*, 135–57. Moncton: The Canadian Institute for Research on Regional Development, 2001.

Daigle, Jean. "L'Acadie de 1604 à 1763, Synthèse Historique." In *L'Acadie des maritimes: Études thématiques des débuts à nos jours*, edited by Jean Daigle, 1–43. Moncton: Chaire d'études acadiennes, Université de Moncton, 1993.

Daigle, Jean, ed. *Acadia of the Maritimes: Thematic Studies.* Moncton: Chaire d'études acadiennes, Université de Moncton, 1995.

D'Amour, Julie (Mère Supérieure Générale). *Les Filles de Marie-de-l'Assomption Sur les Chemins de l'Évangile.* Turin, Italy: Edition du Signe, 1996.

D'Amours, Oscar. "Survol historique de la protection de l'enfance au Québec, de 1608 a 1977." *Service social* 35, no. 3 (1986): 386–415.

DeMont, John. *Citizens Irving: K.C. Irving and His Legacy.* Toronto: Doubleday, 1991.

de Schweinitz, Karl. *England's Road to Social Security.* Philadelphia: University of Pennsylvania Press, 1943.

Desserud, Don. "The Political Economy of New Brunswick: Selling New Brunswick Power." In *Transforming Provincial Politics: The Political Economy of Canada's Provinces and Territories in the Neoliberal Era,* edited by Bryan M. Evans and Charles W. Smith, 110–34. Toronto: University of Toronto Press, 2015.

Dickason, Olive Patricia. *Canada's First Nations: A History of Founding Peoples from Earliest Times.* Toronto: McClelland & Stewart, 1992.

Doucet, Philippe. "Politics and the Acadians." In Daigle, *Acadia of the Maritimes,* 287–328.

Duguay, Rose Marie. *Child Care in New Brunswick: Historical Overview.* Dieppe, NB: New Brunswick Community College, 1996.

Dyck, Erika. *Facing Eugenics: Reproduction, Sterilization, and the Politics of Choice.* Toronto: University of Toronto Press, 2013.

Faragher, John Mack. *A Great and Noble Scheme: The Tragic Story of the Expulsion of the French Acadians from Their Homeland.* New York: Norton, 2005.

Fingard, Judith. "The New England Company and the New Brunswick Indians, 1786–1826: A Comment on the Colonial Perversion of British Benevolence." *Acadiensis* 1, no. 2 (Spring 1972): 29–42.

Fingard, Judith. "Women's Organizations: The Heart and Soul of Women's Activism." In Fingard and Guilford, *Mothers of the Municipality,* 25–48.

Fingard, Judith, and Janet Guilford, eds. *Mothers of the Municipality: Women, Work and Social Policy in Post-1945 Halifax.* Toronto: University of Toronto Press, 2005.

Finkel, Alvin. *Social Policy and Practice in Canada: A History.* Waterloo, ON: Wilfrid Laurier University Press, 2006.

Forbes, E.R. "The 1930s: Depression and Retrenchment." In Forbes and Muise, *The Atlantic Provinces in Confederation,* 272–305.

Forbes, E.R., and D.A. Muise, eds. *The Atlantic Provinces in Confederation.* Toronto and Fredericton: University of Toronto Press and Acadiensis Press, 1997.

Frank, David, and Nolan Reilly. "The Emergence of the Socialist Movement in the Maritimes, 1899–1916." *Labour/le Travail* 4 (1979): 85–6.

Freedman, Jim. *Sissiboo River Redemption.* Ottawa: Borealis Press, 2012.

Fuller, Sandra McCann. "The Loyalist Quaker Settlement, Pennfield, New Brunswick, 1783." *Canadian Quaker History Journal* 74 (2009): 62–79.

Gallant, Cecile. *Les femmes et la renaissance acadienne.* Moncton: Editions d'Acadie, 1992.

Garner, John. *The Franchise and Politics in British North America, 1755–1867.* Toronto: University of Toronto Press, 1969.

Greenhous, Brereton. "Paupers and Poorhouses: The Development of Poor Relief in Early New Brunswick." *Social History: A Canadian Review* 1 (Apr. 1968): 103–26.

Grekul, Jana, Harvey Krahn, and Dave Odynak. "Sterilizing the 'Feeble-Minded': Eugenics in Alberta, Canada, 1929–1972." *Journal of Historical Sociology* 17, no. 4 (Dec. 2004): 358–84.

Griffiths, Naomi. *The Acadians: Creation of a People.* Toronto & New York: McGraw-Hill Ryerson, 1973.

Griffiths, Naomi. *Contexts of Acadian History, 1686–1784.* Montreal & Kingston: McGill-Queen's University Press, 1992.

Griffiths, Naomi. "Perceptions of Acadians: The Importance of Tradition." *British Journal of Canadian Studies* 5, no. 1 (1990): 99–114.

Guest, Dennis. *The Emergence of Social Security in Canada.* Vancouver: University of British Columbia Press, 1980.

Guildford, Janet. "The End of the Poor Law: Welfare Reform in Nova Scotia before the Canada Assistance Plan." In Fingard and Guilford, *Mothers of the Municipality*, 49–75.

Hancock, Lawrence T. *The Story of the Maritime School of Social Work, 1941–1969.* Halifax: The Maritime School of Social Work, 1992.

Havard, Giles. *The Great Peace of Montreal of 1701: French-Native Diplomacy in the Seventeenth Century.* Montreal & Kingston: McGill-Queen's University Press, 2001.

Herrick, John M., and Paul H. Stuart, eds. *Encyclopedia of Social Welfare History in North America.* London: Sage, 2005.

Hick, Steven, and Jackie Stokes. *Social Work in Canada: An Introduction.* 4th edition. Toronto: Thompson Educational Publishing Inc., 2017.

Howe, Miles. *Debriefing Elsipogtog: The Anatomy of a Struggle.* Halifax & Winnipeg: Fernwood Publishing, 2015.

Howell, Colin. "The 1900s: Industry, Urbanization, and Reform." In Forbes and Muise, *The Atlantic Provinces in Confederation*, 155–91.

Howlett, Carolyn. *The Story of Child Welfare in New Brunswick.* Fredericton: Department of Health and Community Services, 2002.

Hoyt, Don A. *A Brief History of the Liberal Party of New Brunswick.* Saint John: Keystone Printing, 1997.

Jennissen, Therese, and Colleen Lundy. *One Hundred Years of Social Work.* Waterloo, ON: Wilfrid Laurier University Press, 2011.

Knockwood, Isabelle. *Out of the Depths: The Experiences of Mi'Kmaw Children at the Indian Residential School at Shubenacadie, Nova Scotia.* Nova Scotia: Roseway Publishing, 2001.

Laliberté, G.-Raymond. *Une société secrète: l'Ordre de Jacques Cartier, Collection L'Homme dans la société.* Montreal: Hurtubise HMH, 1983.

Landry, Nicolas, and Nicole Lang. *Histoire de l'Acadie.* Sillery, QC: Les éditions du Septentrion, 2001.

Larracey, Edward W. *Resurgo: The History of Moncton.* Moncton: City of Moncton, 1991.

Leblanc, François. "Membership, leadership et activisme au sein de l'Ordre de Jacques Cartier en Acadie: le Conseil régional 20 (Moncton), 1950–1965." Master's thesis, Université de Moncton, 2014.

Lewey, Laurel. "A Near Golden Age: The Cooperative Commonwealth Federation (CCF) in New Brunswick, 1940–1949." *Journal of New Brunswick Studies,* 3 (2012): 93–110.

Lewey, Laurel Lee. "Nothing to Fear but Fear: Social Work in Cold War Canada, 1945–1960." PhD diss., University of Calgary, 2006.

Magocsi, Paul Robert, ed. *Aboriginal Peoples of Canada: A Short Introduction.* Toronto: University of Toronto Press, 2002.

Maines, Joy. "Through the Years in CASW." *The Social Worker* 27, no. 4, (1959): 5–45.

Marchildon, Gregory P., and Nicole C. O'Byrne. "Last Province Aboard: New Brunswick and National Medicare." *Acadiensis* 42, no. 1 (Winter/Spring 2013). Retrieved 28 December 2016 from https://journals.lib.unb.ca/index.php/Acadiensis/article/view/20293/23418.

Martin, Gwen L. *Gesner's Dream: The Trials and Triumphs of Early Mining in New Brunswick.* Fredericton: Canadian Institute of Mining, Metallurgy and Petroleum – New Brunswick Branch, 2003.

Massicotte, Julien. "Portrait d'un 'fondateur dans l'âme': Clément Cormier, pionnier des sciences sociales en Acadie du Nouveau-Brunswick." *Acadiensis* 38, no. 1 (Jan. 2009): 3–32.

McKay, Ian. *Reasoning Otherwise: Leftists and the People's Enlightenment in Canada, 1890 to 1920.* Toronto: Between the Lines, 2008.

McKee-Allain, Isabelle. "Une minorité et la construction de ses frontières identitaires: un bilan sociohistorique du système d'éducation en Acadie au Nouveau-Brunswick." *Revue des sciences de l'éducation,* numéro thématique, 23, no. 3 (1997): 527–44.

McKee-Allain, Isabelle. "La place des communautés religieuses de femmes dans le système d'éducation du Nouveau-Brunswick: un bilan socio-historique." *Éducation et francophonie/femmes* 19, no. 3 (December 1991): 3–8.

McKee-Allain, Isabelle. "Rapports ethniques et rapports de sexes en Acadie: les communautés religieuses de femmes et leurs collèges classiques." PhD thesis, Université de Montreal, 1995.

McLaren, Angus. "Stemming the Flood of Defective Aliens." In Walker, *History of Immigration and Racism in Canada,* 189–204.

Meek, Forrest B. *Lumbering in Eastern Canada: Lumbering during the White Pine Era.* Clare, MI: White Pine Historical Society, Edgewood Press, 1991.

Michaud, Marguerite. *Epilogue l'Acadie: La Reconstruction francaise au Nouveau-Brunswick Bouctouche, Paroisse-type, 1955.* Fredericton: Presses Universitaires, 1955.

Miller, Carman. "The 1940s: War and Rehabilitation." In Forbes and Muise, *The Atlantic Provinces in Confederation,* 306–45.

Mullaly, Robert. *The New Structural Social Work: Ideology, Theory and Practice.* 3rd edition. Don Mills, ON: Oxford University Press, 2007.

Mullaly, Robert. *Structural Social Work: Ideology, Theory and Practice.* Don Mills, ON: Oxford University Press, 1997.

Myers, Sharon. "The Governance of Childhood: The Discourse of State Formation and the New Brunswick Child Welfare Survey, 1927–1930." PhD dissertation, University of New Brunswick, 2004.

New Brunswick Government. *Report of the New Brunswick Committee on Reconstruction.* Fredericton, 1944.

New Brunswick Royal Commission on Finance and Municipal Taxation. Report authors Edward G. Byrne, 1963.

Nowlan, Michael O. *A Century of Service: The Knights of Columbus in New Brunswick, 1904–2004.* Moncton: Faye Editions, 2004.

O'Brien, Gerald V. *Framing the Moron: The Social Construction of Feeble-Mindedness in the American Eugenic Era.* Manchester, UK: Manchester University Press, 2013.

O'Brien, Gerald, and Meghan E. Bundy, "Reaching Beyond the 'Moron': Eugenic Control of Secondary Disability Groups." *Journal of Sociology & Social Welfare* 36, no. 4 (December 2009): 153–74.

Olsen, Gregg. *The Politics of the Welfare State: Canada, Sweden and the U.S.* Don Mills, ON: Oxford University Press, 2002.

Pasolli, Lisa. "Bureaucratizing the Atlantic Revolution: The 'Saskatchewan Mafia' in the New Brunswick Civil Service, 1960–1970." *Acadiensis* 38, no. 1 (Jan. 2009): 126–50.

Paul, Daniel. *We Were Not the Savages.* 2nd edition. Halifax: Fernwood Publishing, 2006.

Payne, Margaret. "Social Services for Indians." *The Social Worker* 24, no. 4 (April–May 1956): 25–6.

Peck, Mary. *The Bitter with the Sweet: New Brunswick, 1604–1984.* Tantallon, NS: Four East Publications, 1983.

Pepin, Pierre Yves. *Life and Poverty in the Maritimes.* ARDA Research Report Series No. RE-3. Ottawa: Department of Forestry and Rural Development, 1968.

Phillipson, Robert. *Linguistic Imperialism Continued.* London: Routledge, 2013.

Poirier, Pascal. "La Loi Scolaire de 1871 au N.-B. et ses répercussions." *La Société historique acadienne. Les Cahiers* 34 (1972): 141–52.

Putnam, Bertha Haven. *The Enforcement of the Statutes of Labourers during the First Decade after the Black Death, 1349–1359.* Studies in History, Economics and Public Law, edited by the Faculty of Political Science of Columbia University, Volume 32. Retrieved 6 September 2017 from https://socserv2.socsci.mcmaster.ca/econ/ugcm/3ll3/putnam/StatutesLabourers.pdf.

Rees, Ronald. *Land of the Loyalists: Their Struggle to Shape the Maritimes.* Halifax: Nimbus, 2000.

Rees, Ronald. *New Brunswick: An Illustrated History.* Halifax: Nimbus, 2014.

Renfree, Harry A. *Heritage and Horizon: The Baptist Story in Canada.* Eugene, OR: Wipf and Stock Publishers, 2007.

Rogers, J.D. "A Historical Geography of the British Colonies, Canada – Geographical, 1911." In *So Vast and Various: Interpreting Canada's Regions in the Nineteenth and Twentieth Centuries,* edited by John Warkentin, 230–306. Montreal & Kingston: McGill-Queen's University Press, 2010.

Rooke, Patricia, and R.L. Schnell. *Discarding the Asylum: From Child Rescue to the Welfare State in English-Canada, 1800–1950.* Lanham, MD: University of America, Inc., 1983.

Roy, Muriel. "Settlement and Population Growth in Acadia," In Daigle, *Acadia of the Maritimes,* 135–200.

Rudin, Ronald. *Remembering and Forgetting in Acadie: A Historian's Journey through Public Memory.* Toronto: University of Toronto Press, 2009.

Savoie, Alexandre, ed. "Un siècle de revendications scolaires au Nouveau-Brunswick, 1871–1971: les Commandeurs de l'Ordre à l'œuvre (1934–1939)." Edmundston: Self-published, 1980.

Savoie, Calixte-F. *L'Éducation des petits Acadiens: question d'importance vitale, l'avenir de la nationalité acadienne.* Edmundston, NB: L'imprimerie du Madawaska, 1934.

Savoie, Donald J. *Harrison McCain: Single-Minded Purpose.* Montreal & Kingston: McGill-Queen's University Press, 2013.

Seager, Allen. "Minto, New Brunswick: A Study in Class Relations between the Wars." *Labour/ LeTravailleur* 5 (Spring 1980): 81–132.

Shewell, Hugh. *"Enough to Keep Them Alive": Indian Welfare in Canada, 1873–1965.* Toronto: University of Toronto Press, 2004.

Sinclair, Murray, Nicholas Bala, Heino Lilles, and Cindy Blackstock. "Aboriginal Child Welfare in Canada." In *Canadian Child Welfare Law: Children, Families and the State,* edited by Nicholas Bala, Michael Kim Zapf, R. James Williams, Robin Vogl, and Joseph P. Hornick. Toronto: Thompson Educational Publishing, 2004.

Sirois, George. "Évolution de l'enseignement public au Madawaska pendant le XIXe siècle." *Le Brayon* 5, no. 2, (January–April 1977): 3–31.

Slumkoski, Corey. *Inventing Atlantic Canada: Regionalism and the Maritime Reaction to Newfoundland's Entry into Canadian Confederation.* Toronto: University of Toronto Press, 2011.

Soucoup, Dan. *Logging in New Brunswick: Lumber, Mills and River Drives.* Halifax: Nimbus, 2011.

Soucoup, Dan. *Know New Brunswick: The Essential History.* Halifax: Nimbus, 2009.

Spray, William A. *The Blacks in New Brunswick.* Fredericton: Brunswick Press, 1972. Retrieved from http://preserve.lib.unb.ca/wayback/20141205155416/http://atlanticportal.hil.unb.ca/acva/blackloyalists/en/context/articles/spray.pdf.

Stanley, Della M.M. *Louis Robichaud: A Decade of Power.* Halifax: Nimbus Publishing Limited, 1984.

Strong, Margaret Kirkpatrick. *Public Welfare Administration in Canada.* Social Service Monographs, no. 10. Chicago: University of Chicago Press, 1930.

Struthers, James. "'Lord Give Us Men': Women and Social Work in English Canada, 1918 to 1953." In *The Benevolent State: The Growth of Welfare in Canada,* edited by Allan Moscovitch and Jim Albert, 126–43. Toronto: Garamond Press, 1987.

Struthers, James. "A Profession in Crisis: Charlotte Whitton and Canadian Social Work in the 1930s." In *The Benevolent State: The Growth of Welfare in Canada,* edited by Allan Moscovitch and Jim Albert, 111–25. Toronto: Garamond Press, 1987.

Taillon, Rév. Frère Léopold. "Ce secrétariat permanent d'éducation." Montreal: École sociale populaire: 1943.

Thériault, Joseph Yvon. "The Robichaud Period and Politics in Acadia." In *The Robichaud Era, 1960–70, Colloquium Proceedings,* 37–52. Moncton: The Canadian Institute for Research on Regional Development 2001.

Thorburn, Hugh G. *Politics in New Brunswick.* Toronto: University of Toronto Press, 1961.

Tillotson, Shirley. "Democracy, Dollars, and the Children's Aid Society." In Fingard and Guilford, *Mothers of the Municipality*, 76–109.

Touzel, Bessie. "Public Welfare Services in New Brunswick Survey." Canadian Welfare Council, 1949.

Tremblay, Tony. "Moving Beyond the Urban/Rural Divide in New Brunswick and Atlantic Canada." In *Shaping an Agenda for Atlantic Canada*, edited by John G. Reid and Donald J. Savoie, 338–46. Halifax and Winnipeg: Fernwood, 2011.

Upton, Leslie F.S. "The Origins of Canadian Indian Policy." *Journal of Canadian Studies* 8, no. 4 (Nov. 1973): 51–60.

Walker, Barrington, ed. *The History of Immigration and Racism in Canada: Essential Readings.* Toronto: Canadian Scholars' Press, 2008.

Wallace, W. Stewart. *The United Empire Loyalists: A Chronicle of the Great Migration.* Chronicles of Canada, vol. 13. Ebook #11977, Project Gutenberg.

Walls, Martha. "'Part of that Whole System': Maritime Day and Residential Schooling and Federal Culpability." *Canadian Journal of Native Studies* 30, no. 2 (2010): 361–85.

Weinberg, Merlinda. "Structural Social Work: A Moral Compass for Ethics in Practice." *Critical Social Work* 9, no. 1 (2008). Retrieved 20 November 2016 from http://www1.uwindsor.ca/criticalsocialwork/structural-social-work-a-moral-compass-for-ethics-in-practice.

Whalen, James. "The Nineteenth-Century Almshouse System in Saint John County." *Social History: A Canadian Review* 7 (April 1971): 5–27.

Whalen, James. "Social Welfare in New Brunswick, 1784–1900." *Acadiensis* 2, no. 1 (Aug. 1972): 54–64. Retrieved 25 April 2016 from https://archives.gnb.ca/Irish/Databases/Almshouse/text/en-CA/WelfareNB.pdf.

Whitton, Charlotte. "Agencies Established Under Present Legislation." In *Report of the New Brunswick Child Welfare Survey 1928–29*, 148–50. Canadian Council on Child Welfare. Saint John: Financed by the Kiwanis Club of Saint John City: 1929.

Wilbur, Richard. *New Brunswick: An Annual Review, 1960–2006.* Atlantic Electronic Text Centre, University of New Brunswick, 2008.

Wynn, Graeme. *Timber Colony: A Historical Geography of Early Nineteenth Century New Brunswick.* Toronto: University of Toronto Press, 1981.

Young, Robert A. "'And the People Will Sink into Despair': Reconstruction in New Brunswick, 1942–52." *Canadian Historical Review* 69, no. 2 (1988): 127–66.

Young, Robert A. "The Programme of Equal Opportunity: An Overview." In *The Robichaud Era, 1960-70, Colloquium Proceedings*, 23–35. Moncton: The Canadian Institute for Research on Regional Development, 2001.

Young, Robert A. "Remembering Equal Opportunity: Clearing the Undergrowth in New Brunswick." *Canadian Public Administration/Administration Publique du Canada* 30, no.1 (Spring 1987): 88–102.

Archival Sources

Legislative Library of New Brunswick
Library and Archives Canada
Provincial Archives of New Brunswick

Index